Florence Nightingale's Sister

Florence Nightingale's Sister

The Lesser-Known Activism of Parthenope Verney

Lynn Hamilton

First published in Great Britain in 2023 by
Pen & Sword History
An imprint of
Pen & Sword Books Ltd
Yorkshire – Philadelphia

Copyright © Lynn Hamilton 2023

ISBN 978 1 39906 680 8

The right of Lynn Hamilton to be identified as Author of this work has been asserted by her in accordance with the Copyright, Designs and Patents Act 1988.

A CIP catalogue record for this book is
available from the British Library.

All rights reserved. No part of this book may be reproduced or transmitted in any form or by any means, electronic or mechanical including photocopying, recording or by any information storage and retrieval system, without permission from the Publisher in writing.

Typeset by Mac Style
Printed in the UK by CPI Group (UK) Ltd, Croydon, CR0 4YY.

Pen & Sword Books Limited incorporates the imprints of Atlas, Archaeology, Aviation, Discovery, Family History, Fiction, History, Maritime, Military, Military Classics, Politics, Select, Transport, True Crime, Air World, Frontline Publishing, Leo Cooper, Remember When, Seaforth Publishing, The Praetorian Press, Wharncliffe Local History, Wharncliffe Transport, Wharncliffe True Crime and White Owl.

For a complete list of Pen & Sword titles please contact

PEN & SWORD BOOKS LIMITED
47 Church Street, Barnsley, South Yorkshire, S70 2AS, England
E-mail: enquiries@pen-and-sword.co.uk
Website: www.pen-and-sword.co.uk

Or

PEN AND SWORD BOOKS
1950 Lawrence Rd, Havertown, PA 19083, USA
E-mail: Uspen-and-sword@casematepublishers.com
Website: www.penandswordbooks.com

Contents

Acknowledgments	vii
Introduction	viii

Part I: Ancestry and Childhood — 1

Chapter 1	The Shores	3
Chapter 2	The Smiths	10
Chapter 3	Born on a Honeymoon	16
Chapter 4	The Shore, Smith, and Nightingale Brew	20
Chapter 5	Embley	25
Chapter 6	Educating the Titans	31
Chapter 7	Second Tour of Europe	40
Chapter 8	Florence Refuses to Marry	51

Part II: In the Shadow of Florence Nightingale — 57

Chapter 9	Florence Breaks Away	59
Chapter 10	Parthenope Breaks Down	67
Chapter 11	WEN Gives In	72
Chapter 12	Gaskell Friendship, Spottiswoode Refusal	76
Chapter 13	'All things have … fitted her for this'	79
Chapter 14	The War at Home	84
Chapter 15	The Great Divorce of Pop and Flo	90

| Chapter 16 | 'I never thought to marry anyone but F' | 93 |
| Chapter 17 | 'Principle Object' | 102 |

Part III: Ink-bottle — 107

Chapter 18	Novelist	109
Chapter 19	Lettice Lisle	122
Chapter 20	The Powers of Women and Class Morality	132
Chapter 21	The Miseries of War and the Pleasures of Home	139
Chapter 22	The Death of WEN; Entail Strikes	149
Chapter 23	Continental Travels	152
Chapter 24	Germany	171
Chapter 25	The Defense of Science	174
Chapter 26	Last Years with the Verneys	184
Chapter 27	Death and Epilogue	194

Notes — 197
Bibliography — 201
Index — 203

Acknowledgments

I am hugely indebted to previous Nightingale scholars, especially Gillian Gill, Mark Bostridge, and Lynn MacDonald. Their love of the nineteenth century, preternatural attention to detail, and tireless research are unparalleled. I also owe a debt of gratitude to the Claydon Estate and the Wellcome Library. Their lovingly curated collections on the Nightingale and Verney families make Nightingale research possible.

This book is dedicated to my husband, Joel Parker Worth III, who said, 'Oh, honey, just give up teaching and write. You're only happy when you're writing.'

Introduction

Every fairy tale heroine needs an ugly sister. Cinderella needed her wicked step sisters to throw her own virtues into sharp relief. In Shakespeare's King Lear, Cordelia's honesty shines only because her sisters are so duplicitous. Even the boringly suburban housewife Marge Simpson has two chain-smoking, bitter spinster sisters to ennoble the mother of the long-running animated show, *The Simpsons*.

In turning Florence Nightingale into a symbol of womanly strength and charity, her biographers have frequently employed her sister, Frances Parthenope Nightingale, as a villainous protagonist.

No one did this more forcibly than the feminist literary critic Elaine Showalter. When Elaine Showalter wrote about Florence Nightingale's latent feminism, she reviled Parthenope with these words: 'socially ambitious, intellectually lazy, and emotionally infantile … Parthenope, a year older than Florence, reacted to her sister's superiority in beauty, intelligence, and character with jealousy disguised as passionate devotion'.[1] (It is, of course, interesting that a feminist critic needed to compare the physical beauty of her subject to that of a perceived adversary.)

Showalter paints a portrait of Florence Nightingale patiently waiting for fifteen years to fulfil her destiny while her mother and sister opposed her with every 'emotional weapon' in their arsenal. Time Florence spent with Parthenope was 'sibling slavery' according to Showalter.

Upon Florence's triumphant return from the Crimean war, Showalter writes that she was 'harassed' by her sister and mother who interrupted her work and 'lounged on sofas in her hotel suite' while being 'flighty and demanding'.[2]

This description is heavily extrapolated from a line in one of Florence's letters which says: 'The whole occupation of Parthe and Mama was to lie on two sofas and tell one another not to get tired by putting flowers into water … two people in tolerable and even perfect health lie on the sofa all day and persuade themselves and others that they are the victims ...' which comes from the biography of Cecil Woodham-Smith.

By this time, Fanny, Florence's mother, was in her sixties, and might actually have needed an occasional break. Parthenope was a confirmed invalid, the victim of childhood rheumatic fever. Both of them had spent most of the Crimean War doing errands for Florence, soliciting donations, handling her overflow correspondence, and putting a positive PR spin on all her war-time activities.

This biography will further explore the demands Florence made on people who showed an interest in her work. No doubt, her expectations for what her family members should accomplish during a visit did not align with their expectations that she would socialize with them.

Showalter goes on to subtly ridicule Parthenope for her late marriage:

Only after her marriage at 39 was Parthenope secure enough to relinquish her neurotic attachment to Florence and also to develop some of her own talents as a productive, though never distinguished, novelist and historical essayist.[3]

Showalter's purpose is to configure Florence Nightingale as a feminist even though Florence Nightingale was about as good a feminist as Margaret Thatcher. Nightingale's attitude toward women was often dismissive. She did not even go so far as to wish women to be doctors. She thought of nursing as a sacred profession. Women should seek for nothing better, in her opinion. Attempts to reshape Florence Nightingale as a pioneer in feminism are bound to fail.

Meanwhile, Showalter's portrayal of Frances Parthenope Nightingale, who later became Lady Verney, is unfair and skewed. The astute reader will wonder where Showalter got such a skewed impression of Parthenope.

And the answer is twofold. Showalter got the basic timeline of Florence Nightingale's life from an early biography by Cecil Woodham-Smith. Showalter also refers to an angry work by Florence that she titled 'Cassandra'.

So much Nightingale scholarship has referred to 'Cassandra' that it is worthwhile to consider what this essay actually is and what it says.

Nightingale wrote 'Cassandra' before launching her fabulous career in nursing, and this essay expresses her agonizing frustration with the expectations of well-off young women. These women have no outlet for their intellect, passion, and sense of morality, F.N. writes. As a consequence of their enforced idleness, young women take up daydreaming. In these dreams, girls imagine themselves in heroic endeavours, usually accompanied by a man worthy of their nobility. Nightingale did not see these daydreams as a normal or even excusable part of adolescence. She thought they were unhealthy and sinful.

She goes on to say that most romantic novels are based on these dreams, except that, in novels, the heroine conveniently has no parents ('almost invariably no mother') and is not, therefore, prevented from daring actions.[4]

It could not be clearer that, on some level, Florence wished her mother dead. But Cassandra has nothing to say about sisters, unless one wishes to believe that the 'lizard' in this essay represents Parthenope:

> Look at that lizard—'It is hot,' he says. 'I like it. The atmosphere that enervates you is life to me.' The state of society which some complain of makes others happy ... They do not suffer. They would not understand it, any more than that lizard would comprehend the sufferings of a Shetland sheep.[5]

This passage echoes other commentaries that Florence wrote about her sister. She referred to Parthenope, once, as a bird of paradise that floated above the cruel world, oblivious of its efforts, just enjoying itself. In other writings, Parthenope is a vegetarian whose all plant food diet is killing Florence, who needs meat.

These dismissals, cold as they are, are not consistent with some biographers' descriptions of Parthenope as a spoiled child, flying into constant rages at her sister's ambitions. Either Parthenope was a raving hysteric or she was a cold-blooded reptile with a tremendous capacity for enjoying the life she had. You can't actually have it both ways.

The only other reference in Cassandra that might be taken as describing Parthenope is this one: 'Mrs. A has the imagination, the poetry of a Murillo, [Spanish seventeenth-century painter] and has sufficient power of execution to show that she might have a great deal more. Why is she not a Murillo?'[6]

Florence might have been writing about herself here, but her own great strengths were in science and mathematics, not art. Parthenope, however, was prodigiously talented at drawing from a young age, as her portraits of Embley and Lea Hurst show. It is possible that, in her sister, Florence sometimes saw a wasted talent, not entirely unlike her own.

In her book, *Florence Nightingale*, Cecil Woodham-Smith consistently demonises Parthenope, which seems especially brave as she leaned heavily on the Verney Estate, into which Parthenope married, for the primary sources she needed for her book.

On page 68 of Woodham-Smith's biography, Parthenope is depicted as 'furious, possessiveness and jealousy consuming her with a twin flame'. On page 71 of the same biography, Parthenope is 'passing from fit to fit of hysterics'. On page 72, Parthe explodes.

Most biographers of Florence Nightingale have similarly cast Parthenope in the role of villain to Florence's lovely self-sacrifice. Where Parthenope is not the villain, she is the ugly duckling to Florence's swan or a large boulder in Florence's path.

In a 1985 essay titled 'Florence Nightingale and the Bonds of Sisterhood', literary scholar Sylvia Strauss resurrected all of Woodham-Smith's and Showalter's exaggerated claims about Parthenope. Strauss finds in Parthenopé an acceptance of all the horrible conventions that women of her age were expected to uphold.

Strauss in effect blames Parthenope for Florence's inability to embody a clear model of feminism. Florence, Straus writes, developed a 'sense of uniqueness' and a 'special calling' while Parthenope was resentful and jealous, though unable to express this resentment and jealousy.[7] On page 73 of her short essay: Parthenope 'felt resentment, which she was not able to articulate'.

Why was Parthenope so unable to express all her jealousy and resentment? Perhaps because Strauss was unable to find any good corroboration for it, except in the highly fictionalized Woodham-Smith version of Parthenope and the essay by Showalter based on that biography.

Strauss not only perpetuated the inaccurate Woodham-Smith portrait, she went on to add a couple of imagined evils to Parthenope's villainy. She accused Parthenope of pretending to be sick to get Florence's attention, not once but on an ongoing basis. Only at the end of Parthenope's life did she actually need medical care, Strauss is happy to disclose.[8]

Strauss blithely bypasses the fact that, at the end of her life, Parthenope was supporting Florence financially as well as providing her a home for half the year on an annual basis. And it must be noted that Parthenope was badly disabled, NOT a hypochondriac, for most of her life, as a result of a childhood illness, which may have triggered an autoimmune condition. The fact that Parthenope became a prolific writer in her forties and fifties is not evidence that nothing was ever wrong with her. It is evidence that she could and did wish to be useful in the face of terrible adversity.

Strauss concludes that Florence was the rebel, and Parthenope the Victorian angel of home and hearth who unquestioningly accepted the role that society dictated for her. That, too, is inaccurate. In fact, Parthenope was almost as ambivalent about marriage as her sister. She declined a very eligible suitor in her early thirties and she nearly declined Sir Harry Verney, even though his proposal came with badly needed financial stability along with the social power of an aristocratic title.

Strauss' representation of Parthenope was not the last instance of negativity. As late as 2007, Gillian Gill, in her book, *Nightingales: The Extraordinary Upbringing and Curious Life of Miss Florence Nightingale*, lambasts Parthenope. As readers of this work, our first introduction to Parthenope is a woman who is 'ranting hysterically' alternately with 'half prostrate on the red silk damask sofa in the drawing room'.[9]

The Florence legend and its propaganda machine

To understand why Frances Parthenope Verney, née Nightingale has, for so long, needed to play the demon to Florence Nightingale's angel, we must know something of the Florence myth and how it developed.

Florence Nightingale has been mythologized for a number of reasons. First, she served in a war that was wildly and bizarrely popular for its time. And, by serving in this war, she cast off all the perks and privileges that she was heir to. Plenty of women became nurses, plenty of women served in war-time Crimea, but Florence had other options, options that most women would avail themselves of. This sacrifice, of all she was born to, stimulated imaginations across class lines.

Next, Nightingale paved the way for women to participate in war through medical services. As a leader of nurses in the Crimean War, she was beloved by dying soldiers. She was often the face they saw before dying or making a recovery.

But, how, you might ask, did people in England know about Florence Nightingale's popularity with the soldiers and come to mythologize her as an icon of compassionate nursing? The answer is that Florence's sister, Parthenope, ran a full-time public relations campaign to put a shine on all her sister's activities.

Before the war, when Florence returned home from her travels in Egypt, her sister was busy collating and editing the letters Florence had sent home to family members and getting ready to publish them as a book.

After Florence set off for her war hospital, in a blaze of glory, a mass-produced portrait of the heroine was circulated in shops and became wildly popular. That portrait is, today, still associated with the young Florence Nightingale, a well-born young woman who cast off the trappings of gentility to sterilize bandages and wipe fevered brows.

Down to the present, F. Nightingale enthusiasts are mesmerized by that picture, a simple black and white drawing, but one in which the viewer often feels she sees Florence Nightingale's soul. The drawing is still in print today as an illustration in Cecil Woodham-Smith's 1950 biography of Florence.

A Goodreads review of Woodham-Smith's biography finds the drawing the single most interesting thing about the book. 'You see a sketch of an absolutely striking woman possessed of a round, elfin face and knowing eyes,' writes D.M. Dutcher.

Indeed, some Nightingale scholars have likened Florence to the actress Helena Bonham Carter, her distant cousin. But how did this compelling portrait magically appear just as Florence Nightingale was achieving the pinnacle of her fame?

Her sister, Parthenope Nightingale, drew it to illustrate the novella about Florence that she dashed off after Florence left for war. The illustration shows Florence standing next to her pet owl, Athena. Florence is pictured slightly resting on a classical pedestal which is also a platform for the owl. With these three elements, the woman, the owl, and the half pillar, Parthenope flagrantly compared her sister to the Greek god of wisdom, Athena (Minerva in Roman myth).

The drawing and novella were only the start of Parthenope's home campaign to glorify her beloved sister. She drew another picture of

Florence on horseback facing the battlefield. She wrote carefully crafted letters praising Florence to anyone who inquired about Florence's work. She met with Florence's admirers in person. Often, she invited and hosted important supporters of Florence's work at one or both of her father's homes.

Beauty and talent contrasted

Led by Woodham-Smith, with fresh tinder from Elaine Showalter's scathing criticisms, most Nightingale scholars have thrown Parthenope Nightingale under the bus in order to give Florence someone tangible to fight against, thereby adding more gleam to their heroine's great destiny.

Biographers have generally accepted Woodham-Smith's assessment that Parthenope was less beautiful, less intelligent, and less energetic.

By today's standards, it may seem petty to compare the beauty of two young women who lived over a hundred and fifty years ago. But most Florence Nightingale biographers have made that comparison, combing letters for evidence that Florence was prettier. So this book must note that, in portraits of the two Nightingales, they appear very similar, neither more attractive than the other in these admittedly idealized representations.

Nor is there much hard evidence that either girl was more sought after. Florence received two marriage proposals before going off to war. Parthenope received two marriage proposals before accepting the proposal of Sir Harry Verney.

As to intellect, Parthenope was entirely the equal of Florence. They had the same careful education, at the hands of their father though their gifts were different. Florence excelled at math and Greek while Parthenope learned to speak and write fluently in French, and her writing and drawing were much more skilled and elegant than Florence's. In youth, Parthenope had an artist's temperament. In adulthood, she often put her creative imagination aside in order to report on the social and moral problems of her day.

To call Parthenope 'lazy' is also entirely inaccurate and just plain mean. Neither girl was allowed to sleep in or to dawdle. Ever. Their mother, Frances, saw to that and kept them on a tight schedule of walks, social engagements, and other activities when they were not in the library, conjugating verbs in three different languages.

It is true that Florence received more education, but that is only because the girls' father, William Edward Nightingale (WEN), discontinued Parthenope's study so that he could focus exclusively on educating Florence. Parthenope did not consider this a reprieve. She resented it bitterly and wrote to WEN begging him to reconsider. She continued to read and study on her own, specializing, eventually, in the economic and political climates of contemporary Great Britain, France, Germany, and Switzerland.

It is true that both Frances and WEN hoped their girls would marry and live conventional lives. But it is equally true that both women were highly ambivalent about the institution of marriage.

As children and young women, they were devoted to each other. They enjoyed the freedom that an affluent family with a good library and beautiful grounds can provide, and they often joked about marrying each other. The unspoken declaration was that neither thought their situation would be improved by leaving the family estates.

Parthenope, in particular, had an astonishing capacity for loving what she had and revelling in it. As teenagers and very young women, Florence shared this talent. The important difference is that Florence, in her midtwenties, longed to leave her family and live on her own while Parthenope clung to their childhood fantasy of living the rest of their lives together.

To this separation, Parthenope did object, at least at first. She felt her sister's enormous talents would be wasted in bandaging wounds. She also feared for Florence's health and safety. That fear was well-founded. Florence did, indeed, return from war so damaged by Brucellosis that she never recovered her full strength.

But the jealous fits and constant tirades that Parthenope is supposedly guilty of are largely fictional. The letters Parthenope wrote, and the way people like Elizabeth Gaskell portrayed her, show us a picture of a reasonable, loving, and loyal woman, not a shrewish harpy who was forever blocking her sister's dreams.

How biographers have managed to get agonies of jealousy from Parthenope remains, to some extent, a mystery. Parthenope's letters on the subject of her sister's 'calling' are uniformly measured. The fiercest one that Woodham-Smith could find to quote suggests that Parthenope didn't believe Florence was temperamentally suited to nursing. Parthe herself had recently had a taste of Florence's talent in this field; Parthenope had suffered a nervous breakdown, and Florence was commanded to care for her. Parthenope found Florence a 'shocking' nurse. Shockingly bad, she meant.

Parthenope wrote: 'I wish she could be brought to see it is the intellectual part that interests her, not the manual … her curiosity in getting into varieties of minds is insatiable. After she has got inside they generally cease to have any interest for her'.[10]

The same letter notes that Florence is surrounded by friends ready to praise and rubber stamp anything she wishes to do. Parthenope detects that this kind of sycophancy is potentially dangerous. It prevents people from thinking through their limitations. Parthenope even warns the reader of her letter 'I think it will do her much good to be with you, who, though you love and admire her, do not believe in the wisdom of all she says *because* SHE says it'.[11] Parthenope did not, unfortunately, intuit that inflated ego and success in medicine often go hand in hand.

In a word, Parthenope did not think her sister was up to the cruddy aspects of nursing. In this, it turns out, Parthenope was badly mistaken. But to say that a sister isn't cut out for changing bedpans is not the same thing as pitching a fit, acting hysterical, or collapsing on the floor or the divan.

Since the 1950s, only a few minority voices have strained to correct the record on Parthenope Verney, née Nightingale. In 1958, E.D. Mackerness attempted to undo the demonization of Parthenope in his review of Cecil Woodham-Smith's biography. He is careful to compliment the biographer on her achievement, but notes that Woodham-Smith 'may have been just a little too devoted to her main subject'.[12] Woodham-Smith was 'surely less than just to … Frances Parthenope Verney,' he adds.[13] Mackerness goes on to astutely note that 'there could not be more than one Florence Nightingale',[14] but he does credit Parthenope with the thankless part she played in helping her sister's mission in Crimea.

Mackerness takes definite exception to the assessment that Parthenope was less intelligent than Florence. Her work as a writer showed uncommon talent as well as a deep understanding of the social problems of her day, he writes. Mackerness also points out that, as a writer, Parthenope did not take the path of least resistance by simply imitating the work of other women writers in the nineteenth century.

This book attempts a fair treatment of the woman who became Lady Frances Parthenope Verney. It will examine her childhood, ancestry, relationship and service to Florence Nightingale, and her very real and separate achievements. It will not flinch at Parthenope's reservations about Florence's call to nursing, but it will more carefully examine the reasons for those reservations. Finally, it will attempt an assessment of Lady Frances Parthenope Verney's literary contributions as well as her contributions to social thought and political philosophy.

A Note on Names

Frances Parthenope Verney, née Nightingale, shared her maiden name with three other Nightingale relatives. She shared her first name with her mother, and she shared her married name with her husband Sir Harry Verney and his children.

To avoid confusion among the various players in this biography, the main subject will mostly be referred to as 'Parthenope', and occasionally 'Parthe' and 'Pop', which were family nicknames.

To disambiguate Parthenope's parents from other ancestors with the same names, Frances Smith Nightingale will be referred to as 'Fanny', and William Edward Nightingale will be referred to as WEN.

Florence Nightingale, who has frequently and confusingly been called 'Miss Nightingale', will be referred to as Florence and occasionally 'Flo', Parthenope's nickname for her.

Part I

Ancestry and Childhood

Chapter 1

The Shores

Frances Parthenope Nightingale was born in 1819, in the Italian city of Naples. She was literally born on her parents' honeymoon. She was a small baby, but a huge disappointment. Her parents needed a boy.

She was born in the same year as Queen Victoria, and she lived her entire life in the Victorian era. In many ways, she embodied Victorian values, and in other ways, she quietly, but definitively rejected them.

The era into which this baby was born was a time of exploration, scientific and technical advances, and religious questioning. At the same time, it was an era in which the powerful often resisted change, sometimes with cruelty. It was an era in which some nations recognized and expanded human rights while other nations committed human rights atrocities.

In 1819, for example, the Russian state of Livonia liberated its serfs, and abolitionists formed the African Slave Trade Patrol to stop the abduction of West Africans into slavery. However, in that same year, thirty slaves were thrown overboard from the French slave ship *Le Rodeur*. Many Ashkenazi Jews were killed in pogroms and riots in Bavaria.

In 1819, the outer edges of the world were still unmapped. Captain William Smith and the crew of the tall ship, *Williams of Blyth*, were the first recorded people to see the outer islands of Antarctica. Later that same year, explorer William Parry safely steered his crew around the arctic icebergs and frozen islands of what would become known as the Parry Channel.

The stars, too, offered opportunities for exploration. In 1819, astronomer Carlo Brioschi became the first person to use the telescope at Naples' new observatory. He used that device to measure Cassiopeiae, the alpha star in the famed constellation of the same name.

The arts and architecture also made strides in 1819. On 20 March, London's Burlington Arcade, a collection of shops under a shared roof, was opened, paving the way for malls and department stores. And a few months later, the Museo del Prado was opened in Madrid.

In 1819, the writers John Ruskin and George Eliot were also born. Their analyses of social dynamics became more famous than Parthenope's, but they shared many concerns about the effects of industrialization and religion.

Parthenope was born far away from her parent's English home. It was a lovely convention at that time for newlywed couples, with the means to do so, to travel for a year or two after their wedding.[1] Parthenope's parents chose to travel around continental Europe on their honeymoon. Both their daughters were born on this trip.

Parthenope's life was a struggle from the start. She spent her first weeks on earth literally starving because her mother was unable to nurse her. While still a babe, she would contract a serious inflammation and come close to death. She would be plagued with bad health most of her life. But she would fight through these odds to become one of the most respected journalists and economic analysts of her age. She would become the wife of a baronet and parliamentarian. She would help him fight poverty and injustice. She would stand in the shadow of her much more famous sister, Florence Nightingale, but she would also be highly valued for her own achievements and character by a small circle of friends and family.

What were this child's origins? What DNA went into the particular brew that became Lady Frances Parthenope Verney, née Nightingale?

One of Parthenope's most influential ancestors goes by the moniker, 'Mad Peter'. Born Peter Nightingale II, he might more fairly have been dubbed 'Eccentric Peter'. He was the third Peter in his ancestral line, and he inherited mining money. He was known for hard-drinking, hard gambling, and recklessly driving his horses. But he was, more importantly for the heroine of this story, a savvy investor and entrepreneur, who understood the value of a diversified portfolio.[2]

Peter made his fortune, worth approximately £100,000 at his death, in lead mining and smelting, wool manufacture, hosiery production, a hat shop, and real estate. He died a bachelor, with no children. Because of English inheritance laws, it was this amassed affluence that made Parthenope's father an independently wealthy man, with the leisure time to educate himself far beyond his actual needs and then pass on that learning to his daughters whom he had raised and taught.

Mad Peter died in 1803, leaving his entire estate to his distant relative, the eight-year-old William Edward Shore, who would become Parthenope's father. The Nightingale estate was entailed away from the female line, a specifically European and British tradition that ensured women would never own their fathers' property, not even if they were the only offspring of a wealthy father, as Parthenope and Florence turned out to be.

Estate entailment was, no doubt, described in more flattering terms by the early medievals who invented it. It existed to make sure that a fortune, once earned, stayed in the hands of a solo male heir. One person at a time would hold an entailed estate, but it never belonged to him. It belonged to his descendants. And if he produced no male heirs of his own, it would pass to the closest family that had managed to produce male heirs.

Estate entailment was one of the many ways that Victorians disenfranchised women. But it did not exist for that reason alone. Estate entailment guaranteed that one male family member would always be wealthy and, therefore, well placed to wield social and political power. To divide an estate equally amongst all descendants would quickly fragment the power and influence that is begotten by huge sums of cash and land. Men who stood in the midst of stately mansions with outlying farms, all beholden to the lord of the manor, dreamed of a future after their deaths, when a descendant of theirs with the same name would wield the same power and influence. The entailment of the Nightingale estate meant that the name 'Nightingale' would continue to be associated with wealth and prestige through the ages. It was not the only path to immortality, but it was the most obvious one.

The notion that an entire family should benefit from inherited wealth or that each individual should get a chance to build their own fortune on the seed money of a partial inheritance was entirely foreign to these inventors of the entail, also sometimes called 'fee tail'. By the early nineteenth century, estate entailment was already understood to be an instrument that threw women with no skills or work experience into poverty, but it would not be abolished until 1925.

Through the entail mechanism, estates passed to men who might or might not be ready to take on the management of farms, tenants, palace upkeep, and a staff of servants. The new heir might well piss away the estate through overspending and bad management. It was an imperfect system, obviously, as most systems are those that bestow power and money based on birth rather than merit.

However, the Nightingale estate did not suffer that fate. None of the Shore family was allowed to benefit from the Nightingale estate until William Edward turned twenty-one. In the meantime, the estate was carefully managed by William Edward's father, whose name was also William Shore. He was a mine manager and therefore understood the industry in which Peter Nightingale had been engaged. The estate continued to grow during the younger William Edward Shore's childhood and teen years so that, when he came in control of his inheritance, at twenty-one, he would find himself a very wealthy man. He derived around £7,000 a year from his estate, an amount equivalent to around half a million pounds in today's currencies.

As a child, William Edward Shore lived in the English Midlands with his father and mother, Mary Evans Shore, who would live into her nineties and have a close relationship with her grandchildren Florence and Parthenope.

The Shore home was about two hundred miles from London. The Midlands were, more or less, the birthplace of the industrial revolution in England. Cromford, a town that lay nearby Lea Hurst, the estate that WEN inherited, was a manufacturing town.

The Shores were a Unitarian family which made them 'dissenters' within the prevailing Church of England culture. As such, they endured quite a bit of passive persecution. Their lives were not in danger, but their failure to swear allegiance to the Church of England meant they could not publicly assemble or hold 'Great Offices of State'. Unitarians could attend Cambridge and Oxford universities, but they could not earn degrees from those acclaimed institutions.

Unitarian belief and culture were so integral to the lives of the Nightingales that we must expend some energy understanding this anomalous religion. Unitarianism rejects the notion of a three-in-one god and teaches that Jesus was a good man and brilliant thinker, but fully human. Unitarianism, in its current incarnation, is an openly God-optional religion. By design, it has no creed; therefore, one can be a Buddhist and a Unitarian or an atheist and a Unitarian. However, the Unitarianism of Parthenope Verney, when grown, would definitely cherish belief in a higher external power.

Even in the eighteenth century, Unitarians had been quietly and respectfully radical. The denomination, as Christians have agreed to call it, first sprang up in Poland, Lithuania, and Transylvania at about the same time. Then it swiftly moved to Britain. Britain was fertile ground for such a transformational theory. Essex Street Chapel in London became the first official house of worship for Unitarians in 1774.

Unitarianism embraced science and believed in free will. It rejected the notion that people are 'born into sin', i.e. inherently corrupt and sinful. Unitarianism then, as now, believed that no specific religion or sect has a monopoly on the truth. This means that Unitarians, like the Nightingales, could and still can find instruction for leading a good life from a broad array of religious leaders and philosophers.

The theology of Unitarianism is much less important to the history of Great Britain than its influence on politics and social mores. Unitarianism emphasized education and critical thinking. It appealed to thinking people of education who were almost always people of some wealth. Therefore, many of its members rose to positions of leadership in government. The Unitarian presence in Parliament and the religion's influence on the great political changes of the nineteenth century were astonishing considering the small size of the Unitarian community. The infiltration of Unitarians into government was a huge factor in establishing religious tolerance both in Great Britain and North America.

Unitarianism also played its part in the emancipation of British women. It fought for suffrage and better education for women. It favoured their inclusion in male-dominated enterprises. The great nineteenth-century feminist, Mary Wollstonecraft, was, among other things, a Unitarian.

Unitarianism was one of the pathways to what we currently call 'cultural Christianity', a flexible adherence to church attendance and celebration of Christmas and Easter pageantry, with belief in God a buffet item one is free to pass on. Atheists also claim Unitarianism as a predecessor to public disbelief in any supernatural beings.

It is no coincidence that Thomas Jefferson and George Washington were both avowed Unitarians who often attended more traditional church services in what can only be viewed as an attempt to blend in. Unitarianism was, in other words, the religion of reformers and revolutionaries. Unitarianism was and still is allied with a belief in the equality of all people, a rejection of separatism along the lines of race and creed, and a belief that poverty and disease can and should be eradicated by science and government. We see all these beliefs in Parthenope Nightingale who would become Parthenope Verney.[3]

It likely seems alien to inclusive British minds today that there were religious identities unsanctioned by the country's very government. But religious persecution was only two generations removed from Parthenope Nightingale. In 1792, Thomas Walker, the brother-in-law of Parthenope's paternal grandfather, was the target of an anti-dissenter mob, spurred on by a local Church of England minister. This mob invaded Thomas Walker's house, and he fought them. When the case went to trial, the court sided with the mob. Defending his home earned Walker a magistrate's fine from which he never recovered financially.

This history of religious persecution made the Unitarians a tight-knit community. Young people usually married within this community and long-standing family friendships abided over multiple generations. As is true of small religious minorities, even today, the dissenters were often closer to families living in faraway provinces than they were with their own neighbours.

In 1851, when he turned twenty-one, Parthenope's father, William Edward, legally came into management of the fortune he inherited from Peter Nightingale II. Fortunately for his future wife and daughters, he would turn out to be a good steward of this fortune. As men of England frequently do, he changed his name to match that of his inherited estate. Thereafter, he would be known as William Edward Nightingale or WEN.[4]

It is impossible to overestimate the importance of WEN's windfall inheritance. He was born into a manufacturing family, and it is likely he would have followed in his father's footsteps to become a manufacturer with a staff of perhaps a hundred or more men and women. His inheritance propelled him, in one generation, into the ranks of men whose main job is to manage their passive income wisely.

In other words, at the age of twenty-one, WEN became a gentleman. A gentleman who, if he delegated wisely, would have a great deal of leisure time which could be used on reading, improving his knowledge and character, and educating his children. Without the Nightingale inheritance, there would almost certainly have been no Florence Nightingale, nor Parthenope Verney. There would, no doubt, have been children, but not these children. Our heroine and her sister were very much the product of elite educations that could only have been provided by a WEN with leisure time.

WEN's daughter Florence would, in years to come, describe him, uncharitably, as a man of high energy with not enough to do. It exasperated her that he seemed to have no life work equivalent to her career in nurse management. She noted that he moved around the breakfast room with his plate in hand as if he had important multitasking to do. What she overlooked is that WEN did have a life's work, namely to educate and cultivate the women who would become Florence Nightingale and Parthenope Verney.

Chapter 2

The Smiths

When it came time to marry, the young WEN would look for a wife within the Unitarian community. This custom kept the Unitarian faith strong and culturally relevant. The Shores would marry into the William Smith family to produce both Florence and Parthenope Nightingale as well as their cousins. Let us now take a look at the family that produced Parthenope's mother, Frances Smith, more often known as 'Fanny'.

On her mother's side, as well as her father's, Parthenope had an interesting and distinguished heritage. Her maternal grandfather, William Smith, served in the House of Commons, beginning in 1784. He was then voted in and out of office for the next several decades.

His hard work, devotion to human rights, and idealism won him some ridicule from his fellow Parliamentarians. Smith soldiered right on through this anonymous rhyme, penned at his expense:

> At length when the candles burn low in their sockets,
> Up gets William Smith with his hands in his pockets,
> On a course of morality fearlessly enters,
> With all the opinions of all the dissenters[1]

Of course, this bad poem says more damning things about the person who wrote it than it does about William Smith. Yes, Smith worked long hours, and he was humble. He was true to his religious convictions despite the obvious advantages of trading up to COE. And, yes, he did fight for the principles of Unitarianism. Those principles included an abhorrence of slavery and an insistence on religious tolerance.

William Smith was not solely responsible for the abolition of slavery in Great Britain in 1806, but he was one of its most tireless champions. He was, in fact, the right-hand man of William Wilberforce, the face of abolition in British history.

William Smith was also an author of the Unitarian Relief Act of 1812, which was sometimes referred to casually as 'Mr. William Smith's act'. It is important to understand that Parthenope was born only seven years after the passage of the Unitarian Act which made her a legal practitioner of her family's faith.[2] It would take a few more years for Catholics to get the same reprieve. But the Catholic Emancipation Act of 1829 was also passed during William Smith's time in office.

It is significant that William Smith was also an early feminist who rubbed shoulders with some of the great women writers of his time: Mary Wollstonecraft, Anna Laetitia Barbauld, and Amelia Opie, all of them passionate advocates for the equality of women under the law. To mainstream Britain, these women were outliers, at best, and destabilizing to the status quo at worst. Yet William Smith would pass along his admiration for them to his daughters and granddaughters.

In William Smith, we can definitely see a family role model for hard work and dedication to equality and human rights. Both Parthenope and Florence would possess their grandfather's ability to work tirelessly for positive change.

The William Smith family was a large one. By all accounts, Smith enjoyed a loving marriage, cemented by the couple's shared religious dissension. With his wife, Frances Coape, William Smith had thirteen children. Parthenope's mother, Frances, was born into this brood. She went by the nickname 'Fanny' to help the family keep her separate from her mother. She was the product of a loving, close-knit clan with a surprisingly present father.

Dissenters are, almost by definition, free thinkers. Even though Fanny's mother was socially conventional, she was conventional within the context of a religion that rejected many superstitions and upheld human rights.

From her parents, Fanny and her siblings learned the habit and enjoyment of travel. The Coape-Smiths took many trips, spending four months in Scotland on one occasion and visiting other parts of Britain and Europe on another. The Smith children gleaned a global perspective through travelling. They visited stately homes, but also mines and manufacturing towns. They often got off the well-beaten track and drove their phaeton down roads that were unmaintained and very rugged. They went caving and mountain climbing with vigour. Frances Smith,

Parthenope's grandmother, may have been the first woman to climb Scafell Pike. She did not let her nearly continuous pregnancies slow her down. She could tour the Lake District, riding side-saddle in the rain, stay astride her horse while those about her toppled into streams and mud, then give birth to a healthy child a few weeks later.[3]

Travel is, of course, the enemy of narrow-mindedness, as many great thinkers have observed. For Parthenope's grandmother, Frances Smith, in particular, her journeys were transforming. She entered France a rather narrowly devout dissenting Protestant. The sight of Catholic iconography was, at first, startling to her. The nakedness of the crucifixion, the lavishness of some of the Virgin Mary's dresses were unfamiliar, but she suspended judgment and went back to England a broader and much more global thinker than ever before.[4]

On these journeys, Frances would write and sketch in her journal, a talent and proclivity she passed down to Parthenope for whom art and letters would be all-consuming. Through writing and drawing, Frances engaged more intensely with what she saw and learned than other tourists did. Writing and drawing helped her respect, rather than dismiss, cultural and religious differences. This global perspective would be directly passed down to her daughter Fanny and, from Fanny, to Parthenope and Florence.

From both her parents, Fanny would learn the spirit of adventure and a fearlessness about pitching herself into the unknown that she would pass on to her daughters. She also learned, from her mother, that the delicacy women were supposed to cultivate could be set to one side for the sake of getting to one's destination. Neither Frances, Parthenope's grandmother, nor her mother Fanny were afraid to get mud on their dresses. (It was an era that did not have a line of outdoor clothing and boots appropriate for genteel women on great outdoors adventures. Frances and Fanny would have made all these journeys in the flimsy cloth shoes and floor-length dresses that were the only garb made for respectable women.) Fanny and her mother also understood the value of packing light and being tough in the pursuit of sightseeing.

When not touring, Fanny and her sisters received their education, officially at the hands of their mother, but with important buttressing from their father's library of a thousand or more books. Fanny had access to the great books of her age, including Mary Wollstonecraft's

Vindication of the Rights of Women and Thomas Paine's *The Rights of Man*, which paved the way for democracy and suffrage. Fanny consumed these exciting theories raw, not in watered-down textbook accounts or filtered through the lens of a conservative professor.

Parthenope's grandfather, William, was keen that his children should know more than one language. So Fanny and her sisters learned Italian and French from native speakers who had immigrated to England and were available as tutors.[5]

Unfortunately, while Fanny and her siblings were growing up, the family business that supported them was in decline. William Smith, his wife, and prodigious offspring were all supported by the profits of sugar importation. Like tobacco in colonial America, the sugar industry was profitable only because of the free labour consequent from slavery.

With the abolition of slavery, profits from sugar plummeted. In working to abolish slavery, William Smith had been, all along, also working against his own business and family interests. It would not be long before the Smith family was financially devastated by this change.

Parthenope's mother, Fanny, entered adulthood in a blithe bubble of ignorance. William Smith had sheltered his family from knowledge of their failing fortune. She had no idea how precarious her future and that of her unmarried sisters was. Fanny was, by all accounts, a beautiful and lively young woman, high-spirited and opinionated enough to challenge and attract men, but not unconventional enough to scare them off. She needed to marry someone with his own money because of the failing Smith fortune and also the sheer number of Smith children that had to be provided for. But she was, initially, unaware of this limitation.

Dissenters did not hasten to marry their daughters off as teens. When Fanny entered her twenties as an unmarried young lady, there was no immediate cause for alarm. Nightingale scholars believe that Fanny had her pick of eligible bachelors, but she made an error in her first choice.

Fanny fell in love with James Sinclair, a minor Scottish aristocrat while accompanying her father on a parliamentary trip to Scotland. This young man belonged to a Church of England family, but this did not stop Fanny from forming an alliance.[6] She likely hoped that the Sinclairs would be her admission to the fabled aristocracy. She presented her engagement to Sinclair, an army soldier, as a done deal when she spoke of it to her family.

If a prudent marriage was the business of Victorian women, Fanny was mismanaging her business rather badly. She failed to account for two things. One was that the Sinclair family had entirely different ideas about who their son would marry. They needed to trade on the prestige of their title, and James was expected to marry a young lady of wealth. And preferably Church of England. But definitely wealthy. It appears, though, that James, too, had been kept in the dark about the family fortunes, at least to some extent.

James made approximately £400 a year through his army commission. It was an income that had to be supplemented with gentle infusions of cash from his family. His army salary was definitely not enough money to keep him with a wife and children.

Fanny had also made the mistake of not knowing what she brought to the marriage negotiation table. She assumed that her father would provide a generous enough dowry to smooth over the financial obstacles to her desired marriage. (It appears she also assumed that James Sinclair would have no difficulty working hard for his living which is not so apparent to scholars of the Nightingale family.)

William Smith did attempt to get his would-be future son-in-law a position as aide de camp to a high ranking army leader. But to no avail. It was with great sadness that Smith had to explain to Fanny that he could not provide for her and her trophy husband. Fanny was forced to either marry without a financial safety net or break off the engagement. Eventually, she was wise enough to see how unprepared she was to live by her wits. She had never had to handle or make money, but it was always there, quietly underwriting all her needs for nice clothes and adequate meals. She had never had to worry about food preparation, much less the cost of a meal. She ended the betrothal.[7]

So, at the age of twenty-eight, Parthenope's mother found herself fully ripe for marriage, perhaps a wee bit overripe, by Victorian standards. (One of Jane Austen's heroines, in *Persuasion*, had been declared without hope when she had failed to marry by the age of twenty-eight.) William Edward Nightingale did not actually rescue Fanny from the fate of the spinster. It's likely that she would have married someone else, had Nightingale not been so smitten by her. Nevertheless, it's unlikely that she would have married someone as bright, loving, and dedicated to family as WEN was.

William Edward Nightingale met Fanny when he visited the home of his friends, Octavius and Samuel Smith, Fanny's brothers. Nightingale had studied alongside the two Smith brothers at Cambridge. He was twenty-three, fresh out of college, and wealthy, a perfectly eligible groom.

There is no doubt that WEN married Fanny Smith for love. She was six years older than he, with no dowry and no prospects of inheritance. Though she was at some pains to keep her failed engagement private, it is likely that WEN knew of it, the dissenting Unitarians being a tightly knit community with an efficient grapevine. An unsuccessful climb into an aristocratic Church of England family could have dulled Fanny's patina for other Unitarians, but WEN's enthusiasm for her was unconditional.

WEN knew that he had to have sons or his fortune would blow away from the immediate family. A more prudent choice would have been a woman in her early twenties or even late teens, one with more childbearing years in the bank. His passion for Fanny had him throwing this caution to the wind.

On Fanny's part, it was a good match that delighted her parents and secured her future. No dowry was demanded. In fact, her future father-in-law, William Shore, bestowed a monetary gift on her to alleviate her embarrassment at coming to the church empty-handed. They married on 1 June 1818. WEN was twenty-three, Fanny twenty-nine.

Chapter 3

Born on a Honeymoon

Today, honeymoons are optional and likely to last less than two weeks. Not so, the Victorians. Victorian weddings took place between two young people with compatible social and financial profiles. Knowing one's new husband or wife's temperament, how he/she would handle missing a meal or a nap, was not required prior to marriage. In fact, such intimate knowledge of a new spouse would raise suspicions.

So the honeymoon was the getting-to-know-each-other period. A special, months-long reprieve from social obligations and jobs. If possible, newlywed British husbands took their wives to some warm, sunny place where they could shed a few clothes. The unspoken assumption about the Victorian honeymoon was that young couples needed time and space to start up baby-making production. The young woman was supposed to be a virgin. What better way to coax her into bed on a lazy afternoon than an un-airconditioned hotel room right off the shore of the Mediterranean?

What is not to love about this custom? Continental Europe was enjoying a long spate of peace and stability. Almost immediately after the wedding, WEN and Fanny took off, first to France, then to Naples, where they rented a house. This honeymoon became an unqualified success when Fanny became pregnant and then bore her first child, right there on her Italian honeymoon, Monday, 19 May 1819.

Fanny and WEN named their first child Frances, after Fanny's mother. Her middle name, Parthenope, they whimsically took from the ancient name of Naples. She would rarely be called by her first name. Instead, she became Parthenope or Parthe, sometimes 'Pop' to Florence's 'Flo'.

Baby Parthenope was a disappointment right out of the womb. Had she only been a boy, WEN and Fanny would have been saved from the estate entailment. No discussion of her birth was pure joy or congratulations.

Even Gale, Fanny's servant, participated in dumping on Parthenope for failing to be a boy. To Fanny's sister, Joanna, Gale wrote, 'It was a little disappointment, not being a son'.[1] Parthe's grandfather, the great abolitionist William Smith, strained to say something positive after first noting how unfortunate Parthenope's gender was: 'I am disposed to give the little Female a most cordial welcome … there are advantages to a Mother in having the eldest born of her own sort'.[2]

Parthe's birth was surrounded by other sad portents. WEN contracted malaria, and an inflammation of the breast beset Fanny. On top of all that, the young family got news that the Smith fortune had failed.[3]

Through letters from her sister, Julia, Fanny learned that her father had declared bankruptcy. William Smith now had to sell his home in Parndon, Essex, and his fashionable residence on London's Park Street. The residence on Park Street, in fact, had been a mistake that stretched the Smith family finances to the breaking point. Parthe's grandfather would have to sell his beloved art collection which included some Rembrandts. His exquisite library also fell to his creditors. There was now no hope of a dowry for either of Fanny's unmarried sisters, the already-declared-a-spinster Mary Frances or her lovely sister Julia who would remain single for the rest of her life also.[4]

They were not left entirely destitute. In fact, after the sale of their properties, the Smiths still had an income of £1,000 a year. However, it was nowhere near enough to provide the kind of life they had previously enjoyed. Fortunately for them, Fanny's brother (Parthenope's uncle) Benjamin had become a rich man, principally in whiskey manufacturing, and he was able to subsidize the small income left to his mother and sisters. Frances Smith, Fanny's mother, and spinster sisters relocated to a house near the Welsh border that one of them described as 'awful'.

Parthenope was undersized at birth, and her first three months were rough. Initially, she had trouble obtaining milk from Fanny despite vigorous sucking. Today, a ragged husband would be dispatched to the nearest grocery to procure formula. Husband and wife would then breathe a sigh of relief as the baby imbibed a fluid scientifically designed to replicate all the nutrients of breast milk.

The baby food formula of the Victorians, by contrast, was a makeshift gruel to be shovelled into the baby, not with a plastic nipple, but an oversized spoon. Naturally, Parthe didn't want the gruel, she wanted mother's milk which was not forthcoming. So she basically starved for several days. When both WEN and Fanny got sick, their unfed baby started vomiting blood.

Fanny's married sisters had set the virtuous example of breastfeeding their own children. And they were quite successful in doing so. For that reason, Fanny was quite determined to do the same. Wealthy Church of England families routinely hired wet nurses to feed and sometimes even raise their babies. However, this practice often sacrificed the welfare of the nurse's own children, who also needed breast milk. So, it may have been a matter of conscience and possibly faith for Fanny to breastfeed. If Unitarians raised their children the same way as the godless COE, what was the point of being a mildly oppressed minority?

During Parthenope's infancy, Fanny kept a diary of sorts, which she titled 'Journal of My Little Life'. In this diary, she wrote from Parthenope's point of view, expressing the frustrations of having an empty stomach and a dry breast.[5]

In the 'Journal', Fanny blames the doctor who delivered Parthenope of cruelty and malpractice. In Fanny's mind, this doctor was definitely to blame for her inability to produce milk. Though she does not stipulate that her doctor kept mother and baby apart, it is likely that her dryness came about because the baby didn't attach soon enough. Indeed, some twenty-first-century pediatric specialists say that a mother should start nursing her child within the first hour after birth.

However history may judge Fanny Smith Nightingale for not being the intellectual or moral equal of her husband and daughters, she did not give up on breastfeeding without a fight. Her notes indicate that she tried to get her milk flowing by employing a host of mammals to suck on her breasts—forcefully. Though some mystery surrounds this event, it appears she enlisted women, children, babies and, finally, puppies in the effort to get her breasts producing.[6]

Fanny caved after about two weeks of starving her baby and hired a wet nurse. Once Parthe had a professional nipple, she nursed as if her life depended on it. As it did. Though small, Parthenope was imbued with a fierce life force. Unfortunately, the ongoing saga of haves and have nots played out on this stage. While Parthenope drank deeply and grew strong, the wet nurse's own child, Antonio, weakened and died. While we don't know that Antonio's cause of death was inadequate nutrition, it troubled Fanny enough that she may have tried to breastfeed him herself, and she commemorated his brief life in her diary.[7]

Chapter 4

The Shore, Smith, and Nightingale Brew

Fanny and WEN made a stop in Paris on their way back to England. There they entertained two visitors: Fanny's brother, Ben, and WEN's sister, Mai. Mai was taken with Parthenope whom she described as like a kitten, lisping Italian, 'a pretty piquant little creature'.[1]

But Mai was much more interested in Fanny's charming brother, Benjamin. The instant magnetism between these two mirrored the adoration that brought WEN and Fanny together.

Ben and Mai probably thought, with some justice, that family approval would not be difficult to obtain. Why should either family object to their engagement when their sister and brother had married into the same families? Here Ben and Mai made an error, however.

Ben proposed to Mai without first asking her father for his permission. And evidently, it didn't occur to Mai that she should hold out until that formality had been applied. So she accepted Ben's proposal in Paris. Benjamin could easily have smoothed this over by asking for William Shore's permission to marry Mai upon their return to England. But Ben was a man of independent means who had made his own fortune. Upon the collapse of the Smith fortune, it was Ben who stepped in and provided for his sisters. He saw himself as the head of his own family, not as a child or teenager who had to ask his elders what to do next.

William Shore, however, was a man who believed in tradition, and he was deeply offended at being 'informed' of his daughter's engagement rather than petitioned for his approval. This should have been a small bump in a happy union, but the Shores never got over it and never forgave Ben. The engagement foundered as more family members came to oppose the marriage.

In 1821, the Nightingales returned from their honeymoon with two children in tow. The next year, William Shore died, and Mai's mother effectively kept Mai prisoner in their home, citing the conventions of

The newlyweds, now parents, still on their honeymoon, moved on to Florence, Italy where they rented a furnished house with the lovely name, 'Villa Colombaia'. This villa was beautifully situated in a park-like setting at the edge of Florence.

It was here that Florence Nightingale came into the world on 12 May 1880, named for the city where she was born. Fanny hired a wet nurse from the start. So Florence thrived immediately. The young couple had fewer fears surrounding her infancy than they had with Parthenope.

Unlike 'Parthenope', which was very unusual, the name 'Florence' would ring true to most people as a girl's name though it was not a fashionable one. It would have sounded, to nineteenth-century ears, about as old fashioned and laden with mythological baggage as it does to us.

However joyful a second child was to the Nightingale family, there had to be some despair that Florence was another girl and not a boy. There is no doubt that Fanny and WEN adored their daughters, but a son would have secured the Nightingale estate which was not owned, but merely borrowed from whatever male heir would come to own it on WEN's death.

Of course, the young couple could not have known that they would produce no further children. And history has closed the door on any explanation for that. It is possible that Fanny's two difficult deliveries, under less than ideal circumstances, took a toll on her. She might have survived an infection or two that made her infertile.

mourning. Mai longed to go see the Smiths where she might have reunited with Ben. But she didn't have the fortitude to flout her mother's demands.

WEN's return to his native Derbyshire, in the wake of William Shore's death, was a comfort to his surviving relatives, especially his mother and his sister Mai who was, as yet, stranded by the failure of her engagement to Benjamin Smith.

In 1822, WEN began work on what would be one of his greatest accomplishments: the construction of a house that mirrored his personality and convictions. The Nightingale estate in Derbyshire featured a ramshackle home called 'Lea Hall' that was in disrepair. WEN decided not to invest his wealth in turning it into a house suitable for a gentleman. Instead, he retained it as a farmhouse and bought up a considerable amount of land in the surrounding area. Here, he would build his dream home, using a two-storey house that Mad Peter had bought, as the foundation. Lea Hurst, as it came to be called, was built around the original small house overlooking the Derwent River. WEN admired the original home's mullioned windows and installed more of them into the expansion.[2]

Lea Hurst was ahead of its time. It blended principles of later architectural trends such as Frank Lloyd Wright's usonianism and the Leadership in Energy and Environmental Design (LEED) principle of using local materials. Lea Hurst was a humble dwelling in comparison to the manors and castles that men of similar wealth built. In constructing Lea Hurst, WEN used the same grey stone, called Ashover Grit, that was used to build less grand homes in the area. The building materials were one with the facade. There was no pretentious veneer to convey that this was the home of a great gentleman.

WEN was approximately a hundred years ahead of Frank Lloyd Wright who pioneered the idea that a house should blend into the landscape rather than making a stark horizontal statement to contrast with it.

WEN also pioneered the idea of privacy in home construction. Homes of that time were generally built on or very near a road. This had the effect of making them available for admiration by lesser families. But it was also practical. Deliveries to the home of food and other goods were easier if the house was on a right of way. But WEN built his statement home well off the road. In doing so, he sacrificed practicality for architectural seclusion that would be highly coveted in decades to come. Lea Hurst was, literally, invisible from the road that led to it.

Lea Hurst also reflects WEN's unitarianism. Its design was simple, minimally ornamented, and functional, with clean lines. It was a scholar's house, the home of someone whose joys would be of the intellect rather than the frivolous and social. It was the home of someone who would nurture and devote himself to his immediate family, not squander his resources on 'society', someone who would invest not just money, but the gift of time into cultivating two amazing daughters.

The lack of ostentation at Lea Hurst did not fully extend to the interior. WEN furnished the home with ornate and heavy Italianate furniture of his own design. He hired Italian craftsmen to build it. His taste in furniture may have leaned toward pretension, but these pieces have survived the centuries in excellent condition and are still used by WEN's descendants today. They were built for a longevity mostly unheard of in modern manufacturing. It was upon and among these solidly-built moveables that the small child, Parthenope, would frolic.

Despite the dramatic architectural innovations of Lea Hurst, biographers agree that its best features were its view and its landscaping. WEN had many, many acres on which to build, and the spot he chose was a full day's carriage ride from his mother's house and two and a half miles from his Aunt Elizabeth Evans' home. Close enough that WEN could engage his family on a regular basis, but not so close as to encourage any relatives to spontaneously drop in for a cup of tea.

Every writer who takes on the Nightingale family agrees that Lea Hurst's vantage was magnificent. Novelist Elizabeth Gaskell described it as a haven in the clouds. Outside the house and facing downhill were terraces loaded with flowers, allowed to grow in a jumble, rather than laid out formally. A staircase allowed family and visitors several points of view on these masses of hollyhocks, geraniums, and nasturtiums, flowers that come back annually and require minimal nurturing. This gorgeous garden gave way to a meadow which, in turn, gave access to woodland and from there, the bank of the Derwent River which yielded another majestic view of ranging hills.

WEN had grown up in this natural world and the cloud formations and stiff winds and moors would have seemed familiar and comforting to him. However, Fanny was not at home or happy in this beautiful, remote, and often chilly setting. Furthermore, when it came to day-tripping, Derbyshire offered more in the way of lead smelting plants and mills than scenic views that would attract an artist or a picnicking family.

To be fair, the grand but rugged beauties of Derbyshire may have formed a hard contrast to the warmth and colours of Italy and France where the Nightingales had spent a year. Furthermore, Lea Hurst, delightful in summer and late spring, had no central heating. Residents of these northern homes dressed in multiple layers to keep warm and relied on carpets, window fabrics, and fireplaces to keep warm through the winter months. This is, in part, why the kitchen, which was the domain of the servants, was often the most comfortable and cosy part of the house. That's where the stove was, and meal making would keep the mainstay of the servants' quarter warm throughout most of the day. Also, having a reason to keep moving would help stave off hyperthermia.

Furthermore, if it snowed, the family was essentially locked down until it melted. The roads were unnavigable when snow-covered.

Derbyshire was WEN's childhood home, not Fanny's, and it was near his family, not hers. But what may have convinced WEN that Lea Hurst was not a suitable winter home was the health of his daughters. The Nightingales spent one winter in Lea Hurst after it was built. During that time, Parthenope and Florence were often sick with coughs and colds. By today's standards, this was no place to raise a child. No doctor could access the estate if a child was sick and there was snow on the ground.

Fanny was also used to more of a social scene than what Lea Hurst and its remoteness provided. Parthenope's mother had been much less isolated in continental Europe where British expats frequently got together and kept company. Because of Fanny's famous MP father, these expat communities had welcomed her with open arms.

Yet another source of unhappiness for Fanny was the dislike of her mother-in-law. Mrs Shore was a textbook thorn in the side of Parthenope's mother. Like mothers-in-law everywhere, she did not see in her daughter-in-law what her son saw. Would Mary Shore have thought any woman was good enough for her William? We can only guess. But it definitely was not Fanny.

Mrs Shore never got over the fact that Fanny was six years older than William or that she had been previously engaged to a man very different from WEN. Though Fanny was solidly born into a family of dissenters, her love of creature comforts and a wide circle of friends didn't endear her to William's mother either. Such a creature had entrapped Mrs Shore's son, she estimated.[3] And now she gave him only daughters, no son who could inherit the family emblem or consolidated wealth. Also, it was bitterly clear to Mary Shore that the Smith family was poaching another member of the Shore family, WEN's sister, Mai.

Like WEN, Mai adored Fanny. Mai saw Fanny much the way WEN saw her: charming, lively, beautiful, smart, and a great conversationalist who could talk easily on a wide range of subjects without developing any serious passions to which she would have to commit more than words.

And, really, Mai had every reason to love Fanny. Fanny was, in fact, conspiring with Mai to get the latter out of Mary Shore's house. First, there was the failed engagement to Benjamin, Fanny's brother. Undaunted, Fanny would manage, in 1827, to marry Mai off to her other brother, Samuel, a respectable lawyer, though not a man of wealth.[4]

The Samuel/Mai marriage suited a lot of people, though Mrs Shore was not one of them. Ultimately, though, she did not stand in the way. This union got Mary (Mai) away from a tyrannical mother and into a home that would be truly her own. It also gave her an opportunity to have a son who could then inherit the Nightingale estate and keep it close to the Smith family.

Chapter 5

Embley

WEN might have dug into a scholar's life year-round at Derbyshire, if he had married a different woman. However, it did not suit his still-young wife, Fanny, to winter there. And he could not but notice the hostility of his mother to his beloved wife. Though it must have pained him to move away from Derbyshire, he was a modern man, a feminist of sorts long before that word would be invented, and he was, by all accounts, desperately in love with his wife.

So he spent the better part of a year scouting for locations where his family could live in the winter and spring. He seems to have been largely motivated by Fanny's preferences for he landed on a region with a view of the sea, near several families that were friends with the Smiths, and across the water from Fanny's ancestral home, the Isle of Wight. There were also plenty of hunting opportunities for William and fellow gentlemen to hunt with, in the land that WEN obtained.

This was Embley Park in Hampshire which William bought in 1825. It was satisfyingly rural but with amenities that suited both WEN and Fanny and with a better climate for the children and Fanny. There was, at that time, no polluting manufacture in Hampshire to spoil the beauties of nature for the Nightingale family.

The Embley house itself was a more traditional structure than Lea Hurst. It was Georgian in design and didn't feature any radical elements like harmony with its setting. As she grew, Parthenope would come to love Embley more than Lea Hurst, though she sketched both of them. Parthenope loved the colours of Embley. Flowers bloomed there nearly year-round, the azaleas of spring giving way to the roses and lilies of summer. In her concern for the plight of the poor, Parthenope also saw Embley as ideally located. Its riches flowed easily to the poorest families living nearby.

Here was a place where Fanny could entertain. And she did. She hosted hunting field trips for dozens of families. The men would eat a good breakfast in the morning and traipse off to the woods with their guns, returning only when the dark or their hunger made it impossible to continue. The wives who accompanied these gentlemen would spend their days indoors, sipping tea and entertaining each other with good conversation.[1]

Parthenope and Florence learned their love of books and the great outdoors from their father. But they learned their people skills from Fanny Nightingale. When Parthenope was a young child, her mother was busily establishing the Nightingales as a national force. Fanny Nightingale, née Smith was unapologetic about wanting to establish herself and her household as one of the prominent families of England.

And, without their tireless, social-climbing mother, Florence and Parthenope might well not have had the opportunities they were offered. If she had not been from one of Britain's most influential families, would Parthenope have married Sir Verney? Would she have commanded the attention of prominent magazine and book publishers? Would Florence Nightingale have been offered the opportunity to take a highly-publicized role in the Crimean War if her mother had not been such an accomplished and determined social climber? We can't know the answers to these questions of course. But we do know that history books covering the eighteenth and nineteenth centuries in Britain follow the wealthy and noble families. Those privileged few ran the country, owned most of the land, and made the rules via election to Parliament.

So, when Fanny determined to entertain and be entertained by influential English families, she was, surely, setting the stage for her daughter's successes even though they would both disappoint her in one way or another.

By 1825, the Nightingales had established their routine: Julys, Augusts, and Octobers in WEN's beloved Lea Hurst where he could tend to his mother, the rest of the year in Embley with frequent trips to London, especially in September, where they would stay at a nice hotel. No power couple can rise to social prominence without spending several weeks a year in London. There, Fanny would, in time, present her daughters 'to society'.

After they settled in Embley as their main residence, the marriage of WEN and Fanny started to show some fine cracks. Fanny often went to nearby spa towns (called bath towns at that time), presumably for her health. But such spas were mostly the refuge of wealthy wives who had the means to buy time away from their families without sacrificing any respectability. For his part, WEN often took refuge in his library or at his club in London, two spots that were understood to be sacred, where he was not to be disturbed.

There is a suggestion that Fanny nagged, and a note to her in which WEN asks her, effectively, to 'chill out': 'If I cut a tree, however wrongfully, … disturb not yourself as if I were … destroying what is essential to your existence'. This note goes on to express the view that they should really overlook each other's foibles as much as possible. WEN, in other words, felt a little hen-pecked.[2]

The nineteenth century was amazingly lenient toward couples who spent vast amounts of time apart. When the man of the house went on a three-week hunting trip by himself, no one asked if his marriage was on the rocks. He would not have to declare that he had his wife's permission to do this. Similarly, when a woman of some wealth went, 'for her health', to a village or town by the ocean, no one marked it as a 'separate vacation' that showed the failure of the marriage. To the eyes of their friends and family, the fact that the Nightingale pursuits often led WEN and Fanny in different directions was not the least untoward.

Such couples frequently had their own quarters, even their own bedrooms, and it would occur to no one to question whether they still had a sex life together. What, today, we mark as secrecy and prudery gave couples a wide latitude to structure their marriage as best suited them. Husbands, in particular, benefitted from this freedom.

But women, too, could get some enjoyment from the amount of independence they were granted to run things at home without impediment. The absence of a demanding husband gave some lucky women the space they needed to write, draw, paint, and be creative. (Of course, this refers only to the privileged classes, people who derived what we call a 'passive income'. They occupied a very thin stratum at the pinnacle of the social food chain. There was, ironically, more equality among men and women in the remainder of society. Both men and women in the less ethereal classes had to work, often long grinding hours. And they had no option but to endure the intimacy that small, shared spaces impose.)

During her early childhood in Embley, Parthenope and her sister were frequently watched over by Mai, WEN's beloved sister and Fanny's sister-in-law. We can see that, even at a very young age, there were differences between Parthe and Florence.

For example, Mai enjoyed babysitting both girls, even after her own children came along. But she became increasingly attached to Florence. This attachment solidified when Florence had a bad case of whooping cough which managed to last a year. Mai took in Flo to prevent the transmission of the infection to Parthenope.

Julia Smith, Fanny's sister, made a sketch of WEN, Parthe, and Flo walking together. In this sketch, Parthenope insists on contact with her father. She seems to be holding on to his clothing, while Florence strides at his side, independent and very much her own woman, already.[3]

The two girls were often apart, but they were never alone. And they always had multiple layers of supervision. They had a full-time nurse, Frances Gale. Beyond that, there was always a family member assigned to keep special watch on the Nightingale daughters. If Fanny was away, then one of her sisters or another aunt would keep special care over the Nightingale's most precious cargo. The girls didn't even sleep alone. They either shared a bed with each other, or each shared the bed of another female relative. Until she was eleven years old, Parthenope did not even brush her own hair.

Fanny's theory of parenting included the still common presumption that children need to stay busy at all waking hours. That may be why Florence described the year she spent with whooping cough as the best year of her childhood. While it would be easy to dismiss this as an early sign of hypochondria, it seems likely that Florence needed much more time for reflection than she got as Fanny's child. The year of solitude finally provided a break from the constant bustle and activity.

The Nightingales were sorry they did not have more children. Only two offspring made them a small family among their set. By contrast, Mai and Sam had four children. Fanny, who grew up in a whole tribe of siblings, seems to have been quite determined that Parthenope and Florence would have the huge family experience. To that end, Pop and Flo were frequently surrounded by cousins. Their closest cousins were, of course, those of Sam and Mai. Because the two Shore/Nightingale siblings had married two Smith siblings, these were 'double cousins', i.e. cousins on both the mother's and father's line.

However, there were many other cousins who filled the halls of Embley with laughter and tumbles. Parthenope and Florence frequently consorted with the children of their Aunt Anne and her husband, George Nicholson; the children of Fanny's brother, Octavius, and his wife Joan; and the children of the Bonham Carter family, of which Fanny's sister, Joanna Maria Smith was the matriarch. (Joanna Maria Bonham Carter's direct descendent, famed actress Helena Bonham Carter, is a distant cousin of Parthenope and Florence Nightingale. Some people think Helena Bonham Carter has striking physical similarities to her ancestor Florence.

By contrast, the children of Fanny's wealthy brother, Benjamin, were never invited to Embley nor to meet Parthenope and Florence. Ben's five children were the fruit of his unmarried alliance with Anne Longden. This was considered scandalous, and Ben's children were kept at a long arm's length.[4]

While they were growing up in Embley and Lea Hurst, it is clear that family members already favoured Florence over Parthenope. Florence often travelled with her mother. Florence was allowed to go hunting with her father, though both girls learned to ride. Mai was enamoured with Florence more than Parthenope. Florence played hard and imaginatively with her cousins, especially the boys, while Parthenope often retreated to a couch because she wasn't feeling well.

Despite Parthenope's imperfect health, there were undeniable privileges to being a child of WEN and Fanny Smith. Parthenope and Florence got to live in two beautiful parts of England, the hills and moors of the north and the meadows and seafront of Embley Park.

Both their parents were fans of exercise. Both girls were under orders to take at least two walks a day, often three. Parthenope and Florence were considered skinny, and the walks were supposed to cure skinniness. The concept of calories and how they are burned was not yet understood, any more than germ theory. Luckily, skinny children are often healthy children.

The sisters also did callisthenics. When, as a child, Parthenope injured one of her arms, a doctor prescribed specific arm exercises. These were hard to do and caused her pain.[5] It's possible that she had an undiagnosed broken bone or ligament tear, but one of her governesses accused her of malingering when she resisted doing the prescribed exercise.

Except for weeks spent in London, they were exposed to none of the toxins that accompany industry or human crowding. They had access to medical care and regular trips to the dentist, though these often resulted in tooth extractions at a young age for Parthenope, rather than the less invasive treatments of contemporary dentistry.

They also grew up in two houses with books. They learned to read early and devoured the books that Fanny approved for them. Both girls were encouraged to engage with the world actively by writing down their thoughts and making sketches. We can see that Parthenope, in particular, was a highly talented artist from her sketches of both the Nightingale homes. Florence was already writing complete narratives by the time she was six.

Chapter 6

Educating the Titans

Many of the Nightingale daughters' projects could be called 'citizen science'. They pressed and identified flowers and carefully labelled them in scrapbooks. This way, they developed a keen understanding of the specific botany of Derbyshire and Hampshire. They also collected shells from the seashore and catalogued these. Under the supervision of their family, they were allowed to raise silkworms and experiment with the cultivation of plants. Florence was even indulged in the raising of a baby mouse family which she swaddled and attempted to bottle feed.

Parthenope and Florence were, in other words, deeply immersed in the natural world, not in the passive way of today's students whose experience of the natural world might be limited to a one-day field trip. And they did not just observe. They were largely self-taught amateur scientists. If Parthenope or Florence ever heard the word, 'no', it was not often in reference to the natural world. In their pursuit of messy, untidy truth and science, they were unusually well indulged, perhaps because they had to be both sons and daughters to an interesting couple of people.

Both girls also engaged the local farm folk and tradesmen in conversation, and they developed keen ears for regional dialects which would be invaluable to Parthenope as a novelist who strove to capture the minutiae of country life outside her social circle.

Fanny used a rather ingenious learning method to make sure that her daughters didn't let their minds drift during church services. She required them to take notes on the sermon. This, of course, meant that the girls would further their understanding of the way narratives and arguments are structured. The girls would also have to absorb theological tenants along the way. They both also learned the requisite basic piano skills that were expected of young ladies.

Many people would argue that the informal education that Parthenope and Florence received was the best kind. They learned by doing and engaging their subject matter. Their original research into flora and fauna kept it interesting where learning from textbooks is so often boring.

Educational theorists, from John Dewey to Maria Montessori, have shown beyond a shadow of a doubt that the learning children do with their hands and minds is far more formative than any straight-up book learning. Parthenope and Florence had two tremendous advantages: a well-endowed library and the opportunity to do field work which frequently involved raising wildlife of some sort or another. Short of being able to dissect a human body, it's hard to imagine how two children could have gotten a more practical and meaningful education in anatomy and zoology.

How did Parthenope and Florence get along? Like other siblings, they often bickered and even quarrelled. But they also had a keen understanding of relationship dynamics at an early age. One of Florence's very early drawings illustrates this.

The drawing represents two social dynamics between Parthenope and Florence, one in which the two girls are clearly in conflict. They are standing up, and Parthenope is leaning Into Florence who is leaning back, presumably in an effort to avoid her. Parthenope is saying, 'You nasty thing!' Florence replies, 'I won't give it to you.' Though it isn't obvious from the sketch, the object of Parthe's anger is probably a mislaid book or other belonging that Florence has recovered.[1]

In the same drawing, the second panel shows the same two stick figures in peaceful, loving companionship. They are seated, side by side, and Parthe says, 'Thank you, dear,' to which Florence immediately replies, 'You're very welcome.' However didactic and a little patronizing toward Parthenope this drawing might be, it does show that Florence had a precocious sense of how to prevent escalation of conflict.

Like other highly imaginative children, Parthe and Flo were daydreamers, and this daydreaming often resulted in lost objects, well into adulthood. In just a few pages of Lynn MacDonald's *Collected Works of Florence Nightingale*, we see Florence searching for her cape, her bag, her Venetian chain, and then anxiously asking Parthenope if she has lost her keys.

At an early age, the girls read the Bible on their own. Parthenope read the work of William Gilpin, an Anglican minister who was also a writer and artist.² In 1782, Gilpin published a lavishly illustrated book titled, *Observations on the River Wye and several parts of South Wales, etc. relative chiefly to Picturesque Beauty*; made in the summer of the year 1770. In this book, Gilpin put forth the notes on his travels in the Lake District and also his theory of the 'picturesque'. Today, Gilpin is better known for some foot-in-mouth moments, especially when he said that the ruins of Tintern Abbey would be more picturesque if someone took a sledgehammer to them.

However, there is no doubt that Gilpin had a formative influence on the mind and eventual career of Parthenope Nightingale. His medium was watercolour, and he wrote a great deal about what made a picture beautiful. His influences were other landscape artists. In spending time on Gilpin, Parthenope got some informal training as an artist and illustrator. Later, she would put her observations about art into a series of articles for contemporary periodicals.

Though Florence was often more beloved than Parthenope, their mother feared Florence was not growing up to be an appropriate young lady. Florence was precocious and innovative at a very young age. She was also full of enthusiasm and vigour. She had opinions of her own, one of which was that her wealthy family should do more for the poor. Florence, at six years of age, was a budding communist. She took seriously that verse in the Bible that says it's easier for a camel to pass through the eye of a needle than for a rich man to get into heaven. Parthenope also held precocious moral opinions, but she did not express them as vehemently as her sister.

Therefore, it was Florence that Fanny cracked down on. Fanny may have been angry over some of Florence's offhand remarks. At an early age, Flo knew the word 'booby' and didn't hesitate to use it on relatives.³

Alternatively, Fanny may have been scared. Would such a precocious and outspoken daughter grow up to be the charming but prim young lady who would attract an eligible suitor? The work of women was to marry and have children. Fanny could not foresee any other career for either of her daughters.

Whatever her reason, Fanny resorted to hiring a governess who took it upon herself to 'tame' Florence. The advent of Sarah Christie in 1827 was a bleak period in the life of Florence. Christie immediately favoured

Parthenope, the more docile child, and insisted on the same style of docility from Florence. Parthenope observed this double standard, and it pained her, especially when she looked back on it as an adult. The grown-up Parthenope would blame Christie for Florence's introversion which Parthenope dates to the time that Christie entered their home.

Though both Parthenope and Florence were academically gifted, Christie had little interest in teaching. Actual instruction took up only two, or, at the most, three hours of the day.

The rest of the time, Christie freely tyrannized her charges. She was quite ferocious that their characters should reflect Christie's own ideas of how a child should behave.[4] And she didn't think very far outside the 'children should be seen and not heard' box. The 'Christie plan' for Florence and Parthenope often involved requiring Florence to sit still in a chair which would have been very boring for someone whose brain cells were firing at such a fast pace.

On her visits to see Parthe and Flo, Aunt Mai grew suspicious of the Christie curriculum. She wrote a very tactful letter to Fanny suggesting a more laissez-faire style of child-rearing. In this letter, Mai recommends that Florence should be left more to her own devices. Mai also gave Christie a copy of *L'Ami des Enfans*, a book by Arnaud Berquin that suggests learning could be combined with fun. Mai also, with more success, arranged a little vacation at the Bonham Carters' house which got Florence away from Christie. This visit started out well, but as the months wore on, Florence felt abandoned. One good thing that came out of this separation was that the sisters appear to have renewed their affection for one another.

Despite Mai's attempted intervention, the regime of Christie lasted at least two and a half years. It ended only when Christie formed an engagement with a wealthy German. Fanny was dismayed by Christie's abdication of her role, but WEN did not allow another governess to take her place. He may, after all, have had some idea how damaging the reign of Christie had been.[5]

Biographer Gillian Gill posits that it was the cruel reign of Christie that alienated Florence from her family in an irrevocable manner. As such, the Christie period would also have deeply impacted Parthenope, perhaps not at the time, but when, as an adult, she did not have access to her beloved sister.[6]

By 1831, the sisters were reunited, and so began an eight-year spell of intense sisterly devotion, catalyzed, perhaps, by Flo's stated commitment to being a loving sister. These were intensely lived years for Parthenope, who bathed herself in the love of her brilliant and beautiful little sister and in their renewed freedom to learn at their own fast paces without the strictures of a narrow-minded governess.

The year 1831 also saw the birth of William Shore Smith, the son of Mai and Sam Smith. His family called him 'Shore' which was also his mother's maiden name. The Nightingales and Smiths breathed a huge sigh of collective relief. Finally, there was a male heir to the Nightingale estates and fortune. The Nightingales would, themselves, have preferred to produce their own male heir. Having failed to do so, however, it would come as a tremendous comfort that the estate could now pass through Parthenope's aunt and uncle to her cousin. Florence and Parthenope could be reasonably sure that they would not be abandoned to poverty after WEN's death.

After the Christie reign of terror, WEN took over the education of his daughters. It may, among other things, have provided WEN with a refuge from his wife. As we have seen, WEN and Fanny Smith Nightingale embarked on what seemed, to many, a match made in heaven. For WEN, in particular, it was a love match. However, after many years and two children, their differences in temperament had emerged. Fanny was relentlessly ambitious and social. And she was quick to find fault with the immediate members of her family, especially WEN and Florence.

WEN, meanwhile, cherished peace and solitude. He wished always to nurture his intellect. He was intellectually curious and had a natural inclination for science which he passed on to his daughters. And he had the clarity to see that his daughters were the only people in his extended family who would ever match him intellectually. (Unless we count the unorthodox Benjamin Smith who fathered at least seven illegitimate children with two women. The women in his family felt, perhaps with some justice, that it was a little dangerous to have him around.)

By educating his daughters far beyond Victorian expectations, WEN could provide himself with companions who would be his intellectual equals. And teaching his girls gave him a reprieve from his wife and her social pursuits for several hours a day.

In 1834, WEN took some time off from homeschooling to run for Parliament. Parthenope, then a teenager, was very excited about his news; she believed he would win. Finally, her brilliant father would have some actual worldly work to do. He would have influence outside the home. He would be placed to bring about positive change.

It was the first and only time WEN would attempt a seat in government. He was either very naive, or his run was meant to be merely a token. He was not prepared to go to the mattresses or anywhere close to them. At that time, it was customary for would-be MPs to bribe their voters directly, and WEN declined to do so. So he was easily beaten by candidates who were not above bribery.

Nevertheless, his loss was a disappointment to both Fanny and Parthenope. Parthe, in particular, had hoped that having a father in Parliament would mean more time for her in London. Such was not to be.

WEN was free to continue educating his daughters. One of the obvious benefits of homeschooling is that one can play directly to a child's obvious intellectual gifts while refraining from wasting time on things she will never be good at.

If anyone is in doubt that the Nightingale children were verbal adepts at a young age, know that Florence Nightingale basically invented Boggle which she encouraged Parthenope to play.[7] In a letter to Parthenope, Florence excitedly describes the game. Parthenope is to use two assigned phrases, 'gay ones' and 'great help', and make as many words and phrases out of the letters in those phrases as possible. Florence goes on to specify that the new phrases need not contain all the letters, but the new resultant phrases cannot cheat and repeat any letters. Boggle rules, in other words. And, conveniently, there was already a set of paper letters available to Parthenope to get her started.

When WEN observed that his daughters were already near fluent in French and that they knew some Latin, he added Italian lessons. After all, both girls were born in Italy and given Italian place names. It was only fitting. The girls were frequently assigned to translate the classics. At one point, Parthenope was assigned to translate the entire first canto of Dante's Inferno as part of her day-to-day learning. This kind of intense linguistic work would prove valuable to Parthenope, whose life work would be writing.

To French, Italian, and Latin, WEN then added Greek to his daughters' educational schedule. By the time they were nineteen, Parthenope and Florence could pull books by Homer and Aristotle off the shelves of their father's library and read them in the original language, not just with understanding, but with the ability to form and discuss ideas about them.

Learning Greek put the education of Parthenope on an equal footing with any boy enrolled at one of the elite British private schools, such as Eton or Harrow. From the point of view of the centuries, it would appear that Greek itself was less formative on the intellect than the Greek writers. Parthenope and Florence studied Plato, in part because their father emphasized it. We should not underestimate the influence of Plato on a young mind, especially a girl's, at a time when the main education of girls would be in the arts and religion. Plato opens the world of social dynamics, politics, and the question of what humans owe to each other, which will always be one of the most compelling questions for humanity.

Plato's Republic introduces the idea that government could be better, that institutions could be reformed. And it introduces these ideas in the form of a fictional narrative. It's little wonder that Parthenope developed a talent for narrative and placing ideas about social justice into fiction.[8]

Florence pulled ahead of Parthenope in Greek, possibly because the mathematical nature of the language challenged her in a way that the romance languages failed to do.[9] In WEN's mind, Greek was the pinnacle of academic achievement. It was the language of Homer, Socrates, Aristotle. Even though Parthenope far surpassed Florence in French, her inability to keep neck and neck with Florence in this new endeavour was a sign for WEN. He believed Parthenope was not working as hard as Florence, and he said as much to his younger daughter. He broke the news to Parthenope, in a letter, that she need not bother to continue her education any further. Surely she had matters to attend to that were more consistent with her merry and infantile temperament. In this letter, he betrayed that he didn't know her age. Was it fifteen or sixteen, he asked.

Parthenope had not seen this coming, and it was a shock. To a girl who was just as ambitious intellectually as her sister, the sting was harsh. Here her father basically said that she was wasting her time with academic learning, and he labelled her a merry infant.

Florence had an advantage over Parthenope. She had a sense of what she wanted from a very young age. She wanted an advanced education much more than she wanted to develop the ladylike arts of dressing, conversation, and music. By the time she was in her teens, she was already specializing in mathematics and science. Her sense of destiny was strong and amazingly accurate.

Parthenope did not appear so uniquely ambitious, nor so eccentric, as a child. She sought to win her mother's approval as much as her father's. She was willing and able to be all things to all people. We have already seen that she cosied up to a tyrannical governess. When she was still a teenager, Parthenope showed no profound indication that she sought a future well outside the boundaries of what was customary for well brought up English ladies.

Parthenope, herself, was not ready to be dismissed from her father's instruction or his company. When he dumped her as a student, she knew she was being robbed, and she protested to the best of her abilities, writing to WEN that she considered the discontinuation of her studies to be a severe punishment.

The likely truth is that WEN just wanted to devote himself to Florence, in whom he saw a mind like his own: scientific, exacting, mathematical. He had less use for Parthenope's talents. Her tremendous ability for naturalistic fiction and historical biography, which would emerge as an adult, was not then apparent to him or anyone else.

There is no doubt that Parthenope and Florence were a bonded pair in childhood and in their teen years. But what we learn from pair bonds in the animal world is that one littermate is always more dependent on the bond. One littermate could make it on her own, one could not, at least not with outside help. Parthenope needed Florence more than Florence needed her. This dependency was reinforced all the times that Parthenope fell sick and Florence took care of her. Parthenope was also more emotionally dependent on her sister, which some biographers have interpreted as selfishness, especially when Parthe protested Florence's departure from home.

In 1836, Parthenope became very sick with a wracking cough and fever. Though it is dangerous to diagnose someone who is no longer alive, many signs suggest that this illness left Parthenope with an autoimmune disorder, similar to rheumatoid arthritis which attacks extremities, especially hands and is also systemic and progressive. She never fully recovered her health after this bout with infection. Her mother believed she would die, and she hired a local doctor, one Biddone, to 'treat' Parthenope.

We must understand that this was an era that had not discovered germs, much less antibiotics. While Florence Nightingale did not launch the germ theory, she eventually endorsed it, late in life. Parthenope's illness, therefore, would have been seen as a dysfunction of the humours which resided in the blood.

The treatment for bad humors was bleeding and blistering. Leeches were applied to patients to drink their blood. Hot cups were applied to the skin, and the consequent puckering was thought to be therapeutic. Parthenope was an underweight young woman. She must, we know, have had a strong constitution and will because she survived, not just the influenza, but also the treatment, a treatment which had basically killed Lord Byron twelve years earlier.

Parthenope became the family invalid. She was never as strong as she had been previously. She contracted infections and viruses far too easily because of her weakened immune system. She was now separated from Florence even more often. If there were infection in the house, Parthenope would be sent away to keep her from catching it.

There seems to be a close connection between Parthenope's apparent fragility and Florence's determination to become a nurse. Though Florence nursed many other sick family members, Parthenope was her principal patient prior to her service in the Crimea.

Chapter 7

Second Tour of Europe

In 1837, the Nightingale family began their second grand tour of Europe, the first that the girls would actually remember. There were several purposes for this tour. Mainly, the Nightingales needed to relocate while their beloved Embley underwent extensive renovations, including the addition of six bedrooms and new kitchens. The enlarged house would accommodate a staff of fifteen servants.

With bedrooms for as many as five visiting couples at one time, the expanded Embley would finally meet Fanny's expectations for dominating the social scene in England. WEN also designed a bookcase that hid a secret door leading to his library. In creating a bolt hole for himself alone, he may have anticipated that he would not be able to keep pace with his wife's inexhaustible social energy. It was also hoped that this vacation would put the finishing touch on the education of Parthenope and Florence.

For this trip, WEN put his design skills to work again. He had a carriage custom-built with what we would call 'extras' to make the family more comfortable. The carriage was designed to allow for reading, writing, and informal dining while on the road. Designed to seat twelve people, this land yacht required a minimum of four horses to draw it. It had reasonably comfortable seats on the roof where WEN would sit. Florence and Parthenope took turns sitting next to him and enjoying the unencumbered view. Their horses were steered by postillions on horseback.

They were a large, unwieldy party of travellers who brought along a French maid, to tend to Fanny, as well as Mrs. Gale, the family nurse. Gale hated travel, but she hated being parted from the Nightingales even more, and she had accompanied them on their honeymoon.

The first stop on their trip was Le Havre. Then they made short visits to several tourist destinations in France, including Chartres. They attempted to cross the Pyrenees and enter Spain but the rugged roads and terrible poverty discouraged them, and they turned back.

They passed the Christmas and New Year holidays in Nice. Here is, perhaps, the first indication that Parthenope would, for some years, fail at the business of marriage. Florence's letters name one Mr Plunkett that caught Parthe's fancy. She hoped to dance with him at one of the many expat events. But he made himself unavailable for that exercise.[1]

Later, in Genoa, the sisters were able to go to the opera for the first time. In the Victorian era, the opera was much like a rock concert today, a place where grand passions were acted out in public by larger-than-life celebrities. Parthenope and Florence saw Lucrezia Borgia, Don Giovanni, and Mercadante's Il Giuramento. Young ladies were generally sheltered from even the most sublimated expressions of sexual passion, and a night at the opera was a rare exception to this rule. These operas must have opened quite a window on human experience for Parthenope and her sister.

Parthenope spoke fluent French and was frequently told, by the locals, that she had no annoying English accent. Her mother, Fanny, wondered, out loud in a letter, why she and Florence were not more 'admired'. Parthenope, Fanny noted, charmed everyone everywhere she went, and was 'the world's pet'.[2] But there were no declarations of love or marriage proposals or offers to visit Embley from any of the single young male expats.

The next stop in their itinerary was Florence, where Parthenope and Florence studied Italian, art, and music with cheap local tutors. But, in 1838, they again moved, this time to Geneva, Switzerland. It was in Geneva that Florence and Parthenope read the work of Jean-Charles-Leonard Sismondi. They also got to meet him in person because he was friends with WEN. Sismondi was a political scientist and philosopher whose influence on Parthenope should not be underestimated. He was a historian of the first magnitude. His history of Italy ran to sixteen volumes, then his history of France ran to twenty-nine volumes and took twenty-three years to write.

Sismondi was a radical thinker, and, today, we take for granted many of the institutions he espoused: unemployment benefits, health benefits, a limit to the number of working hours in a day and week, and retirement planning. His work identified the obvious flaws in a purely capitalist, laissez-faire system, unmitigated by what we today call the 'safety net'. His ideas influenced both Florence and Parthenope, but in Parthenope, they seriously took root.

Given that Parthenope's most ambitious work was the history of the Verneys, her future family by marriage, it's likely that Sismondi was her first role model for this kind of achievement. Parthe would also have been moved by Sismondi's personal generosity. He frequently gave money to the poor and even fed the mice who inhabited his rooms even though he was not a wealthy man.[3] He was one of those rare individuals who could reason on a global scale while never overlooking what was happening to the individuals right in front of him. This, too, was Parthenope's great talent.

Before the year was out, political turbulence caused the Nightingales to leave Switzerland and move to Paris. They rented an apartment on the Place Vendome. There, they made the acquaintance of Mary Clarke, a socialite and intellectual who ran a lively and diverse salon. Many of the most interesting minds of the age visited her lodgings. Though Clarke initially doubted whether the Nightingale ladies would contribute anything of interest to her gatherings, they won her over quickly, and she provided an entree to many entertainments.[4]

In her journal, Parthenope lavished praise on Clarke whom she valued as a fellow intellectual and egalitarian. Clarke's salon was not exclusive to ladies and gentlemen of her class, as was so common. Clarke didn't care how much wealth a guest had or didn't have, nor did she care about qualifications of birth and family history. She cared only that every guest contribute ideas to the near constant conversation that occurred in her apartment. Parthenope would absorb information about society from this lively cross-section.

Parthenope was hugely impressed by the Clarke salon.[5] It formed an ideal that Parthenope would later emulate when she became Lady Verney. Clarke and her mother frequently hosted famous socialites such as Jeanne Françoise Julie Adélaïde Récamier. But they also hosted Italian refugees such as Bianca Milesi, Princess Belgiojoso, Count Arrivabene, one of the Ferraris, and General Collegno. The details of this unique sanctuary for intellectuals were not lost on Parthenope. She noted the simplicity of how they made tea. The guest would help, putting the water kettle over a wood fire, amid the brass fire dogs.

The Clarkes and Nightingales formed such a close friendship that 'Clarky', as they called her, came to visit with the Nightingales at Embley or Lea Hurst for up to a month every year. Much later in her life, Parthenope reminisced about Clarke, the way she would curl up in a chair or on a sofa with a huge book on her knees.

Here was a woman who could socialize tirelessly, transforming herself, chameleon-like to suit every social situation. Everyone loved her, rich and poor, powerful and not, young and old. Yet, when not surrounded by company, she cherished her books.

In Mary Clarke, we see the kind of woman Parthenope herself was becoming and the kind of woman she wished to be, someone with rich mental resources, endlessly learning, challenging herself with difficult texts, but always ready to put down a book and prioritize the person who happened to be in the room.

Most of all, Parthenope cherished Clarke's 'trueness', something that, today, we would call authenticity. She admired the way Clarke would never just parrot an idea she had heard or read in a newspaper. All her opinions on politics, poetry, art, and literature were brewed in her own brain, after judicious reflection.

We see this same trueness in Parthenope. She never sought to hide her true feelings or opinions, even when she offended and created resentment in her family. For this, Parthenope has frequently been accused of interfering with Florence's destiny. But, from her point of view, it was dishonourable to be deceptive about one's character and feelings.

In Clarke, Parthenope also saw a destiny one might hope to avoid. By giving so much of her time to others, Clarke had made herself more of a dilettante than a woman of solid accomplishments. She had all the makings of a woman who could achieve something monumental, but her feeling for her friends and her desire to be helpful prevented her from putting her fine intellect to work.

Here we can see Parthenope's fear for herself. Would she ever be more than a well-read, sociable, likeable woman who always had time for others? Clarky was at the same time a model of a well-fed intellect and also a warning to those who wanted to do more than talk.

Clarke's salon was ragingly successful, and her friendships were international, but she showed little inclination to build something of her own. Parthenope's ambitions were greater. Book learning was not enough.

Being a brilliant conversationalist was not enough. Like Florence, she needed achievements that went beyond entertaining her family and circle of acquaintances. She would not settle for simply understanding and discussing the issues of her day. She must take action.

The novelist George Sand was alive and well and living in France at the time the Nightingales visited. They did not meet her in person. By the standards of that day, Sand was scandalous. She wore men's clothes, took lovers, and made no effort to be respectable. Her novels, by contrast, were conventional, if not a little smarmy, but she did make an effort to capture the lives of rural people. Fanny Nightingale allowed her daughters to read these books; there was no reason to prevent it. To read a George Sand novel is to understand how little of the author's originality made it into her writing.

Nevertheless, these books would have had a formative influence on Parthenope. She would undertake similar subjects: rural communities, social dynamics among those who farmed and lived in cottages, rather than splendid apartments or manses.

It seems likely, however, that the Nightingale sisters were more inspired by the life of George Sand than by her fiction. In Sand, whose real name was Amandine Aurore Dupin, Florence saw a woman who could live independently of marriage and apart from her family. Parthe would see a woman whose principal occupation was writing and fictionalizing her understanding of social dynamics, a woman with ties to royalty and yet not defined and curtailed by the stratum of society into which birth had landed her.

In 1839, the Nightingales returned to England. WEN made his way to Embley where he oversaw the last stages of his extensive renovation. The ladies spent May and June doing a London 'season'. They rented a floor of the Carlton Hotel for this purpose. Parthenope had turned twenty-one in April.

At this point, both Florence and Parthenope were 'out' to society and expected to find a husband at one of the many grand social gatherings that they attended. This marriage lottery could not have been less effective at setting up any two people who had companionable temperaments and similar goals: Girls were expected to dance with the men who asked them to dance. They did this under the watchful eye of everyone in the room. Dancing gave men the opportunity to ogle the girls up close, though the ogling was limited to face and upper bosom. The rest of their bodies would be hidden under many layers of clothes.

If a man liked a girl, he could then 'call on her' at her home where he would engage in light conversation in the presence of her mother, sisters, brothers, and possibly companions and servants. Obviously, these conversations had to stay right on the surface, lest anyone be offended or intentions be revealed too soon.

During this decorous and shallow courtship, the families would make polite and discreet inquiries about the girl's financial expectations and the boy's inheritance, trust, or earnings. Their union would be approved, tacitly, by these inquiries. No evidence of heterosexuality or the ability to produce children would be required. It would be assumed that the girl was a virgin unless there was a rumour to the contrary.

The issue of sexual compatibility would not be explored, it would not even be spoken of. Similarly, the young man would not bother himself about whether his chosen bride would enjoy being a mother or whether she had some other ambitions. If they didn't have children, he assumed she would take up watercolours or some other approved lady-like pursuit. There would be no discussion about whether she might have a better head for family finances than he had. He would make all the money decisions by default.

Would the young couple have any real chance to get to know one another before making a decision to wed? Emphatically, not. In fact, if the courtship period lasted too long, the girl would be considered shopworn. It was a little ungentlemanly for a man not to propose if he had been several times to her house for no other purpose but her company. To seek a deep understanding of her mind and character would be unseemly. That's what the honeymoon was for.

This kind of marriage was not designed to produce any kind of long-lasting happiness. It was designed to keep fortunes intact and to keep young ladies 'unspoiled' until some fool took a wild leap of faith and proposed. Both Parthenope and Florence wrote bitterly about these customs and how they led to matches that were no better than a crapshoot.

To work outside this matrix required the kind of verve that Benjamin Smith possessed. After the failure of his engagement to Mai Shore, he formed a relationship with a young woman who bore him several children. They lived together for many years, and their relationship was, by all accounts, a loving one. He was devastated by her death. And yet he never married her. He paid a high price for this originality. He was, in many ways, dead to the Smiths and Shores, even though he saved his mother and sisters from a life of poverty after William Smith died. His children were not allowed to meet or socialize with Parthenope and Florence or with their other Smith/Shore cousins. Benjamin was the proverbial black sheep, and stood as a cautionary tale concerning what happens when a family member strays too far from the path of convention.[6]

And yet Parthenope and Florence didn't have to look much further than their own parents' marriage to see the failure of the system by which young people were thrown together for life, on so little information about what they were getting. WEN fell in love with a beautiful face and a lively mind. Fanny needed to get married because she was almost thirty. These motivations were enough to get them through a few years of togetherness, then they spent most of their remaining years pursuing separate dreams, often in different places.

The only way to get girls married, under this regime, was to marry them off before they had any real time to think about it. The generally poor education of women also contributed to an acceptance of this fate as the 'business of women' about which George Bernard Shaw quipped.

However, Unitarians held a more humanitarian belief in women's rights that ran counter-intuitively to the mainstream habit of stitching girls up into a lifetime legal arrangement before they fully understood what that contract meant. Unitarian families allowed their girls a few years of single adulthood. Unitarian families believed in education for women. Both Florence and Parthenope had time and space to avoid the most disastrous marriages.

As Florence wrote, angrily in *Cassandra*, the only escape from this marriage trap was to marry a friend of the family. Preferably someone the bride has known as a child and grown up alongside. Only then would a well-born woman really know what she was getting when she said, 'I do.' Not only did Parthenope and Florence realize that this was the preferable match to make, they documented this belief in their writings.

What kind of impression did the Nightingale girls make in the drawing rooms and ballrooms of London? Biographers are in general agreement that Florence was a beauty and that Parthenope was 'plain'.

This assumption persists even though a portrait, commissioned during this period of their lives, shows two girls who could be twins. This portrait by William White, which would eventually hang in London's National Portrait Gallery and in the pages of Wikimedia Commons, shows us two young women with fair skin and brown hair. They are dressed according to the fashion, in floor-length dresses with poofy sleeves that taper and bunch up at the wrists. Their dresses are meant to suggest lovely figures without revealing any specifics. Where, in a contemporary portrait, there might be a definite set of breasts and a waist, here there is a fabric curve, starting at the neck and arcing down to the faintest suggestion of a waist. Their hair is similarly conventional, worn up and pulled back to expose their ears and necklines.

Parthenope's dress is gold. She is standing up and handing a book to her sister. In this portrait, Florence is seated and focused on some kind of needlework. Her body is almost entirely obscured by the needlework and an apron.

Florence Nightingale biographer Gillian Gill assumes that Fanny directed the painter on how, exactly, her daughters should be composed.[7] If that is the case, the portrait is perhaps a fantasy of Fanny's. A fantasy that Florence would be transformed into the kind of woman who cares about sewing, which she despised.

It is also clear that Parthenope is the star of this production. She stands and looks directly out at the viewer. Her face and expression are clearly evoked. By contrast, Florence seems like the sidekick. She is seated with her face turned down, with only a three-quarter profile visible.

It's possible that, in composing their portrait this way, Fanny wanted to put Parthenope front and centre to compensate for the obvious preference that Florence was shown in the rooms of wealthy friends. Or maybe Fanny just liked Parthenope better and wanted to picture a more domestic and docile Florence Nightingale in the place of the one who actually existed.

The renovation of Embley was not a complete success as far as Fanny was concerned. There were some mural-like pink roses that she wanted painted over as soon as she saw them. She found fault with some green wallpaper and some green paint which was 'inharmonious'. Florence tried to put a positive spin on the workmanship in a letter to Parthenope, but had to admit the total effect made the rooms look smaller and darker. About the bookcases, she instructed Parthe to abandon all hope. They were a total failure, and the only reasonable comment to make about them was no comment at all. This renovation of Embley and Fanny's disappointment with it points to the increasing rift that occurred between Parthenope's parents.

In the next few years, Parthenope would often be apart from Florence. Fanny sent her eldest daughter to the baths and to the sea for her health. Biographers go back and forth between agreeing that Parthenope was truly sickly and accusing her of using feigned illness to get out of doing things she didn't want to do. In fact, both Parthenope and Florence were sometimes sick when they were called on to do things they didn't want to deal with. Both were also medically fragile during much of their lives.

In the 1840s, some hopes circulated that Florence would marry her first cousin, Harry Nicholson, a close friend of the family along with the rest of the Nicholson tribe. Harry and Florence had known each other for years, seen each other in informal circumstances, and taken something like an accurate measure of one another's characters.[8] Harry fulfilled the Nightingale daughters' belief that an honest marriage could only be undertaken with a family friend, someone with whom one had formed an acquaintance as a child when young women were not so heavily guarded. Parthenope was not invited to the tour of the Lake District that Florence undertook with the Nicholson family. But when the families got together and staged an amateur production of the Merchant of Venice, Parthenope was called upon to paint scenes for the entertainment as well as make hats and costumes.

In 1842, the families got together again, and Florence may have pointedly snubbed Henry, paying more attention to his brother and a single aunt who was on the edges of the Nicholsons' robust happy family. This was the year that it became clear to Fanny and to Parthenope that Florence was trying to break away from them and that she was using her talent as an amateur nurse to do so. Florence had, throughout the previous years, often been at the bedside of an ailing or dying relative or friend.

It has pleased most biographers to assume that Parthenope was too unlovely to attract an early marriage proposal during her optimal childbirth years. They assume this, even though there is little documentation to support the notion. Nor is there any documentation that she wished to get married earlier than she did. We have no evidence that she did not quietly and compassionately rebuff the attentions of any swains who might have looked her way. In her later years, Parthenope wrote that no woman with any sensitivity should ever receive more than two proposals of marriage. As a very young woman, she might not see a proposal coming, but after this has happened twice, she should know the signs and prevent the third and subsequent proposals. She wrote this in a humorous review of Henry James' *Portrait of a Lady* in which the main character racks up the proposals in a way that horrified Parthenope who thought James' heroine, Isabel Archer, was irresponsibly wreaking havoc on men's hearts.[9]

It is impossible to know to what extent Parthenope might have been sought after in marriage while she was in her twenties. What we do know is that she was passionately attached to her family, especially Florence, and copious documents show us that she wanted more time with her father and her sister. What these documents do not show us is that she wished to break away from the brilliant Nightingales and establish a separate household. What biographers, in other words, seem to have overlooked is the possibility that Parthenope didn't care to leave home. Why would she?

Most biographers also seem not to register how dangerous it was for nineteenth-century women to marry. In the absence of birth control, women could not control the number of children they had, and each pregnancy held a death threat. Nineteenth-century childbirth often brought women to the brink of destruction when it didn't kill them outright. Without antibiotics to address the blood poisoning that often occurred during a baby's delivery, the families were basically consigned to standing around the bloodied bed, watching as the new mother gasped her last breaths.

In fact, Parthenope and Florence would both have known several women who died in childbirth and others who suffered terribly from giving birth while still in the prime of life. The girls had the immediate and horrific example of their governess Miss Christie, who left them to get married and died in childbirth shortly thereafter.[10]

There was also the example of Mrs Hope Reeve, the wife of a well-known writer, who died shortly after giving birth. She was a friend of the Nightingale family, and Florence was allowed to visit the family after her death and help care for the newborn daughter.

In the generation previous, Mary Shelley had written *Frankenstein*, a novel that is often construed as early horror fiction, but also sometimes taken as a parable of the perils of giving life. Was Parthenope secretly frightened of the perils surrounding pregnancy? Again, we have no direct evidence that she was. But to assume that young women, generally, didn't notice the high rate of death in childbirth would also be naive.

If Parthenope and Florence were reluctant to start making babies out of fear for their health, they would not have been alone. The great Queen Victoria, who was the same age as Parthenope, privately expressed fears about dying in childbirth. While she turned out to be a sturdy breeder, Charlotte Brontë, author of *Jane Eyre*, was not so lucky. Brontë's father worried that a late marriage would kill his daughter Charlotte, and he was right. She married at thirty-seven and died the next year from pregnancy complications.

Chapter 8

Florence Refuses to Marry

By 1842, it was fairly obvious that Florence sought a life apart from her immediate family. And Parthenope seems to have been broadsided by this. Parthenope's letters to Florence, who was comforting the family of Hope Reeve, politely demand that she come home. If Florence has some kind of as yet undisclosed higher mission, Parthenope does not see it. She thinks that she should be Florence's mission.

Parthenope's devotion to Florence actually became something of a joke in Florence's letters during this period. In one of these missives, Florence writes that she has a new hat, flower-encrusted, and that Parthenope would really want her around if she could see this hat. It's not clear that this letter was purposefully insulting, but it's hard to imagine how it could have been more hurtful to a sister who longed for her missing sibling.

Florence even resorted to making promises to Parthenope that it is obvious she never meant to keep. In one note, she writes that Parthenope 'will have me all your life, for I shall never die and never marry'.[1]

The never dying and never marrying part of the promise she kept. Florence would outlive Parthenope by many years, and she chose medicine over marriage. But she would, in the years ahead, rather cruelly sever ties with her clinging sibling.

There is no point in arguing with Florence Nightingale's decision to live a life apart from her family. She understood her destiny from a young age. To criticize any of the influences that went into her making is also futile. If the ingredients had been any different, we would not have Florence Nightingale. Medicine, especially nursing, might have been set back fifty years. We might still be feeling her absence from history.

But there is no denying that her break from her family broke hearts. Biographers often imply that Parthenope was churlish and selfish in wanting to deny Florence the opportunity to pursue a separate dream and a separate life. And, yes, there is a note of selfishness in young Parthenope, but it is not envy or resentment. No one was a bigger fan of

Florence's achievements. If we examine Parthenope's motives and letters from her perspective, and not that of history, we see an abandoned sibling, an almost twin, who now has to face the world without the one person to whom she has always been closest.

Florence knew that she had an important destiny from a bizarrely early age. Biographers have, perhaps, overstated her mysticism because there must be some explanation for how a young woman, of whom so little was ever expected, accomplished so much. There must be some magic at work. It must have had something to do with all the praying and self-inspection.

Parthenope, by contrast, was a late bloomer. In her youth, most of what she wanted was a closeness to her immediate family which she was increasingly denied, first by her remarkable father, then by her remarkable sister. She was increasingly thrown together with her mother who, for all her social achievements, was clearly a limited woman, and Parthenope would have seen that.

When Parthenope wasn't stuck with her mother, she was often sent to the seashore to collect shells and take baths while the other Nightingales got on with their important work. Her family had decided she was 'sickly' and there was no real coming back from that. Parthenope's own destiny would have to wait until she was nearly forty.

There is no evidence of outrage on Parthenope's part when Florence refused to marry her cousin Henry, even though that rejection cost the Nightingales their close friendship with the Nicholson family to which Henry belonged.

In 1845, Parthenope was reading Thomas Carlisle and formed an opinion, based on his, that self-knowledge is the greatest achievement in life. She tentatively framed this opinion in a letter to Florence. In response, Florence writes that such a belief is mistaken. She proposes, instead, that understanding God is the highest purpose because humans often tire of themselves. In this divergence, we see Florence shaping up to be the woman of action and Parthenope the woman of thought and analysis.[2]

In the same year, Parthenope was already mourning her lost youth. She was all of twenty-seven and Florence twenty-six. Florence wrote a letter cajoling her with the words, 'I never read of "good will towards men" only till [sic] they are five and twenty'.[3]

In 1845, Florence made a detailed plan to train as a nurse and then start up a Protestant sisterhood. The mission of this sisterhood would be, of course, to minister to the sick, dying, and poor, three groups that overlapped a lot because medicine could do so little to save people. This was not a whim. It is now obvious to anyone who studies the Nightingale family that Florence was going into medicine and that trying to stop her was futile. Nevertheless, we operate from the vantage of hindsight. Her family did not see her destiny as she saw it. All of them still assumed she would marry.

So Florence did not immediately get permission to study nursing or to fulfil her dream. She would spend another four years at odds with her family, miserable, restless, frustrated. Parthenope would, likewise, be miserable, clingy, desperate, and hurt. She spent years longing for a sister who was tired of her, and trying to recreate the closeness they had as teens.

The late 1840s found Fanny and WEN quietly desperate to marry off at least one of their daughters. But this desperation was in constant tension with their Unitarian convictions about the rights of women and their basic respect for their daughters. Considering the impossible situation for young women who were deliberately trained to be ornamental rather than useful, both WEN and Fanny Smith Nightingale exercised reasonable self-restraint about not pressuring their daughters to marry early in their twenties. It was assumed that neither girl would marry anyone 'beneath her', i.e. not from the same upper middle class. Neither girl was pressured to marry someone with money, but a poor education or less than admirable manners.

In 1847, a French man declared his love for Parthenope with the hope that she would become his bride. There seems to have been little discussion about this offer. It was dismissed, by Fanny, in writing. He was not even honoured with a letter from Parthenope herself explaining that they were not suited.

In that same year, *Jane Eyre* was published, and we know that Florence read that novel. Parthenope surely read it also. In it, we find a woman who lives independently, earns her own money, resists the temptation to become a kept woman, and finally marries the man she loves, but entirely on her own terms. In the course of her life, 'plain' Jane turns down a marriage proposal from a cousin. *Jane Eyre* forms one of the few literary precedents for a young woman to stay single, rather than compromising her values, rather than letting a man define her life.

In real life, there was the example of Clarkey. However, in the same year that Parthenope refused her French suitor, Mary Clarke, for so many years a model of female independence, married her close friend Julius von Mohl.

The expectation that the Nightingale daughters would marry fell disproportionately on Florence. Florence was the more beautiful and sought after sister, and Parthenope was mostly off the hook because of her ongoing invalidism. In 1848, the whole family went to Malvern, a bath town, so that Parthenope could 'take the waters', i.e. submerge in warm or hot baths.

In addition to her small frame, bad teeth, general fragility, and susceptibility to infection, Parthenope was starting to show definite signs of crippling arthritis. Though it is perilous for biographers to make medical diagnoses of people who lived two centuries ago, it seems more than likely that Parthenope's terrible bout with influenza, in 1836, was the vector for what became a chronic condition.

The Nightingales came to regard Parthenope as an invalid and pinned their hopes of a married daughter on Florence. Unlike Clarke, however, Florence could see no benefits of marriage. In her letters, she mocks women who settle down late in life. She had observed that women who were perfectly happy to stay unwed in their twenties and thirties would suddenly have an attack of terror about becoming old maids at the age of forty. At forty, a woman who had been content to be a virtual nun would suddenly become a wife, she sneered. These observations could not fail to influence Parthenope who was ripe for influence all her life and who mostly shared Florence's ambivalence toward the institution of marriage.

It would not be until Florence turned down a second eligible suitor that her family would finally realize how serious she was about having a career. Florence was systematically wooed by Richard Monckton Milnes, 1st Baron of Houghton, for seven or eight years. Her family looked on with approval as she formed, with Milnes, the close friendship that both sisters demanded prior to marriage, in defiance of Victorian custom. When Florence refused Milnes' offer of marriage, Parthenope despaired. To understand this despair, we must return to the subject of the Nightingale estate entail.

Financially, the Nightingale women were poised and figuratively dancing on the lip of a volcano because their lifestyle was entirely dependent on WEN staying alive. This strange situation existed because the estate was 'entailed' to the male line.

Entailment is a wonderful fictional device because it creates damsels in semi-distress out of well brought up and talented young ladies. The weird and misogynistic custom of entail has been made entirely accessible to the public by the phenomenon of Downton Abbey. In that narrative, three daughters stress out over the lack of a male heir to the very house they have lived in from birth. What shall they do? None of these girls can inherit. The youngest, Sybil, lacks all appropriate caution: broadsides everyone by marrying the family driver and mechanic. It seems the estate will go to a distant cousin whom they have never met. The Earl of Grantham invites this cousin to Downton Abbey with the hope he will fall in love with one of the girls. Breaths are bated. Will he turn out to be a stuffy fool, like the cousin in *Pride and Prejudice*? A totally unmarriable Mr Collins? Whew! No! He is lovely! Through her very convenient marriage to James Crawley, Lady Mary re-diverts the estate back to her own line.

WEN and Fanny had failed to have sons and, by the time her daughters were in their late twenties, Fanny was well past her childbearing years. WEN would be able to leave his wife and daughters only a fraction of his wealth, the part of his estate that passed to him through his father. Lea Hurst and Embley, along with their grounds and furnishings, all belonged to the entailed Nightingale estate. Therefore, upon WEN's death, his wife and daughters would be largely disinherited, and the Nightingale estate would pass, house, money, furniture, and all, to WEN's sister and then her son, Shore Smith, who was WEN's closest male descendant.

Unless.

Unless Florence could marry and have a son before WEN's death. When Florence turned down Milnes, WEN was still in peak condition and probably expected to live long enough to see his grandchildren grow up. In the case of a grandson, the estate would stay within the immediate family. Fanny and Parthenope could then rest easy in the assumption that they would not be dispossessed.

Florence's final refusal to marry, even despite the strong temptation of becoming a baroness, had implications that went far beyond her personal tastes and disposition. Everyone in the Nightingale family felt these reverberations. They dealt with their feelings in distinctly different ways. WEN went to London and hid out in his club, Parthenope retired to her couch to process her feelings privately, and Fanny's screams could be heard throughout the house.

Poor Fanny. She had unintentionally raised two young women of very independent, even eccentric, natures. And yet she herself was not a rebel. She was mostly a conventional Victorian woman who could clearly see all the benefits of marriage. They were patently obvious. Marriage had saved Fanny herself from the disaster of her father's bankruptcy. And her two unlucky sisters, who had not managed to marry before the Smith fortune failed, lived in very reduced circumstances, compared to the lifestyle they had enjoyed growing up.

Martha Frances (most commonly called Patty) and Julia, Fanny's spinster sisters, had few outlets for their superior intellects and educations. Their limited financial resources made it virtually impossible for them to put their fine ideas into action. The lack of dowries also effectively doomed them to an unmarried life. That was a fate Fanny did not want for her own daughters.

She need not have been so afraid. One of her daughters went on to become a powerful force in shaping modern medicine. The other would marry a man much like her grandfather and enact change through partnership with him and through her writing.

Part II

In the Shadow of Florence Nightingale

Chapter 9

Florence Breaks Away

This is not a book about Florence Nightingale, it is a book about her sister. However, in the first half of her life, Parthenope was so dependent on Florence that it is impossible to write about Parthenope without considering what Florence was doing at that time.

Right up to the day of her wedding, Parthenope lived in Florence's shadow, often with good grace, sometimes with anger and a sense of rejection. Until she was nearly forty, Parthenope's life was, generally, a reaction to her sister's. For instance, when Florence got to continue her studies with WEN, and Parthe did not, Parthe's pain at that rejection defined her existence. When Florence rejected her second serious suitor, Parthe agonized over that decision. If one is to believe Parthenope's previous biographers, Parthe agonized more over Florence's rejection of Monckton Milnes than she did over her own rejection of William Spottiswood, a more than eligible young man with whom she had a great deal in common.

When Florence travelled the world apart from Parthe, the pain of Florence's absence defined Parthenope's existence. Parthenope would eventually learn to sublimate her pain by documenting Florence's achievements and then becoming her volunteer aide-de-camp.

With Florence's refusal of Milnes, WEN gave up hope that Florence might ever conform to expectations. Instead of forcing her to attend more parties, he let her make a long and semi-perilous trip to Greece and Egypt with family friends. Florence wrote letters home about everything she saw and did in Egypt. Some letters were for all her family members and she headed these with the words, 'My Dear People' and sometimes 'Dearest People'. But she also wrote letters just to Parthenope. In these letters, she sometimes invites Parthenope to join her in her imagination.

For instance, in a letter Florence wrote from Rome (7 December 1847), she invites Parthenope to 'go and kiss the little temple of Vesta for me'.[1] She takes her reader through the olive groves outside Tivoli and invites her to smell the sulphur mines. Later in the letter, she transports Parthe to a cave covered in maidenhair where the waves of the Teverone River crash.

'Your face is wet with spray,' Florence writes.[2] She wanted to baptize herself in this river. She wanted Parthenope to be exhilarated with her.

Some of these letters were so warm and enthusiastic, they must have reminded Parthenope of the loving years they spent together, studying with their father, taking walks through the meadows near Embley and the forests of Lee Hurst, identifying wildflowers, and playing word games.

Florence was so prolific in her letter writing that it seemed to Parthenope a waste that only a few people should ever read them. So she collated Florence's letters and found a publisher for them. In doing so, she gave herself the job of editing and giving literary shape to a collection of otherwise beautiful, but random thoughts. By saving these documents, Parthenope unwittingly contributed a great deal to future Nightingale scholarship.

Parthenope may have nursed the hope that Florence would find her grand destiny in the literary arts. She may have dreamed a dream in which the two of them would collaborate, Florence the writer and Parthenope the coach, illustrator, and editor.

What Florence was not writing home about was her ambition to study nursing in Kaiserswerth on the way home to England. This training was more or less sprung upon Parthenope after the fact. If we consider Parthenope's hopes for a sister who stays safe at home, writing, we may find it easier to understand why Parthenope blew up so hard when she learned that Florence was training as a nurse.

Florence arrived home from abroad with an owl in her pocket. While she was exploring the Athens Acropolis, she had noticed some boys tormenting an owlet. She rescued this baby and made it her pet. It grew up tame, bonded with Florence, and passed much of its life content to nestle in her pocket while she went on with her amazing life.[3]

She named the owl 'Athena' after the Greek goddess of wisdom. It is not a coincidence that the Parthenon, the focal point of the acropolis, was built in honour of Athena. So the owl was named, as were both Flo and Pop, after a mythic creature and also named after the temple where she was rescued.

Florence also brought home several bracelets that she bought in Egypt. The bracelets she gifted on Parthenope. Parthe was horribly conflicted.

On one hand, she was proud of her sister's bravery in sojourning to other lands. On the other hand, she was angry and frustrated that Florence had privately been training as a nurse, without informing her family. Parthe reacted to this by taking the Egyptian bracelets and throwing them back at Florence. Florence, also capable of drama, fainted dead away in reaction. In a private note, she said that Parthenope would be the death of her.

Florence met the announcement that Parthe was publishing her letters with a combination of contempt and indifference. She had little to no use for Parthenope's literary talent. According to Edward Cook, Florence 'regarded her elder sister's contentment in the beauties of art and nature, and in the world as she found it, with the tender pity which one may feel for a happy child'. He quotes Flo as saying, 'It would be an ill return for all her affection … to drag down my White Swan from her cool, fresh, blue sea of art into our baby-chicken yard of struggling, scratting, life. How cruel it would be, as she is rocked to rest there, on her dreamy waves, for anybody to waken her'.[4]

However, Florence did not derail the publication of her letters. The book went forward without her further input. This may be the first indication that Parthenope would rise to become a woman of letters, with a particularly keen eye for what was culturally important. Parthenope has frequently been accused of envy, but Parthenope was jealous of Florence's company, not her achievements. When it came to her sister's achievements, she basked in them. She found settings for her sister's diamonds. She documented, glossed, and framed Florence Nightingale and took pride in doing so. Nothing better illustrates the way Parthe subordinated her talents to those of Florence than Athena, the owl.

Owls were already associated with wisdom at that point in time. Who could not fall in love with an owl named Athena? Who could resist the narrative of a wise woman who rescues an owl?

Certainly not Parthenope. Athena would immediately call out to Parthenope's imagination. Her drawing of Florence and the owlet would make it into the Egyptian memoirs that Florence thought so little of. In fact, the drawing would be the most successful part of the travel diary. While the diary was printed and read by a few people, the drawing was so popular that it was printed separately and sold in shops across London.

The care of Athena fell to Parthenope when Florence was travelling or visiting. In one letter, Florence enjoins her sister not to let Athena drink ink or make ink blots.[5] Parthenope was perfectly content to care for Athena and undertake other errands for Florence. But she had still not taken the full measure of Florence's determination to break away from her family.

Neither Fanny nor Parthe had what we would, today, consider a healthy reaction to Florence's ambitions. Imagine a mother today kicking up a fuss because her daughter wanted to be a nurse. Such a scenario seems possible only if the mother preferred her daughter to become a doctor or an engineer.

We can understand Fanny only in the light of her social ambitions. Fanny was a social climber, and she needed her most eligible daughter to fall in line with the aim of social climbing. An advantageous marriage was obviously more prestigious than a vermin-infested hospital or a battlefield. An advantageous marriage would, in Fanny's estimation, raise all Nightingale boats.

But there's little evidence that Parthenope was similarly interested in climbing a status ladder. All signs point to Parthenope being much more like her sister than her mother. Like Florence, Parthenope was interested in books and ideas, not in weddings and babies. Parthenope, like Florence, was appalled by institutional poverty. Like Florence, Parthenope would rather be taking a basket of food to the poor family in the village than scheming for an invitation to a grand manor.

There is a little-discussed psychological phenomenon called 'dependent personality disorder'. It is what it sounds like, an overdependence on other people. People with DPD cannot comfortably be alone. According to the Cleveland Clinic, they are perceived as clingy and needy. They fear abandonment and feel helpless when a relationship ends.

The chief causes of DPD include childhood trauma and childhood sickness. Parthenope experienced both. Consider Parthenope's inability to breastfeed from her mother. While both Parthenope and Florence were fed by wet nurses, Parthenope experienced days of near starvation before Fanny hired a wet nurse. Parthenope also had rheumatic fever and some kind of arm injury as a child. These events could easily have caused childhood trauma.

Florence Breaks Away 63

The Cleveland Clinic goes on to say that DPD often interacts with cultural expectations such as 'reliance on authority'. Nobody could claim to have reliance on authority drilled into her mindset more than Parthenope Nightingale.

Biographers do hindsight psychoanalysis at their own risk. But dependent personality disorder does explain a lot of Parthenope's behaviour toward Florence. Parthenope never withheld her admiration for Florence and often stepped up to the plate to burnish Florence's achievements. But she also flew into rages at her sister. And these rages do seem mostly related to Parthenope's fear of losing Florence. Or fear for Florence's safety.

In any event, Parthenope's relationship with Florence was more complex than most Florence Nightingale biographers want to concede. Parthenope has been dismissed as mostly just a hurdle that Florence had to clear. To say that they often got in each other's way would be fairer. They also inspired and supported each other especially as Parthenope came into her own powers. They were, in other words, sisters, and not fairy tale antagonists.

Upon her return from Egypt, Florence wrote a description of Parthenope that claimed to note her good qualities with her bad. It is, however, a cruel description. Florence writes that Parthenope is not a Nightingale at all. She is, instead, a bird of paradise, with gorgeous feathers, who floats above the world while not engaging it. She acknowledges Parthenope's obvious talents, her artistic ability and talent for words. She also concedes that Parthenope is devoted to family and, in particular, discrete. Historians need to note that Florence herself wrote here that she saw no envy in Parthenope. Almost as if Florence knew how closely her family would be examined and wanted to steer her biographers away from that too easy conclusion.

She states that Parthe hates to see anyone suffer, but then goes on to state that Parthe prefers not to engage anyone's suffering and would prefer not to see it. Florence also says that Parthenope has no ambition and no love of any individual, just a generalized love of humankind.

It seems a little perverse to say that Parthe didn't love individuals. Florence surely knew better. Parthe's passion for Florence herself was a near-constant annoyance. If Parthenope had written an honest description of Florence at this time, it might have said that Florence was too overwhelmed by her own ambitions to notice anyone else's.

In 1851, Florence went on yet another trip, this time to Germany. When she came home, Parthenope was sick, as she so often was. Sick, and still single, despite being a debutante for a humiliating fourteen years. At thirty-one, she now had a heart condition and the beginning of disabling arthritis in her hands.

Fanny assigned Florence to babysit Parthenope in no uncertain terms. And she demanded that this babysitting stint should last at least six months. This caused a chain of reactions now typical of the Florence/Parthenope connection. Florence was resentful about being stuck with her sister when she (Florence) should be pursuing her divine mission. Parthe was sensitive to this resentment, and it raised her anxiety level. She would cling even harder to Florence, and Florence would then pray for death.

During the next three months, Parthe and Florence had the privilege of meeting George Eliot and Elizabeth Barret Browning. In being happily married or partnered up, Eliot and Browning established a template for the successful woman writer, one whose financial and emotional needs were neatly taken care of, allowing her to focus on her work. If Parthenope was ever guilty of envy, it seems more likely that she envied these women, and not her eccentric sister.

We do know that Parthenope's future life as a writer was heavily influenced by both Browning and Eliot. Eliot's broad view of English society, which captured the points of view of country squires, the middle class, servants, farmers, labourers, and even Jewish minorities no doubt influenced Parthenope to undertake writing about England's northern rural farming communities. Elizabeth Barret Browning's poems on love also inspired Parthenope, as readers can see in *Stone Edge*, the novel Parthenope would write in the future.

Florence spent three months with Parthenope out of the six that Fanny had ordered. Then she found an excuse to leave. Parthe found herself in the unhappy position of wanting a close sibling relationship with a sibling who didn't want the same thing. Could she have handled it more bravely? Yes. But her desperation warrants more sympathy than condemnation.

Later in 1851, Fanny travelled to continental Europe with both her daughters. The main purpose of this trip was for Parthenope to do more hot water therapy for her arthritis and debilitation. Unlike many Victorian medical treatments, hot water therapy was not all hokum and superstition. In fact, medical experts today recommend hot water therapy as a treatment for rheumatoid arthritis; hot water is thought to loosen up the fingers, providing more flexibility and use of the hands.

Unfortunately, there is no indication in any of Parthenope's writings that she enjoyed this therapy or believed in it. When she wrote of it, she cited it mostly as an assault on her person.

It was arranged that Florence would accompany Fanny and Parthenope part way and then make a detour to a hospital establishment where she intended to study. The sisters wrote back and forth to each other during this separation. Parthenope wrote about how much she hated Frazensbad, the bath town where she was getting therapy. Part of her misery may have been caused by the separation from Florence.

Parthenope was still having a very hard time accepting Florence's ambitions, at least in part because the world of nursing was so toxic. Parthe would have been happier if Florence's ambition had been painting or writing. Those pursuits would not necessarily have taken her away from Embley, unless she married. Likewise, if Florence had only established a school in the nearby village, she and Parthe could have worked there together.

But nursing was not, then, a job for women who were as well brought up as Parthenope and Florence. It was a desperate profession, undertaken by women who had no better opportunities. Even young gentlewomen who fell on hard times were generally expected to become governesses or school teachers or, if they had talent, artists or writers. Florence was not the first woman to notice what a trap this was.

So while Parthenope was enduring the bath therapy, she received a number of letters from Florence pleading for understanding. She writes that she knows Parthenope loves her: 'I have had too many proofs of it'.[6] She also writes, 'I am very glad to hear that you like people to be happy in their own way and hope that means that you mean to let me be happy in my own way. Indeed, I know of no other in which people can be so'.[7]

Parthenope wrote back, pouring out all her fears about a future that involved becoming a nurse in the nineteenth century. To that Florence replied that worrying about the future would prevent her from being able to benefit from and enjoy the present. She went on to write these rather heart-breaking words: 'I look again and again if there be any light to rescue those who so dearly prize each other from the sad sorrow of grieving or injuring each other'. Florence declared that she tried to find a path of destiny that didn't involve trying something completely new, but could not find it. In other words, she had definitively declined the life of wife and mother, of the artist or writer, of the content daughter and sister.[8]

In a letter dated 9 September 1851, Florence wrote a parable about two women, A and B. They ate a diet of fruit, vegetables, and modified meat. (Florence did not say how the meat was modified, but Victorians frequently ate meat-soaked grease and lard.) While apart from A, B ate real meat and found that it made her stronger, more energetic, and more capable of doing God's work. This new diet frightened A, and she feared for B. Florence used the words, 'terrified' and 'miserable'. So B went back to starving on A's diet, paralyzed at the thought of hurting A.

The parable goes on for another page. If B were capable of doing nothing, she would be content to wait for death, and a shot at her dreams in the next life. But no. She was a woman of action. Nature would not let her sit still. A was miserable. B felt like she was in prison. A never figured out that she was making B unhappy. Instead, A believed that B wanted something sketchy. A thought the mostly vegetarian diet was delicious.

Though Florence may have intended A and B to be equals, her assumption of superiority over Parthenope is clear when she writes things like B is 'the idol' of A's imagination.[9]

Chapter 10

Parthenope Breaks Down

In 1852, Parthenope suffered a nervous breakdown which she might have weathered, on her own, except that the treatment turned out to be worse than the disease.

Florence was away from home again. To Parthenope, fell the job of being a full-time companion to her mother, and Fanny had no capacity for reflection or solitude. She insisted on constant social activity, no sleeping in. Moments of introspection were, for her, idle daydreaming, not to be tolerated. In Florence's absence, the full weight of Fanny's disapproval would also fall on Parthenope who, like Florence, had disappointed her mother in failing to make an advantageous marriage.

WEN and Fanny decided that Parthenope needed professional help. As a consequence, she fell under the care of one Sir James Clark, a doctor who was friends with WEN. Clark was the kind of doctor that, today, we would dismiss as a charlatan. His mistakes would have been exposed, there would have been death threats on social media, and he would likely have changed his name, possibly his appearance, and moved somewhere very quiet. That was not to be, however. Clark's mistakes never came home to roost in any meaningful way, and he was allowed to continue practising medicine for an appallingly long time.

Clark's greatest claim to fame was his part in the scandalous Flora Hastings affair. Clark examined Hastings, one of the Duchess of Kent's ladies in waiting, without noticing that her baby bump was, in fact, a malignant liver tumour. He thought Hastings was pregnant and participated in a cover-up. The rumour of Hastings' pregnancy reached Queen Victoria anyway. At that time, out-of-wedlock pregnancies among the aristocracy were scandalous. To get pregnant, unmarried, while serving in Buckingham Palace was more or less equivalent to treason.

Queen Victoria believed Hastings was pregnant out of wedlock and denounced her. A subsequent diagnosis revealed that what looked like pregnancy was, in fact, a malignant and fatal tumour. The media of that time got hold of the story and shamed Victoria for falsely accusing an innocent and dying woman. So Clark's oversight filled Hastings' final days on earth with misery. It also combined with young Victoria's poor judgment to tarnish her early reign.[1]

Clark is also notorious for having treated the poet John Keats who was dying of untreated tuberculosis. Clark hastened Keats' death by bleeding his patient, overdosing him on laudanum, and starving him.[2] Though it is true that the last stages of tuberculosis are mostly fatal, and Clark could have done nothing to save Keats, he could certainly have made his dying days more comfortable.

This was the man to whom Parthenope's father entrusted her treatment. The conventional practice of the time was to blame sick women for being sick. Either they were spoiled from having too many luxuries and too much free time or they were nervous wrecks from being single. Clark adhered to this model of treatment in dealing with Parthenope. In no way did he consider the likely impact of Parthenope's obvious arthritic condition on her mental health. To be fair, no medical expert of that day had the tools to treat rheumatoid arthritis. Today, the first line of care is judicious use of corticosteroids.

Clark initially thought that Parthenope's condition was organic, i.e. her fault because she was rich and had too much free time. This condition he called 'neurasthenia'. He took her to his home in the Scottish highlands and prescribed exercise.

Neurasthenia was a catch-all diagnosis that was often applied to women who were well educated. In the opinion of some doctors, too much education, or even athletic achievement, could ruin a woman, for life. Freud thought that neurasthenia was caused by lack of orgasms. For that reason, among others, unmarried women were often the target of neurasthenia diagnosis.

It is quite possible that, with careful diet and the right exercises along with hot baths, Parthenope could have found some relief from the symptoms of RA as well as the nervous breakdown that she endured at this point in her life. Talk therapy might also have helped her achieve an appropriate emotional independence from her family members. But these treatments were not forthcoming.

Removed not only from Florence but also from her mother and father, Parthenope did not improve: instead, she got worse. Of course she did. She had never learned to be alone. The idea that a well brought up young woman should learn to be independent to the point of enjoying solitude was not a contemporary value. For Parthenope, there was no 'me time'. If there had been, Parthenope's writing career might have begun much sooner.

Though she was often the least popular Nightingale within her own immediate family, she had previously always been with her mother, father or her sister. If not, she was at the home of a cousin or aunt or a family that was close to the Nightingales, like the Nicholson family or the Bonham Carters.

It has been noted that the elder Nightingales kept up their break-neck paced social agenda without interruption the whole time Parthe was in Clark's care. This is surprising because WEN and Fanny were extremely loving parents. They had never before neglected the health of either of their daughters. If anything, the Nightingale offspring were some of the most carefully cosseted and nervously monitored young ladies in the empire.

Parthenope was always blessed (or cursed, depending on how you value it) with keen self-awareness. She was aware that her state of mind was not normal. In her letters, she describes herself as alternately swept around by a flood and beset with fancies as numerous as the grains of sand at the beach. Her letters speak of a brain fog and difficulty concentrating, which are classic signs of nervous breakdown.

Florence got tagged to go see her and dutifully raced to Scotland, shockingly unaccompanied except by a single servant. Upon her sister's arrival, Parthenope immediately improved. Florence wrote home to say they were both eating well, sleeping well, and taking walks.

This sudden recovery could not be lost on Clark. Though it's hard to imagine he had much face to save, he decided he needed to change his diagnosis. He determined that she was not, as he had believed, neurasthenic. She was, instead, a hypochondriac. A hypochondriac who needed to be separated from the one person in the world for whom she would positively rally. He literally prescribed separation from Florence as her treatment.

A letter that Clark wrote concerning Parthenope's poor mental health does make one shudder. He wrote, specifically, that Parthenope's nervous condition could lead to imbecility and recommends separation from her family and placement in care of some well-wishing group of friends or relatives.[3]

One trembles to think: What if Parthenope had not been so befriended and beloved? Would she have been 'separated' and sent off to an asylum, as so many Victorian women were who became inconvenient, angry, or bitter, with or without good reason? In that era, women could be pronounced 'mad' for having an affair or even for asking for a divorce. Many of the women so committed spent the majority or remainder of their natural lives in indifferently-run institutions.

So, when Fanny wrote that too much fuss was being made of Parthe's breakdown, she may have been less a negligent mother than we think. She certainly pulled Parthenope back from any wholesale removal from her happy home.

On their way back to England, the two sisters had to make many stops along the way to accommodate Parthenope's exhaustion and pain. On this journey, Parthe was frequently crippled, whether from her chronic arthritis or from mental anguish, or a combination of the two, we will never know. Clark had declared, in advance of this trip, that she would fake being unable to walk. And his conjecture gets some credibility from the fact that Parthenope was walking around Scotland—with Florence.

It took four days just to get from Birk Hall, where the Clarks lived, to Aberdeen, Scotland. By the time they arrived, Parthenope was praising Sir James, with the clever tongue in cheek that makes her novels so readable for twenty-first-century audiences. She describes Clark as 'so great a man that he enabled me to do this journey'.[4]

In the next phrase, she credited him for the speed of the horses between Aberdeen and Aboyne. On the rest of her time with Sir James Clark, Parthenope chose to remain silent and discreet, not inflicting any opinion about her care on her parents or friends, who would have been hurt to think that she was experimented on by a charlatan with her full self-awareness intact.

Florence summoned an employee of Lea Hurst by the name of Watson to provide extra security and muscle for the remainder of the trip. Sir James insisted upon a male attendant, claiming that Parthenope 'may fancy she can't walk, and then a man will be of use'.[5] Watson never showed up, however. Florence coped by employing a porter to carry Parthenope when she could not walk.

Back in Embley, Parthenope composed a poem in which she reflects on her time in Scotland. It is clear from this poem that she is coming to terms with her feelings and actions toward Florence. She describes herself as a plant growing between rocks and a rushing river. In other words, she finds herself trapped with no real choices except to adapt to unfavourable conditions.

The lines: 'God has broken down my idol for me/ That I might to His raise up my will' are intriguing.[6] The reader is highly tempted to construe the broken idol as Florence. But, in what sense is she broken down? It seems likely that Parthenope was beset with a sense of loss mixed with fear about what Florence was choosing. Regardless, Parthenope hears a call, similar to Florence's, to align her life with God's will.

She also writes about the difficulty of discerning what is truly 'right'. Is she right to oppose Florence? She isn't sure. The storm and strife that she refers to in her poem have made it difficult for her to find her path.

At the end of the poem, though, she indicates that she has learned a lesson from the 'storm and trouble'. And that lesson is that she cannot choose where to grow, she must accept her position, caught between the rock and river. She cannot choose where she can spread her roots or blossoms.

This poem definitely speaks of the struggle Parthenope underwent to let her sister go. But it also suggests that Parthenope was already in the process of accepting Florence's calling. This process did not progress smoothly, but it is definitely the beginning of Parthenope's conversion from naysayer to full supporter of Florence's work. It is interesting to note that, after escorting Parthenope home from Scotland, Florence often took the tone of a mother in her letters to Parthenope, using the heading, 'My dear child', despite the obvious fact that Parthenope was the elder sibling.[7]

Chapter 11

WEN Gives In

For Florence, Parthenope's breakdown and Clark's jumbled prescriptions were a godsend. Clark's prescription of separation from Parthenope was a ticket to the freedom she had sought for at least the past ten years. It also gave WEN the excuse he needed to give Florence her independence. This came in the form of a small income of £500 a year. This small sum allowed Florence to live alone in rented London rooms.

During Florence's painful breakup with her family, WEN condemned all of Parthenope's actions. At one point, she opposed Florence's plans; at another point, she supported them too fervently for her father's taste. He himself obsessed over this obsession, drafting letters to Parthenope that he never sent. He considered sending Parthe off to a place in the country and got so far as to write commanding her to pack her books, but then reconsidered and did not send the letter. WEN himself took refuge in his London club, as he had done when Florence refused to marry Monckton Milnes. It was his bolthole against family drama.

To the impartial observer, it looks very much as if WEN redirected his anger and frustration against Florence to his older daughter. He had trouble admitting that he himself resented Florence's dreams of a larger life, so he blamed Parthenope for her expression of those fears. As events unfolded, it became clearer that WEN's fears about Florence revolved around the possible damage to his reputation of having a daughter who travels at will and takes employment when she isn't forced to by financial straits. Parthenope's fears about Florence, by contrast, concerned her sister's safety and the possible waste of such a fine mind on bedpans and bandages.

In 1853, Florence accepted a job directing a sort of retirement home for financially desperate ladies called the Institution for Ill Gentlewomen on Harley Street. Parthe was not surprised by this acceptance. She was, however, concerned for Florence's safety. She would be around sick people, unprotected, in the heart of London. Parthenope still felt that the job was a terrible waste of Florence's tremendous intellect. But it was never her decision to make.

There is no need to pretend that Parthenope ever truly stood in Florence's way. Under English law of that time, a woman could not work outside the home without the permission of her father. While Fanny and Parthenope were welcome to shout their opinions and feelings from the rooftop if they liked, they did not, nor could not command Florence. WEN, as Florence's father, was the only individual who, by law, could allow or prohibit the actions of his daughter.

Florence's decision to take a full-time job outside the home was a highly eccentric move. And the discussion that took place between Florence and various members of her family was intense and fraught with strong language and feelings. However, when Florence went off to work in London, she did so WITH the public blessing of her entire family. We know this because of the interference of Marianne Nicholson.

Marianne Nicholson was the sister of the spurned Harry Nicholson. Florence had politely declined Harry's marriage proposal several years previous. Harry went on to make another, perfectly respectable marriage as did Marianne whose last name now was Galton.

But it seems she had never fully forgiven Florence for not becoming her sister-in-law. Marianne spoke to one of the committee members who were in the process of hiring Florence for the position in Harley Street. To this lady, Marianne stated confidently that Florence did not have the consent of her family to take this job. The committee withdrew their offer of employment, forcing WEN to commit his permission in writing, at which point the job offer was restored, and Florence was free to start work.

Parthenope was outraged that a private quarrel had made its way into the public sphere where it could materially hurt Florence's ambitions. It was one thing for Parthe to resent those ambitions and quite another for any word she said to actually thwart them.

Parthe first committed her concerns in a letter to Lothian, Marianne's brother. In this letter, she condemned Marianne's interference as 'dishonored'.[1] Next, she wrote to Marianne's aunt in order to set the public record straight, using the plural first person to represent the entire family. A job tending to the sick in Harley Street was not what 'we' wanted exactly, she explained, but our principle concern is and will always be to make sure Florence does exactly what she wants to do, was the drift of the letter.[2]

Parthe had learned a valuable lesson here. She had learned that her private thoughts and tantrums could quickly and easily become public fodder. She had a famous sister, and that changed things. Parthenope was no longer a fully private individual. She could fall into the limelight without warning. She could not rely on friends and family to keep anything she said confidential. From this point on, Parthe was more circumspect. She made sure that the public always saw the side of her that supported and championed her sister, not the peevish side of her that just wanted Flo to come home and share her life.

Parthenope's life in the shadow of Florence officially begins at this point. From here until the time of her marriage, she mostly served as Florence's secretary, supply chain supervisor, and mopper upper. She also tried to be an advisor, but her advice was mostly dismissed; in fact, Florence was often enraged by it.

Parthenope began this work as Florence's unappreciated assistant by furnishing her sister's Harley Street apartment. For this work, she received a letter, addressing her as 'Dear Pop'. However, when Florence went in person to Covent Garden to buy produce for the Harley Street establishment, Parthenope protested against the unnecessary danger, earning herself a sharp rebuke.

Around the time that Florence started her job at Harley Street, Parthenope wrote her a letter of contrition. This letter speaks, with some agony, of her (Parthenope's) mistakes, by which she means her opposition to Florence's career. To Florence, she poses the question whether human mistakes are ordained by God, just as are human misfortunes.[3]

There's a good deal of evident soul searching in that question. Parthenope doesn't see how she can blame God for her own, personal shortcomings. But how can an all-powerful God permit well-intentioned people to do the wrong thing? Florence, who was going through a short-lived period of philosophical determinism replied rather roughly that God wills everything, and that nothing is a mistake, not even Miss Ryder, a superintendent of a charitable organization, who made the news for unintentionally poisoning and killing one of her clients.[4]

By August 1854, the rift between Florence and Parthenope was largely healed. In that month, Florence sent Parthenope a letter, confiding that she was determined to resign her position on Harley Street and accept a job of more power and prestige at another hospital. This information was to be kept a secret. Florence ridiculed the men who came to gawk at her. She wrote to Parthenope that they had no idea what she was capable of. Florence also recommends that Parthenope read Frederick Hill's book, *Crime, Its Amount, Causes, and Remedies*.[5]

This letter clearly shows that, as early as mid-1854, Florence considered her sister a full ally and even a fellow activist who would enjoy a good laugh at the expense of the unwoke. Many biographies have unfortunately conflated Florence's wrath with her family, AFTER her return to England from a war zone, with the initial resistance posed by her family, which was rather easily overcome, once Florence had determined to do so.

Chapter 12

Gaskell Friendship, Spottiswoode Refusal

In 1854, both Parthenope and Florence were in Lea Hurst, where they hosted Mrs Elizabeth Gaskell. Gaskell was not as wealthy as the Nightingales, but talent and accomplishment are their own assets. She was a celebrity whose novels were quite popular.

Gaskell and Parthenope developed a friendship that was close enough to exchange confidences over many years. For instance, to Elizabeth Gaskell Parthenope confided that Florence was motivated by ambition more than compassion. To Gaskell, Parthenope confided her famous comparison of Florence to a swan among common ducks: 'Miss Nightingale says— with tears in her eyes/ alluding to Andersen/ that they are ducks & have hatched a wild swan…'[1]

Gaskell's word picture of Parthenope is at odds with the common perception that she was envious, sickly, and grouchy. Gaskell found Parthenope busily relieving Florence of all the little humdrum chores: tending to her parents, managing the servants, caring for the community's poorer members. Gaskell considered Parthenope good-natured and absolutely devoted to Florence, to the point of worrying that Florence would be blamed for any local duty left undone.

Gaskell observed that Parthenope's very existence was lost in Florence's. Gaskell, it seems, was one of the few observers who were able to get an emotional distance from Florence and see the sisters' relationship from Parthenope's point of view. The friendship between Gaskell and Parthenope would last for the rest of Gaskell's life.

The Nightingales urged Gaskell to stay on at Lea Hurst after they had decamped. And Gaskell accepted the invitation. She was able to use the solitude of that grand establishment to grind away at and finally finish *North and South*, her great novel about Britain's northern manufacturing industry. Gaskell portrays industrialization as both a rather gruesome way to make a living and as an opportunity for men of great ambition and work ethics to obtain wealth, however desperate the circumstances of their birth.

North and South substantially influenced Parthenope's work as a writer. The novel's hero, John Thornton, is a self-made gentleman who has earned a fortune in manufacturing. He is a devoted and loving son and brother to the several women in his family who depend on him financially. But, to his workers, he is often merciless. The triumph of *North and South* is its objective treatment of the industrial revolution, which examines all sides of the ongoing battle between factory owners and workers.

At one point in the novel, Thornton contemptuously acknowledges that he sought to filter and ventilate his factory to protect his employees from breathing in cotton fibres and getting respiratory illnesses. But then the workers complained. The floating cotton had ended up in their stomachs and made them feel full. They felt that ingesting cotton was a perk of the job that had been taken away from them.

As an anthropological analysis of its time, *North and South* is unmatched. It is somewhat flawed by the last chapters which are wholly taken up by Thornton's rocky romance with the heroine, Margaret Hale. But to be fair to Gaskell, she was a popular writer making a living from her novels. As such, she was expected to deliver romantic drivel by the folio. She also realized that social issues would only be ingested by some readers if those issues were heavily infused with melodrama.

Gaskell must be understood within the context of her time. She was brave not to confine her novels to romantic topics as did most women novelists of the nineteenth century, including Jane Austen and all three of the Brontë sisters. Gaskell always tackled bigger subjects: especially poverty, the plight of working women, and ruralism that most female novelists avoided.

Parthenope would read *North and South* and, in her own time, build on its ideas by considering how industrialization impacted the lives of rural women. Parthenope, too, would write novels that were an exposé of poverty, and the lives of country folk who are otherwise almost completely absent from nineteenth-century fiction.

Gaskell provided a template for the kind of career that Parthenope would eventually have. Here was a fellow Unitarian, a happily married woman and mother. Yet she somehow balanced her conventional duties against her prolific writing career.

Gaskell formally credited Parthenope with the timely invitation to occupy Lea Hurst off-season, calling it a 'happy happy pause of life'.[2] She was still at Lea Hurst when the housekeeper found the dead body of Athena, the owl. Gaskell had the pet stuffed. Florence blamed Parthenope for not caring adequately for her pet.

Sometime in 1854, Parthenope received a marriage proposal from William Spottiswoode.[3] They had formed a friendship over the publication of Florence's Egypt chronicle. Spottiswoode, a mathematician, was also a publisher whose firm, Eyre and Spottiswoode, reviewed the letters from Egypt though they were published only privately in Florence's lifetime.

Parthenope's refusal of Spottiswoode is mystifying. From this vantage in time, he seems perfect for her. He was a scholar, like her father and like herself, lively, a good conversationalist. He was an avid traveller. Having failed to marry Parthenope, he undertook a great journey to eastern Russia in 1856 and then to Croatia and Hungary in 1860. In 1861, three years after Parthenope's wedding, he finally settled down and married Elisa Taylor Arbuthnot with whom he had children.

Spottiswoode's willingness to serve Florence may not have been wholehearted enough for Parthenope. While Parthenope did eventually marry, it was to a man who did not just serve Florence, he served her slavishly, taking her out for carriage rides, making deliveries, researching her ideas for reform, and presenting some of them to Parliament.

Still, it is difficult to understand why Parthenope declined such an eligible young man who was several years younger than she. Parthenope's chances of having children would have been greater at this time than at thirty-nine when she did finally marry. It looks as if Parthenope deliberately annihilated her own agenda and happiness to do the behind-the-scenes grunt work of Florence's great vision.

Florence and Parthenope Nightingale, well dressed. Located in the National Gallery. (*Public domain*)

This popular image of Fanny Nightingale with Parthenope (left) and Florence as children was originally painted by Swiss artist Alfred Chalon. (*Pubic domain*)

Frances Parthenope Nightingale drew this beautiful portrait of her sister, Florence (left), with her cousin Marianne Nicholson. Marianne hoped to become Florence's sister-in-law by marriage, but those hopes were dashed when Florence determined to stay single and pursue nursing. Courtesy of the Florence Nightingale Museum in London. (*Public domain*)

This portrait of Florence Nightingale by her sister Parthenope has captured many imaginations. Florence is pictured here with her owl Athena. The image has been enhanced by engraver F. Holl. (*Courtesy of Wellcome Library*)

Fanny Nightingale holding her daughter, Frances Parthenope, by an unknown artist. Courtesy of the Florence Nightingale Museum. (*Public domain*)

Frances Parthenope Verney is here pictured with the bay of Naples in the background. The artist is believed to be Rocco Lentini. (*Courtesy of Wellcome Library*)

This caricature of Sir Harry Verney appeared in Vanity Fair in 1882. The artist, known by the pen name "Spy," was really Leslie Ward. (*Public domain*)

This plaque is a memorial to Sir Harry Verney, Member of Parliament, liberal reformer, and husband of Lady Frances Parthenope Verney. (*Public domain*)

Parthenope Verney (left) pictured with her sister Florence Nightingale and husband Harry Verney on the grounds of Claydon House. Sir Harry frequently consulted Nightingale about issues of health and public welfare. Photographer unknown. (*Public domain*)

Frances Parthenope Nightingale's drawing of the Nightingale winter home, Embley, courtesy of the Wellcome Library. (*Courtesy of Wellcome Library*)

This photograph of Lea Hurst, the Nightingales' summer and autumn home, is believed to have been taken by Richard Keene. Reproduced here courtesy of the Wellcome Collection, London. (*Public domain*)

William Edward Nightingale built Lea Hurst to blend in with its natural surroundings. This wood engraving is reproduced courtesy of the Wellcome Library. (*Public domain*)

Sir Harry (top, left of center) and Parthenope Verney invited the nurses studying under Florence Nightingale (center) to enjoy recreational outings at the Claydon estate. (*Photo courtesy of the Wellcome Collection*)

Claydon House was the home of Frances Parthenope from the time she married Sir Harry Verney to the end of her life. (*Courtesy of Wikimedia Commons*)

Claydon Chapel, also known as All Saints Church, nestles on the grounds of the Claydon estate. It dates back to the 1200s. (*Photo courtesy of Mark Murphy and Wikimedia Commons*)

A view of the Claydon Estate, including All Saints Church. (*Courtesy of photographer Mel Braithwaite / CC BY-SA 2.0.*)

Pictured here is the interior of Claydon House, where Parthenope lived with the Verneys, helping to raise the two youngest. (*Public domain*)

Elizabeth Gaskell was a fellow Unitarian and lifetime friend of Parthenope Verney. Here, Gaskell is represented in a miniature by Scottish painter William John Thomson. (*Public domain*)

Elizabeth Gaskell became a novelist a few years before Frances Parthenope Verney did, and Gaskell's attention to the lives of rural English men and women inspired Parthenope to take on the same subject. This portrait of Gaskell was drawn by George Richmond. (*Public domain*)

William Spottiswoode, a Victorian mathematician, scientist, and publisher, was a great admirer of Parthenope Nightingale and proposed marriage to her. (*Courtesy of Wellcome Images, a website operated by Wellcome Trust, a global charitable foundation based in the United Kingdom*)

Frances Parthenope Nightingale was born in the same year as Queen Victoria who drove Victorian style and manners. This carbon print by J.J.E. Mayall was commissioned by the queen in 1860. (*Public domain*)

The abolitionist, William Smith, was also a leader in obtaining religious freedom for dissenters from the Church of England. He was Frances Parthenope Nightingale's maternal grandfather. (*Public domain*)

In All Saints Church sits the memorial to the Verney family into which Parthenope married. Documenting the history of her husband's family became a life project. (*Image © Acabashi, Creative Commons CC-BY-SA 4.0, Wikimedia Commons*)

Harry Verney, a Victorian member of parliament and Parthenope's husband, often consulted Florence Nightingale on matters of health and public interest. They are pictured here on the grounds of the Claydon estate. Photo courtesy of the Wellcome Library. (*Public domain*)

A colorization of Embley Park, after the drawing by Parthenope Nightingale. (*Courtesy of Wellcome Library*)

Chapter 13

'All things have ... fitted her for this'

Today, the Crimean War is largely forgotten. The most notable thing about it, for many people, is that it was the stage for Florence Nightingale's derring-do. It made her the lady of the lamp. So it may be difficult for readers to understand the tremendous support that this war received from the British public at large during its time.

The imaginative human wants to believe that wars are sparked by a trifle. The Trojan War was launched by the beautiful face of Helen, Menelaus' wife. King Arthur was conceived during a war sparked by his mother's beauty. Henry V attacked France over some tennis balls.

In this vein, the Crimean War was started over a key, the key to the Church of the Nativity in Bethlehem. Built to honour what was considered the birthplace of Jesus Christ, this church is sacred to several Christian sects, including the orthodox sects and the Roman Catholic Church. Instead of just sharing, Napoleon III of France wanted it to be under the stewardship of the French Catholics. The Russian czar, Nicolas I, wanted it for the Russian Orthodox. Who held the key to this church became hotly contested. The rights of the Ottomans who lived all around the church, to live in peace, were not part of the war room discussions.

Differences in religion were only the pretext, however. Russia wanted to expand its territory and power into Turkey and the middle east, while Britain and France wanted to maintain the strength of the declining Ottoman Empire in order to protect British trade routes and rights.

The French, British, and eventually the Sardinians showed up to side with Turkey and the Ottomans after Russian troops invaded and occupied a few Ottoman territories in what is now Romania. These allies targeted the port city of Sevastopol in the Crimean peninsula. The choice of target shows to what extent the allies did not understand the scale of Russia's landmass. Horrific mistakes were made, among them the battle described in Alfred Tennyson's 'Charge of the Light Brigade'. Stripped of its poetry, that charge was a suicide mission to the wrong location with the wrong weaponry.

In the short term, the allies won; in the long term, Russia won and then lost. Why, one might reasonably demand to know, was this first modern war so celebrated by the British when it did not even involve their own land or colonies? In a *New York Times* book review, Douglas Porch has an interesting theory about that. He notes that the war in and around the Crimean peninsula was the first war to be covered by war correspondents using the telegraph to provide fresh updates. The telegraph turned out to be so useful in disseminating information rapidly that British politicians often learned what had just happened in the Crimea when they opened their newspapers. Their own military dispatches from the front were much slower.

The pioneer of telegraph-to-newspaper content production was arguably William Howard Russell, a reporter for the *London Times*. When the Nightingale family opened their copy of the *Times*, perhaps over morning tea, they took in Russell's news about British soldiers fighting the Russians over a patch of land in the Black Sea.

Like other British citizens, the Nightingales would have been thrilled by the bravery of their soldiers, but also aghast at battlefield conditions, especially the casualty rate. Florence reported, later in her life, that it was Russell's daily reports on the war that inspired her to become a battle nurse.

The British public knew only the iceberg tip of the chaos happening in Sevastopol. The Crimean War was a massacre of which Florence saw only a small fraction in her time as head nurse in Scutari, the location to which wounded British soldiers were taken. More than half a million Russian soldiers died, mostly from disease; the allies lost a little less than half that number. The war could not help but wane in popularity as it dragged on from one to two years. However, Florence Nightingale's reputation did not suffer; instead, it went from good to great, as she reformed the military, wrote a new curriculum for nurses' training, and redesigned hospitals.

When Florence received her commission to head up nursing in Scutari, the entire Nightingale family swung into action, none of them more than Parthenope. The family relocated to their London house where Parthenope stayed busy packing supplies that would accompany Florence when she sailed to Turkey. She simultaneously undertook the work of locating nurses fit and courageous enough to go into a war zone while she also organized donations of clothing and supplies that came to their London rental on Cavendish Square.

A letter from Parthenope shows that she now fully accepted Florence's destiny: 'All things have … fitted her for this … None of her previous life has been wasted'.[1] In another letter, to Gaskell, she wrote that Florence 'seems led by something higher than I can see, and all I can do is to move every obstacle in my power out of her path'.[2]

Gaskell's friendship was a comfort to Parthenope, Gaskell being one of the few people who understood the extent to which Parthenope had sacrificed her own happiness to support Florence's dreams. In a letter to Parthe, Gaskell wrote, 'dear Miss Nightingale if it had not been for your careful performance of the quiet home duties, she would not have been at liberty for what she is now free to do'.[3]

To another correspondent, Gaskell noted that Parthenope was not as ordinary as she seemed: 'Parthe is plain, clever and apparently nothing out of the common way as to character; but she is for all that'. Gaskell saw Parthenope's commitment to Florence as an amazing thing.

> She is devoted—her sense of existence is lost in Florence's. I never saw such adoring love. To set F. at liberty to do her great work, Parthe has annihilated herself, her own tastes, her own wishes in order to take up all the little duties of home, to parents, to poor, to society, to servants, all the small things that fritter away time and life, all these Parthe does, for fear if anything was neglected people might blame F. as well from feeling these duties imperative as if they were grand things.[4]

If anyone had a balanced view of Florence Nightingale, it might have been Elizabeth Gaskell. She had a proper respect for Florence's accomplishments. But she could also see the price of such accomplishment. Florence was somebody who saw forests, not trees. She saw global suffering, not local needs. Florence, who was something of an actuary, lost her interest in individuals and focused on reforms that would benefit many, not actions that would immediately benefit a family. Florence Nightingale's closest friends and family were the ones who paid the price for this grandeur.

Gaskell quotes Parthenope as saying, 'F. does not care for individuals … but for the whole race as being God's creatures'.⁵

As an insider, Gaskell was ever so mildly shocked at how 'F.N.' treated her family. About this, Gaskell tactfully wrote, 'F.N. has very seldom told her family of her plans till they were pretty well matured'.⁶ Gaskell noted that, on one occasion, Fanny was still nursing Florence's toothache and was very worried about her daughter's health when Florence announced her imminent departure from home. Then, and only then, did it emerge that Florence had already planned this departure down to the last detail, thereby pre-empting any family discussion of whether she should leave while still in such poor health.

In the same letter, Gaskell credits the entire Nightingale family for adapting to necessity (something they had been trained to do over the years): 'they had nothing to do but yield', Gaskell wrote, adding, 'it struck me that, considering how decidedly this step of hers was against their judgment as well as against their wishes, it was very beautiful to see how silently and diligently they all tried to 'speed the parting guest'.

Gaskell was also one of Florence's few contemporaries to notice a coldness in her that was agony to Parthenope. Gaskell tells the story of a sick village boy in whom Florence at one point took an interest. The boy died, but, in his mother's mind, Florence was an angel. Parthenope felt, very deeply, that Florence should visit this woman when her husband later died. Florence, always torn between the personal and the professional consented to visit, but only once.

Gaskell saw this kind of behaviour as somewhat Machiavellian and used a Bible verse to both justify and question it: 'Who is my mother and my brethren?' That's actually something Jesus says in the Gospel of Matthew (12:48). Scholars generally agree that Jesus was right in prioritizing his important mission over the needs of his family, especially their need for a close relationship with him. Gaskell hit the nail on the head with this quote. Florence, like Jesus, could cold shoulder her family whenever she had an opportunity to effect positive change. Still, it bothered Gaskell, who mostly saw Florence through the lens of her affection for Parthenope.

Vetting nurses fit for wartime service was a huge undertaking for Parthenope. Because of the high wages, there were many applicants. The job paid twelve to fourteen shillings a week, rising to eighteen to twenty-four shillings after a solid year's service with good performance.

Those wages were quite high compared to the wages that nurses were paid for domestic work. So finding applicants was not difficult. What was difficult was sifting through the unqualified candidates to find that one who was not just in search of high wages, but also had actual character and credentials.

As Nightingale scholars have noted, ad infinitum, the nursing profession during the Nightingale sisters' time was neither prestigious nor respectable. This problem was not lost on Parthenope who described the vast majority of applicants as 'rubbish'.[7] Nevertheless, she was able to find the needles in that haystack. She hired Eliza Roberts, for instance, a nurse with twenty-three years' experience. Roberts would do her part to burnish the reputation of the nursing forces in the Crimea.

Just before she boarded ship for the war zone, Florence requested to see her dead, stuffed owl. Upon taking it in her hands, she shed a sad tear. She shed no tears upon parting with her sister.[8]

Chapter 14

The War at Home

While Florence was pacing the halls of the hospital in Scutari, legendary lamp in hand, Parthe's less grand destiny was to manage the fallout on the home front. Among other duties, she checked on the families that the nurses had left behind. When the nurses returned to England, it fell to Parthenope to find jobs for them.

A letter to one Mrs. B—, reportedly an American friend of the family, during this period shows us how subsumed Parthenope was in Florence's work. Parthenope needs to make sure that Mrs. B—, all the way across the ocean, knows that Florence has undertaken the 'true crusade'.

She goes on to write that she has organized a B-team of reserve nurses 'in case she [Florence] writes for them'. At last count, the number of nurse applicants was 367, she writes. Though she confesses to being, 'overdone with writing', the tone of the letter is relentlessly upbeat, if a little hurried. She briefly alludes to the massive work of donations for shipment overseas: 'old linen, books, money, knitted things, etc'. Then she goes on to write that the support for Florence's work has been amazing: The railroads had refused to accept payment for transporting the donations. 'The enthusiasm for her has been something wonderful'.

In this letter, Parthenope offers absolutely no information about herself, apart from her servitude to Florence's mission. She apologizes for the 'monotheme' of the letter. In other words, the letter offers only information about the war effort and Florence, but at the same time, Parthenope assumes that is the reader's only true interest. She signs on behalf of herself, 'Partho', her father, and mother.[1]

This letter is representative of the hundreds of letters that Parthenope undertook for Florence in the 1850s. She spent years channelling Florence, putting a positive spin on everything she did, and keeping track of the fans and donors.

Parthe poured over Florence's letters from the Crimea and took up her drawing tools to illustrate Florence's career once again. Her drawing of Florence on horseback gazing at the war-torn field of Sevastopol was mass-produced and very popular. Having never been to the Crimea, Parthenope had to use her imagination to come up with this ennobling piece of propaganda. Parthe also stayed busy writing *The Life and Death of Athena, an Owlet of the Parthenon*. She mailed it to Florence and then had it published.

For her part, Florence sent Parthe several symbolic gifts. In October 1854, when she had been in Scutari for nearly a year, she sent a comical letter to Parthenope along with a wedding scarf. The two had an ongoing joke about marrying each other, and this scarf picked up the thread of that humour.

> I send to you by Σ [use of the Greek letter unencrypted, so far] a bridal scarf for Parthe, the meaning of which is that the *new* "me" she has wedded which is really the old original "me", now thirty-five years old, acknowledges the eternal union with a wedding garment.

Florence also sent a jug and some rose water. Pouring rose water over the hands is still a part of some Indian and Greek wedding ceremonies, though Florence confessed she didn't know much about that tradition. And, for some reason, Florence also sent Parthenope a bullet that she picked up off the ground as well as some native wildflowers.[2]

Once embedded at Scutari, Florence was not content just to nurse the bodies of fallen soldiers; she also sought to improve their minds and souls. To that end, she established a sort of artist's coffee-house where the men would perform plays, read, draw, and otherwise engage in intellectual pursuits rather than idling and drinking.

It fell to Parthenope to drum up donations of supplies that would engage the soldiers who were in constant mortal danger of misusing their time. Florence commanded her to get donations of books, including copies of Macbeth, copybooks, sheet music, sports equipment, maps, board games, even a stereoscope, i.e. the early version of three-dimensional photography.

Queen Victoria was not exempt from donating. She sent a portrait of Duke Wellington presenting a bouquet to Prince Arthur. To our ears, this gift might sound a little tone-deaf. Did she really think wounded soldiers would care about this moment in royal history? But the print was, after all, very popular with the men. Perhaps it fed their starved fantasies.

While Parthenope was tirelessly working on behalf of the war effort, WEN preserved his manly ambivalence about the whole adventure. Even though the media coverage of Florence's efforts was overwhelmingly positive, he hated it. While Parthenope worried about whether Florence would return to England in one piece and whether her fellow nurses could reintegrate into their former lives, WEN fretted about the potential damage to his reputation of having such a famous daughter, one who was so out of sync with convention. He wrote that, upon reading about Florence, he would tremble for his own name. Even as Florence's accomplishments piled up, he wrote a sardonic letter to his wife, quipping that Florence's next act would be bringing the dead back to life. WEN's cherished privacy had been well and truly breached.

Parthenope bore the burden of reflected glory more graciously. In 1855, she accompanied her mother to a social event hosted by Richard Monckton Milnes, Florence's rejected suitor. There, Parthe and Fanny were besieged by Florence Nightingale fans who wanted to meet them. Among those admirers were Charles Dickens and William Makepeace Thackery.

By 1855, Parthenope had clearly become Florence Nightingale's fulltime secretary, writing twelve to thirteen letters a day on her famous sister's behalf. Some biographers claim that Parthenope had finally found a 'purpose' by which they presumably mean that she gave up writing, sketching, and caring for her nearby villagers in order to be Florence's amanuensis.

Parthenope almost never complained about this dreary work. However, when Florence became terribly sick, with what we now believe to have been brucellosis, Parthenope's work increased substantially. In a letter to Ellen Tollett, she wrote, 'I am quite done with writing, a second blast of linen and knitted socks was nearly the death of me'.[3]

Lynn McDonald's *Collected Works of Florence Nightingale* contains a letter from Florence in Parthenope Nightingale's handwriting, suggesting that Parthenope was reduced to ghostwriting for Florence on occasion. The letter, written to Richard Dawes, responds to earlier correspondence from him. In this letter, Parthenope channels Florence as she makes some very specific demands of Dawes. The problem, Parthenope as Florence writes, is that the soldiers get drunk upon receiving any paycheck. They don't redeem their time as Florence would have them do, by improving their reading and writing skills. To that end, well-wishers need to put their donations where their sentiments are. While this intriguing letter is written entirely from Florence's point of view, it possesses aspects of Parthenope's wit, suggesting that Parthe had the rough outline of what was needed from Florence to which she added some flare:

> I often hear of kind friends at home asking what they can do with wisdom for us. The best thing they can do for us is to give us something more tempting than rum and water, or rum without water. I have often been told by commanding officers that the only conversation which can be overheard among the men is about the comparative merits of rums. We want copybooks, pens and ink, Chambers's Educational Series or some reading books, which will enable us not to use the Bible as a textbook, and not to offend the priests, one third of the army being R. Catholic.

The letter goes on to ask for diagrams, by which Florence seems to mean lecture outlines; the Kenny Meadows illustrated complete Shakespeare; Milton, but not any Milton, it must be the version illustrated by Martin and Darby. Not content with this shopping list, Parthenope as Florence adds *Pilgrim's Progress*, *Household Words*, and illustrated magazines.

The letter goes on to ask for human resources. Specifically, Florence needs a trained schoolmaster for Scutari, not for the soldiers in the Crimea who are getting ready to bug out. This schoolmaster will ideally be trained in trigonometry.

Parthenope closes this do list with a skilfully brazen admonition, mixed with fear-mongering: 'I know that I need not apologize for thus trespassing upon your time, because you live only to do us good. And the poor soldier may well come within the number of your children. For he is a sad, silly child'.[4]

Why did Parthenope pose as Florence in the writing of this letter? Could it be because she began to find Florence's demands so imperious that she didn't want to pose them in her own person?

In a letter dated 11 November 1855, Florence sent Parthenope a list of things she wanted from Queen Victoria and the Duchess of Kent. She refers to the queen with a level of informality that might have been disrespectful if the letter had been shared directly with that sovereign: 'Should H.R.H. condescend to wish to know that which will most benefit the British soldier now —it is every kind of interest and amusement which will tend to draw them away from their besetting sin—drunkenness'.

Then Flo gets down to business with the specific list of things she wants these high-born ladies to provide. The queen needs to send chess boards and pieces, dominoes, draughts, backgammon gear, educational books, especially 'Chambers' Educational Series', in which Florence put great faith and mentioned it in several letters, and, again, the lecture diagrams. Not just any lecture diagrams, however. These must include lessons on 'elements of astronomy and the orrery, natural history, mechanical powers, elements of physiol-ogy, stratification of the earth, etc...'

The same letter assigns the Duchess of Kent (Queen Victoria's mother) to send copies of *Pilgrim's Progress*, the *Penny Post*, and 'miscellanies'.[5]

It also fell to Parthenope to manage or at least attempt to manage some personal quarrels that Florence undertook. When Florence broke ranks with Mary Stanley, Parthenope suggested calm and putting anger aside. Parthenope managed this breach with a series of letters back and forth to Stanley.

When Florence developed a morbid suspicion of Henry Edward Manning, who sent fifteen nuns to the Crimea to support Florence's work, she assigned Parthenope to research, cut out, and send any article in which Manning mentioned Florence's name. Parthenope was also to note the name of the publication from whence this clipping came along with the date. Florence was determined to know what, where, and when Manning had made any mention of her.

Parthenope's work as Florence's biographer, secretary, and supplier soon gave way to fielding contributions to the Nightingale fund. This was a fund set up by Florence's fans to fund whatever work she chose to do back in England.

One need only read a few of the letters Parthenope wrote during this period to understand how dull and unrewarding this correspondence must have been. Columbia University's archive of Florence Nightingale documents includes a dozen or so letters from Parthenope to Mrs S. C. Hall, thanking her for her hard work on the fund, inviting Hall to visit Embley, thanking her for her sketch of Florence, detailing Florence's poor health, detailing her own poor health, etc. Thanks in large part to Parthenope's tireless correspondence, the Nightingale fund was successful in raising £44,039. It was closed in 1856.

That was also the year that Parthenope moved in with Florence and became her full-time gatekeeper. Florence had taken rooms at the Burlington Hotel in London. By this time, both Parthenope and Florence were badly disabled, Parthenope with rheumatoid arthritis and Florence from a bout with Brucellosis that she contracted in Turkey. Neither woman ever enjoyed full health again.

Upon her triumphant return to London, Florence almost immediately became adept at deflecting any unwanted attempts to drain her energy, and, for a brief time, it was Parthenope's full-time job to vet visitors and correspondents. The letter writing continued. Now, the tenor of her letters was to politely refuse access to celebrity mongers and people who wanted money. Parthenope's mission was clear: Save Florence from wasting time on anyone who couldn't directly advance her goals. Florence's goals, from this time forward, were to reform medicine through the elevation of the nursing profession and hospital design.

But Parthenope would not enjoy the role of Florence's protector for long. Florence soon recalled all the reasons she was angry and resentful of her sister and the other members of her family. They had opposed her independence, and they had not supported her decisions. Florence had to do some historical revision to get to this conclusion.

Chapter 15

The Great Divorce of Pop and Flo

Florence's writings from this period are the work of a woman struck down with illness in her prime. They show little perspective and less reason. Utterly forgotten were all the fundraising, the indefatigable letter writing, the virtual propaganda machine that Parthenope ran with occasional help from her mother and little to none from her father. At this moment in time, Florence bitterly complained that Parthenope and Fanny were hypocrites who only now cared for her because she had succeeded on the world stage.

She developed this theme at length, claiming that people regard others, especially their family members as their property. When someone leaves her family to accomplish something in the world through pain and diligence, the world flatters the family for 'giving her up', Florence rants. And the family praises themselves for giving up their family member, as if it were their decision.

Florence felt that she was called by God to serve in Harley Street and in Scutari. It was not, in retrospect, the job of her family to 'let' her serve in this way. (Even though they did give her their full support.) It was their job to get out of her way. Some of her thoughts about this are admirably feminist; others oversimplify the complex relationship she had with her immediate family.

The tension Florence Nightingale describes, balancing the concerns of a loving family against one's own needs, exists as much today as it did then. To what extent do we owe it to the ones who love us to stay safe, for their sakes? Every family answers this question for themselves. But Florence felt she had been thwarted, and that now her sister and mother were basking in her reflected glory.[1]

Aunt Mai was called in to replace Parthenope, and Mai became Florence's new gatekeeper. Part of her job was to keep the gate mostly closed against Florence's immediate family. It was Mai who told Fanny and Parthenope to find lodgings in a different hotel, not the Burlington.[2]

It was Mai who instructed them never to visit at the same time. It has been suggested that Mai believed Florence was not long for this world when she (Mai) accepted this job. As the years wore on and Florence continued to steer medical science from her chaise lounge, Mai might have felt trapped.

We have little documentation of the emotional impact her banishment must have had on Parthenope. We know that she expressed some degree of indignation at being shut out from Florence's life, however, because Florence enlisted other people to tell Parthenope to back off.

One such personage was the famous poet Arthur Hugh Clough who was drawn into Florence's circle. In May 1858, Clough wrote to Parthenope, telling her, in so many words, to stay away. He acknowledged that the separation was harder on Parthenope than on any other person, but called on her to make the sacrifice and 'stay away'.[3]

Parthenope found refuge, finally, in the company of her father. Having both been rebuffed by the most popular Nightingale, they found some comfort in each other. Parthenope finally had the closeness to her father that she had sought when she was a schoolgirl. For WEN, who no longer had access to Florence, Parthenope was the next best thing: a daughter he had hand raised and educated to be a worthy companion to himself.

Through 1865, Florence remained partially estranged from her family. Though she lived off an income provided by WEN, she rarely saw Fanny or Parthenope. She infrequently wrote to her sister or her parents during this period. Mai nursed Florence and wrote to the Nightingales on Flo's behalf.

The effect of losing Florence was basically the same for Parthenope as if she had lost her spouse and her job at the same stroke. She not only lost her most beloved person, to whom she was jokingly married, she also lost her life's work. For the past several years, she had been Florence's secretary and aide-de-camp on the home front. All those letters petitioning funds, games, and books, thanking people for their contributions, politely denying them access to Florence! Those letters not only had to be handwritten, they had to be carefully and legibly written, with flawless use of the English language, so as to reflect well on Florence and her work. They had to capture just the right tone, and omit no detail of politeness that was due to the recipient.

Parthenope no doubt felt that her tireless and uncomplaining support had earned her a place in Florence's drawing-room. Through hours of thankless letter writing and troubleshooting Florence's human resources problems, surely she had fought her way back to the sisterly connection they had enjoyed as young women, studying, hiking, and travelling together.

That was not to be. Parthenope was shut out. Cold.

So.

It was an ideal time for a Prince Charming to ride onto the stage and sweep Parthenope off her feet or at least provide an alternate object of devotion.

Enter Sir Harry Verney.

Chapter 16

'I never thought to marry anyone but F'

The recently widowed Harry Verney knew of Florence Nightingale as did everyone in England, literate and illiterate. She was a nationwide celebrity. Verney's first wife, while still alive, had expressed the wish that her daughter might meet the famous Florence Nightingale.

The request of a dying woman is a mighty thing, but there is some debate about whether the meeting was ever granted. Sir Harry, himself, however, had the power and influence to help Florence with her work, so he was regularly accepted into the inner sanctum of her Burlington rooms.

If someone had Florence's confidence and trust, it was nearly automatic that he or she be invited to meet the rest of the Nightingales at Lea Hurst or Embley, and Sir Harry was no exception. Harry, as might be predicted, fell in love with the Nightingale clan. Who would not want to marry into the Nightingales?

Harry Verney was a tall handsome man of fifty-six to Parthenope's thirty-nine years. He had been born Harry Calvert and took the name Verney when he inherited the estate of that name. Like WEN, he was the recipient of an inheritance that was entailed away from the female line. The seat of the Verneys was Claydon House, a mansion that survives today, now owned by the National Trust. It is an ancient family that traces its ancestry back to the fifteenth century. The estate that Verney inherited, however, was indebted and in a state of neglect, even semi-ruination.

By the time he met Parthenope, Verney had led a varied, often thrilling life. As a very young man, he chose the military and attended the Royal Military Academy Sandhurst from the age of fifteen. In 1819, he joined the 31st (Huntingdonshire) Regiment of Foot. He was sent to Germany where he learned that language as well as Italian and French. He then served in other regiments and, in 1826, became private secretary to the Commander-in-Chief of the Forces.

He accompanied Lord William Bentinck to Brazil, but fell ill in Rio de Janeiro where he was left to live or die as the fates might have it. When he recovered, he explored the Andes Mountains and the Pampas that extend through Argentina and Uruguay. In 1929, he sailed around Cape Horn on his way back to England. He was promoted to Major in 1831.

In 1832, he became a member of Parliament, and he represented Buckinghamshire and Bedford off and on, for the next several decades. He married his first wife, Eliza Hope, in 1835, and she bore him seven children. Most of Eliza's surviving children were grown and living their own lives, but her youngest, Frederick William, was but twelve when Parthenope came to Claydon. Eliza's daughter, Emily, was then fifteen.[1]

Here was a man who was worthy of a Nightingale daughter. He had travelled widely, read prodigiously, not only hoped for positive change, but was prepared to put it into law. His ideas were progressive, by the standards of his day. It was this respectable and accomplished man who chased after Parthenope with all the valour and enthusiasm of Shakespeare's Romeo. Fanny actually used the words 'hot pursuit' to describe Verney's romancing of her daughter. She went on to say he was like a soldier, making a mad dash to get married before going into battle.[2]

According to Fanny, Parthenope was initially 'alarmed' by Verney's honourable, but direct and unmistakable advances. Well, Verney was, after all, a man who had served bravely in the military, been left for dead, recovered, travelled the world, held a chair in Parliament, and took on the renovation of an indebted estate. He was not going to be scared off by a Nightingale, no matter how reserved, accomplished, and hemmed in on all sides by family and servants.

Parthenope and Sir Harry bonded over a chapter in the Old Testament book of Isaiah.[3] Both of these people were champions of new readings of the Bible. A rejection of inherited wisdom is practically a tenet of Unitarianism. Though Sir Harry was officially an evangelical within the boundaries of the Church of England, he was also a reformer and rationalist. To people like this, a shared interpretation of even one chapter of the Bible would be enough to look at each other and think, 'Hm. Could he/she be the one?'

Sir Harry would have known about the Nightingale estate entail. There's little doubt that he could have made a more financially advantageous marriage, one that would have put the Verney debt at rest.

Was there some pity involved in his proposal to Parthenope? Did he fancy himself the knight rushing in to aid a noble but saddened young woman? Did he want an excuse to be close to Florence and the other amazing Nightingales? Probably.

But Verney also saw in Parthenope a woman much like the lovely, young lady he had first married. Her character, pursuits, and education reminded him of the mother of his children. Furthermore, he thought that his first wife would approve this choice.

But this particular course of love did not run perfectly smooth, especially at the beginning. Parthenope initially accepted Sir Harry's proposal, then withdrew it. She admitted to having a deficit of romantic feelings for him, and worried that a marriage under that circumstance would be dangerous. She also expressed the concern, as have other women for the past two hundred years, that she might end up like a caged bird.

But the most insuperable obstacle that Parthenope saw to happiness with Verney was their religious differences. He was Church of England; she was Unitarian. He believed in a literal hell; she found that idea repugnant. He accepted the Calvinist underpinnings of most Protestant theology; she thought Calvin was a dangerous individual and responsible for more than his share of the world's suffering.

In fact, by this time in her life, Parthenope had developed a whole set of unique and independent religious ideas, not all of which can be explained by a strict adherence to Unitarianism. While she was careful not to directly formalize or declare any religious doctrine, it is patently clear to anyone who does a close reading of her work that her beliefs would not pass the test of orthodoxy, not by a long shot.

Parthenope suppressed this theology. Her letters avoid the subject. In her non-fiction essays and articles, she is deliberately vague about religion. Nightingale scholars arrive at her belief system only by reading her novels, where a definite theology emerges, uttered by a host of fictional characters. She could not be prosecuted for these ideas, cloaked as they were in the personas of various rural characters of different social strata.

To understand why Parthenope would suppress her unique theology, except as comedic asides or flustered declarations by fictional characters, we must understand the historical context. The second half of the nineteenth century was not, in fact, a good time to have ideas about God and faith that departed radically from the state religion. Queen Victoria and the short-lived Albert had certainly set an example of civility and decorum, but that did not prevent some very real religious persecution from taking place.

In 1860, for example, a collection of essays modestly titled *Essays and Reviews* appeared on library and bookstore shelves. It was a compilation of new interpretations of the Bible that, at some points, challenged the received wisdom preached from Church of England pulpits. One essay openly questioned the need for an actual hell where sinners would burn in eternal damnation. The author of this essay and one other contributor to the anthology were hauled up before an ecclesiastical court and found guilty of blasphemy. Though a civil court overturned the decision, it was a disturbing setback in the progress toward religious freedom because it set a precedent for civil authorities to try people on the subject of religious compliance.[4] Ever to do so jeopardizes church and state separation, the basis, some would say, of a fair and just state.

The Unitarians, to whom Parthenope belonged by birth and taste, occupied a state of precarious grace within the Victorian era. Their wealth, intellect, social standing, impeccable conduct, and frequent leadership positions earned them a place safe from being branded as heretics, even though there were and are major departures from mainstream Christianity in Unitarian doctrine, both historically and in the present time.

When Parthenope confessed to religious differences from those of Sir Harry so profound that they constituted a reason not to marry, she was not acting on a whim. She had, in fact, thought long and hard about the way Christianity was taught and practised. Though Parthenope had not begun her serious writing career at the time of Sir Harry's proposal, her thoughts were well-formed. And she would give voice to these ideas in the near future.

By having fictional characters speak of and act out religious ideas, she was able to point out a range of hypocrisy and muddled theological thinking. And she was able to do so from the safe vantage of imaginative literature. Cartoonists and animators today can put forward outrageous images and ideas, because they are just drawings, not representational, and how can you take offence at an art form originally designed for children? Similarly, Parthenope was able to put forward a fairly coherent theology in her combined books without risking scandal and denunciation.

We know from her novels, for instance, that Parthenope had read Darwin, as had most serious thinkers of that time. In *Lettice Lisle*, she summed up his work with the words, 'There are many ways in which Mr Darwin's "struggle for life" is carried on; and in many things the meanest, shabbiest, and cheapest win the day'.[5] The author goes on to point out that poorly designed rental properties are surely the basest form of architecture possible. Their cheapness of construction had won the day against the kind of beauty that the Middle Ages, Renaissance, and Enlightenment had left the world with.

Though her use of Darwin's theory of evolution is mostly humorous (and, therefore, how could it be heretical?), it is worth noting that she does not repudiate him. Instead, she expands his theory to cover the productions of mankind.

And, when one sums up the *Origins of the Species* as the 'struggle for life', it becomes impossible to argue with. All Parthenope's characters are poor, on the brink of becoming poor, or struggling to maintain a foothold in the class to which they were born. Parthenope had never kept herself separate from the communities of farmworkers and labourers who lived near her father's estates. She was often involved in caring for the sick or hungry. Who could repudiate a theory that is based on so evident a fact as the struggle for survival?

However, the religious doctrine of her time that Parthenope most struggled with was predestination. Few people in our time, or in Parthenope's, thought about or cared about predestination, but it is a theological doctrine that has wormed its way into most Protestant denominations. Predestination is the brainchild of exactly one man, John Calvin, whose influence, through this one doctrine, has been understated.

Predestination is not difficult to understand. It notes that everything that happens is God's will and was ordained to happen. Therefore, Adam and Eve had no real choice about eating the forbidden fruit and getting kicked out of paradise. Jesus was destined to die on the cross, and the Romans who persecuted him were likewise without any real choice to do as they did. They will be punished with eternal damnation, nevertheless. The few hundred or thousand people who will go to heaven are the 'elect'. It was always their destiny to be saved, long before they were born, and it was always the destiny of the damned to reject salvation. Free will is a very strong illusion, but it is just an illusion, according to the tenet of predestination.

Predestination is the distinctive quality of Calvinism, and most Protestant sects are founded on Calvinism. Most Protestant ministers choose to soft-pedal Calvinism and predestination as one of 'God's mysterious ways' that we need not understand in order to be saved. After all, if church congregation members each started seriously and individually questioning whether or not they were truly 'elect', doubt might empty those pews along with the offering plates.

One cannot seriously study the writings of Parthenope Verney without eventually noticing that she has a problem with predestination. However, she throws up a screen of humour over the horror of theology.

In *Lettice Lisle*, Parthenope uses the character of Mary Edley to ridicule Calvinism. Mary, herself, is the perfect Christian: patient, loving, tactful, always, always giving away her material possessions and her time to the sick or in other ways needful.

Mary's husband, Jesse, understands Calvinist theology, so when he prays, he prays to be at peace with God's will. When Jesse's brother, Calvin, is taken prisoner for smuggling, Jesse needs a lot of time to pray 'that it might be made a blessing to his [Caleb's] soul'.

Then Mary protests, 'But I could ha' wished as it had a been God A'mighty's pleasure he should save his soul like outside in the world as 'twere'.[6]

In the same scene, Mary says, 'but it weren't to be, ye see, and we can't go agin' what's set down up there, ye know … But what wi' prevenent grace and pedestrination, and all them things, why, I'm quite muzzed by times, I am'.[7]

Through Mary's garbled understanding of accepted doctrine, Parthenope gets at the problem with predestination. It leaves us nothing to do. There can be no point in obtaining justice, righting wrongs, or even praying, really, if everything bad is God's will.

If predestination is repugnant, how much more so the idea of a devil who stalks us omnipotently and is constantly drawing us to the dark side. Parthenope rejected this idea rather thoroughly in her book, *Cottier Owners, Little Takes and Peasant Properties*.

The book is mostly an assemblage of observations about the lives of French people, the current politics, and random thoughts. Within this innocuous set of memoirs and random thoughts, the future Lady Verney would find a reason to tell the story of Saint Kado, an obscure personage who currently seems to reside mostly in unsanctioned apocrypha and a few gift stores. In Parthenope's retelling of the story, Kado wants a bridge built across a troublesome river. He applies for aid to the Virgin Mary, but she says that it's not women's work. So Kado takes the project to the Devil (capitalization Parthenope's). The Devil, being a skilled engineer, draws up a solid blueprint. He then agrees to build the bridge on the condition that he is allowed to harvest, for hell, the soul of the first person who walks across it. Kado gets his bridge built, then sends an unwary black cat across the bridge whose presumably already lost soul the Devil has to accept for payment. Parthenope concludes this tale with the words, 'one cannot help taking the Devil's side, who has honestly completed his bargain, and is defrauded rather indecently by the wiles of the holy man'.[8]

The reader can see a lot of theology rejected in the way Parthenope tells this tale. The devil is the clear man of talent and action. He is the only one capable of getting an important infrastructural project completed. The so-called 'holy man' is both manipulative and dishonest. Most importantly, true ability and accomplishment are devalued in the traditional narrative while lazy cunning is held up as a model of behaviour. By association, people who sum up their beliefs with stories like this are also devaluing projects that advance civilization while admiring scoundrels.

These are just some of the thoughts that were rolling around in Parthenope's head when she held out against marrying Verney. But at the time that Parthenope was deciding whether to marry, she had not yet put these ideas into publication. That would have to wait for the next chapter in her life, the chapter in which she became a successful novelist.

Verney was a brave man, and he would not give her up. He begged her simply to put her doubts and their differences out of her mind, and he claimed that he had lost his heart to her. He may have gone so far as to suggest that he would waste away if she would not have him. His second proposal carried the day, and Parthenope put her engagement back on the calendar.

Most people who marry have complex feelings toward one another, so we should not attempt to sum up Parthenope's feelings for Verney or his for her too quickly or simplistically. It is fairly obvious that Verney saw a different Parthenope from what Florence saw. He did not see the panicky, crippled, useless, emotionally dependent woman that Florence saw or the barely adequate substitute for Florence that WEN saw. Nor did he see the child of lesser beauty who had failed to find a husband even after years of London parties and dances, as Fanny saw Parthenope.

No, Verney saw an immensely talented woman, fluent in French, a published artist and literary editor, knowledgeable about politics and philosophy, able to keep up with any Member of Parliament in conversation. He would have also seen a woman of good humour, loving to those nearest to her, and genuinely compassionate to the less fortunate.

It may be hard for students of the Nightingales to understand why Parthenope would hesitate so long to marry such an eligible man. Women of that time and ours frequently make much worse marriages just to escape their parents. Just to escape the humiliation of being the thirty-nine-year-old child in her family might have been enough.

The rights of Victorian British women were so few and far between that marriage was really the only way for a woman to have any say in the way her household was run. Even then, she was often running a home to which she had no legal claim.

But Parthenope did not come from a typical Victorian family. Her parents were William Edward and Fanny Nightingale. They had educated Parthenope far beyond what was ordinary for a young woman from a well-born family. They had given her the gift of travel and books and private tutors. They treated her more or less as an equal, not just as an asset. Parthenope had always been attached to her father. And of late, their relationship had flourished.

Parthenope's letters from this period show that she felt tugged in two directions. On one hand, she hated leaving home because she felt a debt of gratitude to her parents. At the same time, she knew beyond a shadow of a doubt that Harry Verney was a good man to whom she could safely entrust her future. She was positive that he would be an affectionate and sensitive husband.

She continued worrying about Florence who was not well, and during the summer, the heat made her symptoms worse. She was under doctor's orders to take a carriage ride (presumably for the fresh air), but the motion of the carriage made her even sicker. She was not sleeping or eating. And her doctor said she needs absolute silence when not talking to the people who could make her ideas manifest. Parthenope had all this information from Aunt Mai, who was still the only family member allowed to come and go in Florence's rooms.

As usual, Parthenope's sense of humour did not spare herself as its target. Once she had finally agreed to marry Verney for the second time, she wrote to Elizabeth Gaskell that, 'I never thought to marry anyone but F'. In the same letter, she mourns the loss of her sister: 'life has cut me off from her. I cannot help her now'.[9]

Gaskell wrote back, and her enthusiasm for the marriage must have been heartening for Parthenope. Her relief that Parthenope was finally out from under Florence's shadow was obvious. She expressed it very tactfully, however, saying that she had worried about the future of someone so subsumed in another's existence. Parthe would now be someone's 'principle object' and not just an unappreciated, even despised satellite, Gaskell wrote.[10]

Parthenope and Verney were married at Claydon on 24 June 1858, with little fanfare. There was no cake, no brand new clothes, no honeymoon. Two people were conspicuously absent from this quiet wedding: Florence Nightingale and Verney's eldest son Edmund.

Florence begged off on the grounds of being too busy. Edmund, however, had listened to quite a bit of gossip about Florence Nightingale, and he disapproved of the marriage. He had gone so far as to warn his father that a woman from that family was not his idea of marriage material. Florence's religious 'ideas were all over the place, he noted, giving rise at one point to a suspicion of atheism. (An astute observation, actually. Nightingale scholars are still trying to pin Florence down on the subject of God, and she keeps eluding them, long after death.) But Edmund had an even more scathing judgment to deliver. He suspected Florence and, by association, Parthenope of being 'self-willed', with 'strong prejudices', and, gasp!, a 'strong and imperious mind'.[11]

Chapter 17

'Principle Object'

Despite these apocalyptic forebodings, Sir Harry and Parthenope were wed, and they embarked on a marriage that was both happy and productive. Parthenope found herself the stepmother to twelve-year-old Frederick and fifteen-year-old Emily, both of whom expressed great affection for her in their letters. Emily started writing to her new mother before the wedding and said that she knew Parthenope would be a great comfort to 'papa'. Over the years, Emily and Frederick would come to address her as 'mama'. One year after the wedding, Edmund was doing the same. Upon acquaintance with Parthenope, Edmund came to fully appreciate her.

As mistress of Claydon and Verney's London residence, Parthe had a whole new and absorbing set of duties. Conventions of the time dictated that her first duty was to her new home and family. No longer could she be saddled with all the clerical duties surrounding Florence's projects. The days of packing Florence's bags, organizing her donations, mailing trunks of supplies and clothing overseas, and running human resources were over. Parthenope had yoked herself to a less ruthless master. In fact, Harry Verney had no real interest in dominating his wife at all. She entered marriage, free to become her own person, at last.

One of Parthenope's first self-appointed duties as Lady Verney was to participate in the renovation of Claydon. The estate was in terrible decay and disarray, due to no fault of his own, when Verney inherited it. Parthenope was able to contribute financially to the renovation of Claydon, though perhaps not to the extent she would have liked. The financial situation of the Nightingale daughters had improved over the last forty years. The Nightingale estate was still entailed to the male line. But WEN had done a good job of investing the funds he managed that came to him from the separate Shore estate. Funds from this estate formed Parthenope's dowry.

This meant that the Verneys had at least some of the money needed to repair Claydon as well as funds to improve the homes of their tenants. However, Parthenope's marriage settlement was all the money she could ever use to help Claydon. The remainder of monies was entailed away from her in the form of a trust assigned to the Shore line, when she failed to produce an heir.

This did not dampen Parthenope's enthusiasm for creating a warm and inviting home for Verney and his guests. One task that she took up was the cataloguing and displaying of many valuable paintings. Among them were portraits of the Verney family by Peter Lely and Anthony Van Dyck. One especially valuable painting had been used to cover a hole in the wall to prevent the entrance of rats. Parthe did not stop at renovating the existing structure. She supervised the construction of a new library and furnished a drawing-room that would allow the Verneys to entertain.

Parthenope began a biography of Florence Nightingale during this period. It has never been published, largely because it takes the reader up to only the point of the Crimean War. Parthenope may have abandoned the project out of fear of Florence. The latter had, by this time, developed a withering contempt for women writers to whom she referred as 'female ink-bottles'.

Parthenope became pregnant with surprising speed after her wedding. In one letter, she reveals that she hoped for a girl, a 'little Flo'. This, indeed, would have been Parthenope's greatest tribute to her beloved sister. But it was not to be. She miscarried as 1858 was ending, and was unable to get pregnant again.

Parthenope's new exciting life looked a lot like her teenage years. Verney actively cultivated the friendships of intellectuals, and Parthenope's principle social duty was to run a salon for these guests and promote stimulating conversation. This she did, with vigour, despite ongoing troubles with rheumatoid arthritis and flare-ups of rheumatic fever. The marriage worked, in large part because Verney respected his wife's education and intelligence, consulting her on his work on the estate and in Parliament.

Florence was initially sardonic about Sir Harry, calling him a 'pompous princess',[1] but she changed her tune fairly quickly and expressed joy over her sister's marriage. In point of fact, the addition of Sir Harry to the family meant that Florence now had, not just a sister ready to do her bidding, but also a brother in law.

The ice that had formed over the sisters' relationship began to thaw almost immediately upon Parthenope's marriage. With the pressure off her to be Parthenope's soulmate, Florence was ready to let her sister back into her life in small ways. Sir Harry was immensely instrumental in reuniting the Nightingale siblings.

One year into the Nightingale/Verney marriage, it became clear that the Verneys and Florence Nightingale could be a powerful force for positive change. In 1859, Harry Verney, Parthenope Verney, and Florence Nightingale collaborated on the extensive renovation of a hospital in Buckinghamshire. An issue was the design. Florence had developed new models for hospital structure that were based on the need for good hygiene and the reduction of contagion. Harry and Nightingale fought for their choice of an architect to do the remodel which was heavily influenced by Nightingale's structural reforms. Lady Verney would lay the cornerstone for the addition in 1862.

In 1860, the Verneys consulted Florence on a problem closer to home. Florence was shocked to learn that the Claydon residence was close to the cemetery, and that the Verneys believed their health was suffering as a result of this proximity. Florence swung into action (or at least writing) and told them to get an inspection and gave directions for preventing further contamination of their living quarters. Jokingly, she told the Verneys that the Burial Act applied to this situation and 'I hope you will be tried and transported for the terms of your natural lives, Freddy and all'. She also declared she would swear out a warrant against them if they didn't take action. She even tells them to withhold a relevant charitable contribution until they get action on their structural problem.[2]

Harry and Florence enjoyed a mutually beneficial friendship. Through him, she had a voice in Parliament. For his part, Harry had unique and privileged access to Florence Nightingale, one of the great thinkers and reformers of her age. And direct access to Nightingale had become extremely rare. She continued to protect her time, health, and energy by seeing very few people. Most of her communication was in the form of letters and blueprints.

Nevertheless, she was, by now, a recognized health expert. So when Sir Harry became interested in the possibility of prisoners growing some of their own food, he consulted Florence on the health aspects of 'earth closets' and whether they could be used to grow vegetables in prison. Florence sent information to Sir Harry and then backed it up with a letter to Parthenope. She explained that earth closets and the use of manure as fertilizer were linked to fever and cholera. She hints that the 'liquid system' which employs water instead of rained on manure is better. She was advocating for hydroponics, in other words, as a way of growing food indoors.[3]

Verney took Florence for rides in the park, ostensibly for her health. Parthenope sometimes complained that Harry spent more time with Florence than he did with her. However, Verney understood that his wife's happiness still depended to a great extent on having a relationship with her sister. The unspoken price of his assistance was that Florence would reconcile with Parthenope and grant her at least an occasional visit. In this he succeeded, though Florence at first put strict boundaries around these occasions, being clear about what time they would begin and what time they would end. Parthe continued to crave her sister's company and sent her little gifts, like asparagus. Florence preferred to conduct this relationship, as she did most relationships, through letters. In 1860, for instance, she wrote a letter to Parthenope asking for advice about what periodical she should submit a specific article to.[4]

When they were in London, the Verneys lived in close proximity to Florence. Both had residences on Park Street. Despite the physical closeness, Florence continued to keep Parthe at arm's length, preferring to send and receive notes and exchange food and other gifts.

We know something about the Verney's London residence from Florence who advised on hiring a housekeeper in 1862. It was a big house, by the standards of independent dwellings in busy London, with front and back entrances far removed from each other. Also, the house was so beautiful, Florence was quite fearful that it would be robbed and advised against having only one woman there. She recommended 'Fletcher', a woman she knew who was respectable and could live there with her sister for fourteen pounds a week.[5]

While she was renovating Claydon, Parthenope made an important discovery. At the top of the house, in a forty-foot long gallery, were the Verney papers, dating from the time of King Henry VII. Here was the history of the Verney family, beautifully preserved in bundles of letters, long parchments, 'rent-rolls' stitched together, pardons, and charters with the seals of great men stamped on them.

In these papers was the fourteen-generation history of a great English family, one that had fought and loved and lived as the world changed around them. An amazing time capsule spanning hundreds of years, documenting the minutia and the macro events of a family that was deeply woven into English history as a whole.

For Parthenope, who was intensely interested in history and had a knack for storytelling, this was better than finding a pot of free gold. Here were primary sources, waiting for an expert writer and researcher to give them a voice and a shape. Eventually, Parthenope would write a book titled *Memoirs of the Verney Family During the Seventeenth Century*, a book that is still in print and sometimes goes under the title *Memoirs of the Verney Family During the Civil War*. It would not be until near her death that Parthenope would complete this grand project, but it would occupy a part of her thoughts and time almost to the end of her days.

Parthenope stayed busy through the next years, writing novels, magazine articles, and sifting through the copious Verney documents. But meeting Florence's needs still took a very high priority in her life. She would, it seems, drop everything else to take a mission from her intimidatingly famous, but still cherished sister.

Florence routinely asked Parthenope and Harry for donations. For instance, she asked for 'hampers with large flowers' to decorate the rooms of patients during an outbreak of infection at St Thomas'.[6] In general, Parthenope and her husband were very generous about meeting these requests.

Part III

Ink-bottle

Chapter 18

Novelist

By 1864, Parthenope's parents, William Edward and Fanny Nightingale, had badly declined in health. In that year, WEN was seventy, and his wife seventy-six. William was stricken with hearing loss, and Fanny with a loss of vision as well as the onset of dementia. Though they still lived independently in their huge house, they were shadows of the powerhouses they had once been. Rarely did anyone visit. When they did, they were struck by how dignified, but diminished the couple were.

Fanny was, for a time, painfully aware that she was losing her cognitive abilities. She wrote to Parthenope, describing herself as a thoroughly broken wreck. She went on to lament the sad state of affairs that had left a blind wife with a deaf husband.

Fanny strove to retain a sense of order over her life and home by writing copious notes. She also devoted some of her last remaining moments of lucidity to attempting to clear Parthenope's name. Specifically, she felt that Parthenope's copybook had been blotted by accusations that she opposed her sister's ambitions: 'most painful and most untrue', Fanny wrote.[1] Sadly, this revision to history was never published or dispatched as a letter.

Florence visited her parents for several weeks to several months a year, and they were invalids altogether. Though she was the primary caregiver to the ageing Nightingales, Parthenope took a substantial interest in her parents' care. The Verney home was available for a stay. Florence and Fanny recuperated there, and Florence praised Claydon House for its beautiful, silent, and peaceful atmosphere.

Parthenope also took an interest in hiring care for Fanny and WEN. However, the Miss Parish that she and Florence had agreed to hire was suspected of alcoholism or madness and dismissed. Luckily, Parthenope's younger cousin William Shore saved the day. He invited the Nightingales to live with him, his wife, and their children for six months of the year.

Florence Nightingale's contempt for women writers is well known among her most well-read fans. The derogatory term that she coined, 'female ink-bottles', dates to a letter she wrote to Macmillan's magazine in April 1867.[2] She uses the term loosely to describe all women writers, but in particular the one who most recently wrote an article referencing Florence Nightingale's influence on nursing. Florence disliked the article, strongly enough to write in protest to it, because the writer, she felt, had not treated the nursing profession with enough respect. She had put it, Florence felt, on the same level as cooking and dusting.

By her late forties, Parthenope had already braved one custom that Florence was known to ridicule: the marriage made when a woman is approaching forty. So, when Parthenope decided to try her hand at fiction writing, she was tackling another institution that Florence was known to deride.

However, Parthenope had all the makings of a novelist. She had not only read widely, in fiction, non-fiction, and poetry, but she had also observed. And, most importantly, she had the disposition of a writer. She had always been more of an observer and less of a doer. She had always had a fascination with community dynamics and a subtle wit that could find the ludicrous in almost anything, including herself.

Interestingly, most of Lady Verney's fiction does not take up the subject of her own social circle, with the exception of *Fernyhurst Court*. Instead, she writes mostly about the rural poor and middle class, especially rural women who made bad marriages. Does this mean she did not write about what she knew? Not really. From her philanthropic work, Parthenope was well acquainted with the life of villages, farming families, and families living on charity or only a few shillings away from living on charity.

The same auditory genius that allowed Parthenope to learn French as fluently as if she had been raised in France gave her also the gift of reproducing dialect, word choice, and turns of phrase that were unique to the parts of England that she lived in. Where another novelist would have produced a false sounding narrative that only condescended to rural lives, Parthenope's accuracy of characterization through speech is hauntingly real.

Avenhoe, Lady Verney's first novel, published in 1867, is difficult to assess. The World Catalog finds no copies in existence. Nor was the Claydon estate able to produce a copy. And, while extensive efforts have been made by various publishers to reproduce other novels by Lady Verney, no such facsimiles exist for *Avenhoe*.

Llanaly Reefs, published in 1873, is similarly difficult for scholars to access, though not impossible. Copies exist at the Universities of Oxford, Cambridge, Yale, Texas, New York, and Exeter; the National Library of Scotland; the British Library; the Boston Athenaeum, Germany's Badische Landesbibliothek; and the University of North Carolina at Chapel Hill.

However, *Stone Edge* (1868), *Lettice Lisle* (1870), *Fernyhurst Court* (1871), and the novellas *Grey Pool* and *Hasty Feet Sorrow Meet* are available as paperback facsimiles. Presumably because of copyright expirations, they are also published in their entirety on Google Books.

Starting out, Parthenope published her work with no byline. As she gained confidence, as a writer, this changed. She first claimed credit as 'Lady Verney' and later as 'Frances Parthenope Verney'.

Alexandra Virginia Scamahorn has described Parthenope's fiction as 'feminine realism'. By that, she means that Parthenope never challenged the basic infrastructure of patriarchy, but she did argue, forcefully, for more opportunities for women: better education, better jobs, and opportunities leading to independence. Parthenope expressed these ideas both in her novels and as a regular contributor to Cornhill, Fraser's, *Contemporary Review*, and MacMillan magazines.

The earliest novel available for general study is *Stone Edge*. In this narrative, Parthenope painstakingly recreates and preserves the Derbyshire dialect spoken by villagers she grew up around. The novel is set in a remote Derbyshire farm community in the early days of the industrial revolution, when mills were opening and offering off-farm employment to both men and women. Derbyshire, you might remember, is the setting for Lea Hurst, WEN's wild and wonderful summer home.

In writing *Stone Edge*, Parthenope put to work all the conversations she had had with local farmers and villagers. Her ear for dialogue was masterful. Her influences include Gaskell's *North and South* and *Mary Barton*, and George Elliot's *Adam Bede*.

The first chapter takes up the story of Lydia, an orphan from the age of fourteen who must earn her meagre living as a hired hand at whatever farmhouse will take her. German Ashford, a lazy farmer, forty years older than she, sees her at church and is then impressed by the way she moves around the 'cheese room'. A widower, he decides she has the right amount of youth and energy to take care of him. He confronts her on the road one day and basically demands that she marry him. His proposal is phrased, 'Lass, I've settled for to ma' me thee my wife'.[3] Just in case there was any suggestion of romance in this liaison, he clears that up in the next sentence: 'thou'rt a housekeeping wench and a tidy, and I think thee'll do'.

Lydia, a teenager with no other options, and no one to lobby for her interests, accepts him. She's used to being given orders, Parthenope writes, and the proposal was worded mostly as an order. Though Ashford marries Lydia for the free housekeeping, he does get her pregnant very quickly, and she bears a son.

Within the first nine pages of the *Stone Edge*, Ashford gets drunk and throws his two-year-old son across the room where his head lands hard on an iron fender. The boy dies within seconds. At this point, the average reader will be expecting some kind of judicial inquiry. But none is forthcoming. Ashford gets away with killing his own two-year-old, and his womenfolk accept this as a sad inevitability. There is never even a discussion about justice for the child.

Lydia is in a daze of depression for weeks, but comes out of it eventually, due to the tender care of Cassandra, Ashford's daughter by his first wife. When she comes out of her depression, Lydia bonds with Cassandra, transferring all her maternal devotion to her stepdaughter and stepson, German, Jr.

From this point in the story, Cassandra emerges as the central character. Ashford is estranged from his sister-in-law, Bessie, who has not been allowed to see Cassandra and German for many years. This breach between the families occurred because Bessie inherited a sum of money that had been promised to Ashford's wife.

Cassandra, now a young woman in her teens or early twenties, journeys six miles to Youlcliff to mend the rift with Bessie. She is welcomed with open arms by both Bessie and her husband, Nathan, to whom Parthenope often applies the epithet, 'the wise'. In Youlcliff, Cassandra meets and falls in love with a handsome young man, Roland, who returns her affections in full.

In *Stone Edge*, Parthenope both glorifies and questions the folkways of rural Derbyshire. These traditions are at the same time charming and also terrifying. For instance, Cassandra's visit to Youlcliff dovetails with the annual football game played by the 'Upwards' and 'Downwards', names that signify two teams who live on different parts of the mountain.

During Cassandra's visit, the two teams are already under a legal injunction not to kill each other during the game because of the number of fatalities that have occurred in past years. In fact, if anyone dies during this game, law enforcement officials have said they will shut down the game altogether. So when the ball falls into the river rapids, and can't be retrieved except by risking lives, the two teams agree to call it a tie. This occurs, however, only after two hours of very rough play, during which the team kicks the ball all over Youlcliff and its environs in a game that seems to have two geographical goals but no further rules of any kind (save the 'no one must die' injunction).

There are no boundary markers, no distinction between private property and public land. The game starts in the town market where the spectators take shelter on high walls to stay out of the slaughter. Then, only the most hardy fans risk life and limb to follow the players as the ball is kicked out in the surrounding dales and forests. Because Roland is in the game, Cassie follows the action, much against the advice of her aunt who calls after her, 'Ye munna go i' a' that riot, Cassie child. Ye'll just get murdered!'[14]

Parthenope was not an athletic woman, but her description of the football game is some really excellent sports reporting. It neither quivers at the brutality of the game, nor condones it. She does capture some of the savagery with which the fans enjoy the game's violence in the dialogue of an unnamed 'red-armed milkmaid' who casually mentions that the part of the river where Roland is trying to retrieve the ball is where 'Tom Baines was drownded last year'.[5]

Parthenope reveals her well-tuned sense of irony just moments later when she has the same character declare, 'They mun be drownded, and nothing can't save un ... 'tis a vera fine sight, to be sure!'

By the end of the game, there's one broken leg, three arm injuries, and one player has been trampled. Community consensus is that it was a fine game with only moderate collateral damage. The milkmaid remains unsatisfied, however: 'I likes a smartish bout, where they breaks each other's heads a bit'.[6]

The football game also provides an opportunity for Parthenope to touch on the human female's sexual attraction to raw masculinity. Roland emerges dripping wet, clothes torn and muddy, with scratches and blood all over his arms and face. Cassandra's aunt tells him to get home and repair the damage while Cassandra stands there, speechless, flushed, with eyes sparkling.

It's a rare moment in nineteenth-century literature, which tends to stay focused on female beauty and the male reaction to it, even when women like George Eliot and Charlotte Brontë are writing the story. Of course, Parthenope's depiction of this attraction is very chaste, but the meaning is clear when Cassandra wordlessly reaches out her hands to touch Roland.

'She thought he looked beautiful!' is the way Parthenope puts it.[7]

From here, *Stone Edge* turns into a story of star-crossed lovers. It emerges that Roland's father, Joshua, and Cassandra's father, Ashford, have a feud going on. The source of the feud is about as trivial as the initial trigger for the Hatfield-McCoy war. Joshua went around Ashford, who was bargaining for a horse, and offered full price for it.

Both men are unrepentant scoundrels. Ashford has committed homicide and somehow never been brought to justice. Joshua's bad faith business dealings are never spelt out in detail, but he teeters on the edge of bankruptcy for many pages.

Both fathers prohibit the marriage. Twenty-first-century readers might chafe some at the failure of the young people to defy their fathers, run off together, and start their lives somewhere else, especially when Bessie sweetens the deal by declaring that Cassandra will receive sixty-eight pounds upon signing the paperwork to marry Roland. To readers today, this obedience to bad fathers looks much like a failure of character and determination. But, if we put the novel in the context within which it was written, the young people show an appropriate loyalty and obedience.

Parthenope's outlook is at least partly shaped by Florence's determination to leave home and pursue a career. Yet she never did so against her parent's express wishes. Florence spends years, in fact, as a grown woman, chipping away at her parents' and sister's resistance to her divine calling. Her leap to Harley Street, her occupation of her own apartment, took place with the permission (if grudging) of her father and even his financial support. This is the kind of patience urged on Cassandra and Roland by Lydia who, at this point in the novel, seems to channel Parthenope directly.

Both bad fathers are eventually hoisted on their own individual petards. Ashford demands that Cassandra cash out her £68 inheritance from Bessie, upon the latter's death, and give it to him. Here, again, today's reader might chafe at Cassie's compliance. But that money is due to their landlord. Otherwise, Lydia, German, and Ashford face eviction.

Ashford piles on some more cruelty by granting permission to marry Roland, but also predicting, at the same time, that Roland will not take Cassandra without her money. This terrible prophecy is fulfilled when Cassandra meets with Roland and tells him she is free to marry. Roland's father, however, has made a similar deal. Roland may marry Cassandra only if she brings the money over to Joshua to save him from bankruptcy.

Joshua and a shady horse dealer murder Ashford as he is crossing the moors, and the two killers split Cassandra's gold which Ashford had in his pockets along with local currency he had acquired from selling livestock.

Joshua confesses his bankruptcy, though not his commission of murder, to his son and asks Roland to flee town with him. Much to the reader's surprise and chagrin, Roland agrees to this. He cannot abandon his father. The two of them go to Liverpool where Roland supports Joshua through warehouse work. When Joshua shows up at Roland's place of employment drunk and belligerent, Roland is dismissed and cannot find other employment because he has no references.

Roland finds difficulty in adapting to city life. The bleak streets of Liverpool are vastly different from the hills of Derbyshire, and Roland experiences something we might today call culture shock. Parthenope takes this opportunity to compare the lives of the poor in the country with the lives of the poor in the city. In the country, people with few means are still surrounded by natural beauty and clean air. In the city, Roland finds the pollution and lack of visibility nearly unbearable. In the country, as Parthenope portrays it, people take some care of each other. A murder is rare, but crusts of bread and pitchers of milk are frequently shared. In Liverpool, Roland moves through noisy, dirty, crowded streets where he knows no one and no one knows him. He is friendless, anonymous, disconnected.

Roland's suspicions about his father's participation in Ashford's murder are confirmed when Joshua wraps up his half of the gold and takes off, telling Roland that he's on his own. His father's departure does come as a rare gift to Roland who can now return to Derbyshire, with the hope that Cassandra still loves him. He finds that, having been turned off the farm, Lydia, Cassandra, and German, Jr. have made a comfortable life for themselves. They rent a small cottage, and Cassandra and Lydia freelance for the nearby mill while German works as a hired farmhand.

Industrialization is much kinder to Cassandra and Lydia than it is to Roland. They maintain a connection to their community, and they pick up work at the mill and do that work in the comfort of their own home, returning it to the mill and getting paid when the work is complete. Parthenope makes it very clear that Lydia and Cassandra are much better off working for the mill and making their own income, without having to constantly placate a violent man. The flawed industrial revolution is actually kinder to them than the work into which they were destined by birth, marriage, and agrarian culture.

German feels he has come down in the world, from farmer to cowkeeper, but the women do not feel the change the same way. 'They hardly dared to acknowledge, even to themselves, the relief it was to live under their own roof-tree with none to make them afraid'.[8]

This is where we see Parthenope's feminine realism most pervasively. While men of the nineteenth-century countryside are motivated by their perceived status in the community, women are motivated by the need for financial security and safety, often from the men. While Roland finds the encroaching industrialization disheartening and depersonalizing, for Cassandra and Lydia, the local mill offers stability and freedom. The opportunity to work is so transforming that Cassandra is able to politely decline Nathan's offer to come live with him as his housekeeper. And Lydia is able to decline his offer of marriage (in which she would, again, become a man's housekeeper.) Though Parthenope is clearly not a feminist along the lines of Gloria Steinem, the point she makes is insightful: given the opportunity of employment, women can often make better lives for themselves than they make by marriage.

And then Roland returns.

Here Cassandra rises to the level of heroine. She never once looks at her safe, comfortable life and regrets its disturbance. They quickly sell everything, and leave town just as the local law is closing in on Roland for complicity in Ashford's murder. Parthenope transports all four of her characters, Lydia, Cassandra, Roland, and German, to Canada, where they settle on the shore of Penetanguishene Lake. Parthenope caved to the temptation of using some very common new world tropes, at this point in her tale. Eight years into their immigration, Roland and German are pictured muscular and heavily bearded, wielding axes. (The reader has to imagine the checkered flannel shirts, however.) Cassandra has borne several children on whom Lydia can pour all her maternal talent.

They are content, but Parthenope concludes the novel on a surprisingly ambivalent note. The men and women still see things differently. As the sun sets on a glorious Canadian evening, rich with the colours of leaves in Autumn, Roland notes, 'Yer wouldn't hae seen such a sight as that in England', but both women reply, 'there were fair things too in the dear old land … though things mebbe werena all so gaudy for the look'.[9]

It does not take intensive research to discover Parthenope's literary influences because she quotes many of them at the beginning of the chapters. We can see the value of her thorough literary education at the hands of WEN, who loved books, when she quotes William Wordsworth, Robert Burns, Elizabeth Barret Browning, and even the contemporary poet Arthur Hughes Clough who had been instrumental in rebuffing her attempts to see her sister.

Parthenope discloses early on in her novel that she has placed a Romeo and Juliet story in rural Derbyshire. When Roland first lays eyes on Cassandra, the narrator shrewdly observes: 'A beautiful girl is very interesting to most people … so is the daughter of one's father's enemy; but to combine both attractions is to be charming, both before and since the days of Juliet'.[10]

Parthenope even contrives to have Cassandra and Roland just missing each other, crossing each other's paths on different roads, as do Romeo and Juliet. But Parthenope was a Victorian, and Victorians were, amongst other things, realists. In real life, Romeo and Juliet would probably have kept trying to work things out, as do Cassandra and Roland. Options other than self-slaughter are found, and tragedy is averted.

Parthenope also reveals a close study of Wordsworthian landscape depiction. Her descriptions of the Derbyshire hillsides make use of her encyclopedic knowledge of wild flora, knowledge gleaned on her forays into the grounds surrounding Lea Hurst. Contemporary readers might find the landscape descriptions a little tedious and overly detailed, but there is no denying that they are very fine specimens of nature writing, heavily influenced by Wordsworth.

The flaws of *Stone Edge* will be obvious to most readers. The ending glosses over the travails of ocean voyages, during which many travellers died, due to contagion or accident or poor nutrition. If Parthenope understood the difficulties of surviving a Canadian winter, she did not refer to them at all. Her ending verges on the deus ex machina. The difficulties of such a journey and resettlement are palmed off in one sentence: 'They had a hard fight to begin with, but they won their way to a farm in the backwoods in time'.[11]

One might be tempted to see *Stone Edge* as an unfinished novel, one that deserved at least another hundred pages depicting that hard fight. But Parthenope took the advice of many sage writing teachers to stick to what she knew. She knew Derbyshire. She did not know Canada.

Another tendency that today's readers might find annoying is the way Parthenope reaches for a Christian message and then overwrites it, as in the scene following Bessie's death when Lydia says: 'There's a something a comin' for to take us all away—one's only got to be right for't; but she were a well-livin' 'ooman as iver were, and set her heart and her trust steadfast i' th' Lord'.

And, then, as if the author is unsure whether she has sermonized enough for the conscientious reader, she adds: 'She'd a found her savior, she hadn't to look for him not at the last, but just only to lie there and be still'.[12]

That said, it would be difficult to find a Victorian novel without flaws, unless, perhaps, it is George Eliot's *Silas Marner*. Charles Dickens was paid by the word; wading through minutiae, irrelevancies, excessive sentimentalities, and digressions is in-built in the Dickens experience. By contrast, Lady Frances Parthenope Verney's prose is a marvel of economy.

The masterful moments in *Stone Edge* far outnumber the minor disappointments. Parthenope's sense of humour was far ahead of its time; today's readers might appreciate her wit more than did Parthe's contemporaries. In her novels, and really only in her novels, Parthenope reveals an intense delight in the frequent follies of human existence and social interactions. One is sore pressed to find a page without a quip or a speech like this rant that Bessie makes after Nathan quotes the Book of Proverbs one too many times:

There thou'st got to thy proverbs agin! I believe my master thinks more o' King Solomon nor a' the rest o' the Bible put together fro' Genesis to Revelations, Kings, Lords, and Prophets put together,' said Mrs. Broom with some slight confusion between the constitution and the canon ... 'I dunna think as Solomon knowd much about women either ... he'd but a bad lot to deal wi'—that Egyptian huzzie as had the temples and high places and things.[13]

Parthenope even turns her incisive humour on her own class and gender, finding that working-class women frequently cope better and more practically, with life's slings and arrows. For instance, when Cassandra is uncertain whether Roland returns her affections in kind, she finds distraction from her grief in making the cheese. And Parthenope comments: 'No doubt cheese is a great help when one is crossed in love. It is much more so, for instance, than lounging in an arm-chair with some ugly worsted-work, and then taking "an airing" in a carriage'.[14]

In fact, Parthenope seems to break away from her story here a bit to make a biting commentary on the way her own griefs and ills have been handled. She seems to downright envy the working-class woman's freedom to do hard work with her hands while women in Parthenope's stratum of society are forced to be idle and useless. Here she strongly identifies with her sister's frustration at the lack of opportunities for women to make a mark on the world.

In one very telling passage, Parthenope even goes so far as to reject the common Victorian assumption that successful marriages are made only when the bride and groom both bring valuable assets to the marriage, all of which should be fully disclosed and weighed prior to the wedding. For examples of this materialistic undercurrent, one need only read William Makepeace Thackeray's Vanity Fair or Eliot's *Daniel Deronda*.

Parthenope, in direct contrast to this ideal, expresses the very twentieth-century notion that women marry men for their flaws and weaknesses. There, Parthenope notes, the 'true woman' will see an opportunity to nourish and heal. In proposing to Cassandra, Roland declares his basic poverty and deep need with the words, 'Ourn ain't a comfable, pleasant place, Cassie ... and a man's a poor creatur' wi'out a woman to love him and see to him'.

In parentheses, Parthenope discloses this intensely personal observation:

a man does not offer the woman he loves his comfort, or his wealth, or his position, even if he has them; he knows better, and he offers her his loneliness, and his distress, and his sorrow, and his work, and his poverty, and tells her she can help him. With all these things he will her endow, and these are the things, flavored with love, which tempt a true woman to marry.[15]

The above passage helps us understand why Parthenope flourished so brilliantly in her marriage to Sir Harry. It's not the status he offered her or a refuge from her family's bizarre entail that made her happy, it was the opportunity to transform his ramshackle manor into a home, the chance to positively impact public welfare through parliamentary actions, the need to fill the void left by a beloved wife and mother that made Parthenope happy in her marriage.

Roland's proposal anticipates the way post-Second World War Britain and America saw marriage: a partnership between two people with no particular assets who would both, in their own ways, work very hard to create a joyful and meaningful life for each other. Many a James Stewart movie captures this ethic as do a slew of stories where, after chasing the wrong girl for weeks, a man finally notices the woman who has been working side by side with him, who has endured all his bad decisions and knows and loves him for exactly who he is. For her time, Parthenope had an almost revolutionary idea of what marriage should look like and what women should look for in a marriage.

Why, one might wonder, has a novel like *Stone Edge* fallen by the academic wayside when novels by Anthony Trollope, Elizabeth Gaskell, Wilkie Collins, and even George Meredith were reconsidered with fresh eyes by scholars and educators in the twentieth century?

One likely culprit is the Derbyshire dialect in which most of the novel is written. Parthenope did not cut corners on the authenticity of the local speech. In fact, her use of dialect was not a whim, but a researched consideration. In her preface to *Lettice Lisle*, she writes that: 'Mr. Max Muller, in his *Science of Language*, observes that if the dialectic varieties, the proverbs and traditions of a district, were collected, much that is interesting and even useful to the history of our English tongue might be preserved'.[16]

This painstakingly accurate attention to the nuances of dialect can, indeed, be perceived as making the novel of greater historical value. But it does slow the reader down. Also, since the mid-twentieth century, writing instructors have generally urged fiction writers not to use dialect extensively, for the reason that it is not reader-friendly. Instead, fiction writers are supposed to use word choice and grammar to place their characters geographically and socially. The accurate recreation of dialect has been devalued.

One might also speculate that being the sister of Florence Nightingale had both its perks and disadvantages. While interest in Parthe's work might, in its day, have derived some spark from her relationship with Florence, it is also clear that Parthenope was widely considered the lesser of two sisters. From society's point of view, she was always the less beautiful, less energetic, and less noble foil to Florence. This shadow fell upon Parthenope's work while she lived and has remained across her reputation to this very day, making it difficult to obtain an objective critical assessment of her work.

Florence was not immediately supportive of Parthenope's new role as a serious writer. In 1869, Florence wrote Parthenope a recriminatory letter which pits the reader, in medias res, into some kind of argument. It appears Parthenope had sent a tepid letter to Florence, noting that people were talking about her (Florence's) latest article.

In reply, Florence writes in rage mixed with contempt, 'I have never seen *any* "reviews" at all of the only two "magazine articles" I ever wrote'.

She needed to put 'magazine articles' in quotes to convey her contempt for that kind of writing, the kind of writing that Parthenope was currently excelling at. This contempt for magazine articles is only matched by her contempt for anyone who would dare review her.

Florence follows up these sentiments by hinting that Parthenope should be sending her any reviews of her work, then demanding to know if the *Pall Mall* has published any reviews of Flo's work. Finally, 'if you send me in the *Pall Mall*, would you kindly mark what I am to read[?]'.[17]

We can see from this letter that Florence continued to regard Parthenope as tolerable only when the latter could be useful to Florence. However, the two sisters continued to communicate through letters, and Parthenope remained conscientious about keeping ties with Florence at all times, never sending back any in-kind recriminations.

Chapter 19

Lettice Lisle

The early 1870s were kind to Parthenope. She was at the height of her powers as a writer, and her ideas had found an audience. There is every reason to believe Parthenope was at her happiest. Any doubts she had about marrying Sir Harry had melted away. Only with him had she found the courage to write and publish on serious subjects.

We know this because, in her article, 'The Powers of Women and How to Use Them', Parthenope frames a marriage of two equals as the absolutely happiest 'use' a woman can find: 'That the "highest result" of life both for men and women is a really happy marriage there can be no doubt; where each is improved by the other, and every good work is helped, not hindered, for both'.[1]

She quotes the great feminist John Stuart Mills, whose own marriage seems to have mirrored that of Parthenope and Harry Verney:

> [E]ach can have alternately the pleasure of leading and being led in the path of development ... where the two care for great objects in which they can help and encourage each other, so that the minor matters on which their tastes differ are not all important, ... here is a connection of friendship of the most enduring character, making it a greater pleasure to each to give pleasure to the other than to receive it.[2]

Parthenope was writing about her own experience here, and perhaps that of some of the happier marriages she had witnessed: that of Sam and Mai, that of Mr and Mrs Gaskell, for instance. It is unlikely that she was writing about her own parents. The chinks in their union would have been obvious to Parthenope, now in her fifties.

In 1870, Great Britain was enjoying the many fruits of peacetime. England had its first international football match, with Scotland. The British Red Cross was formed. Oxford University saw the opening of

Keble College, the first new college added to that esteemed institution for over a century. And the Tower Subway, a transportation system which united London by tunnelling under the Thames, took its first passengers.

It was not, however, a time of peace and prosperity for Britain's neighbours on the continent. In 1870, when Britain was enjoying the invention of the postcard and halfpenny postage, secular Italy was at war against the Pope and Vatican, Spain's prime minister was shot and died two days later; his murderers were never caught. France and Germany, the playgrounds of the Nightingales, both in Parthenope's infancy and again when she was a teenager, were locked in terrible combat. The Franco-Prussian war, sometimes referred to by Parthenope as the Franco-German war, came to a head in and around the cloth manufacturing town of Sedan with disastrous results for both forces.

For Parthenope, who had passionately enjoyed her time on the continent with her parents and Florence, it was as if two old friends, never forgotten, had now fallen out and were slowly destroying each other. She began the process of collecting letters that would serve as primary sources for her article, 'The Miseries of War', which would be published in *Saint Paul's* the next year.

Despite the ugliness of war, 1870 was a highly productive year for Parthenope. She was able to see *Lettice Lisle* through to print as a complete book, and enjoy the positive feedback she got from that novel. The novel had been first published in *Cornhill*, serially.

Lettice Lisle tells the romantic adventures of the title character who grows up among virtuous and honest farmers, then, through an unhappy twist of fate, falls in with smugglers (euphemistically called 'fair traders' in Lady Verney's narrative).

As we enter the world of this strangely engrossing book, we find that Lettice is a child of about eight, living on a beautiful, but indebted estate with her four uncles and stern grandmother. The setting for this blonde gem of a child is a magical blend of nature given its free reign combined with the fixtures of agricultural life: cows, sheep, and a kitten. Woodhouse, the farm in question, is also crossed by a waterway rich in fish and plenty of game to hunt.

Lettice's mother is dead, and her father has apparently abandoned Lettice, but she is beloved by her four uncles who live under the same roof as their mother. The head of this family is Amyas, a man with book learning far more advanced than is practical for a farmer. He was educated away from home in preparation for a life as a clergyman. However, upon the sudden death of his father, Amyas finds himself needed back at the farm.

Upon his head, then, falls the terrible burden of the farm's debt. Yeomen farmers, such as Amyas and his family, lived on such beautiful estates in a state of constant jeopardy. They did not own the land or home under their feet, but, instead, rented it from an owner who often lived far away.

The Wynyate family had lived at Woodhouse for generations. But the land and farmhouse are heavily mortgaged. When Amyas 'inherits' this precarious establishment, it is already years behind on payments, including the interest on the loan.

When the reader first sees Woodhouse, in fact, it is through the eyes of a sinister landlord who has come, much in the manner of less literary Victorian melodramas, to demand payment of the rent.

It does not help that Amyas is far too charitable for his own good, to the point where his own immediate family is in constant danger of losing the roof over their heads. He lets people fish in his stream without demanding the payment of fishing rights. He employs a blind farmhand, who is useful for little more than eavesdropping and making butter. When he stumbles into an inheritance, he immediately gives it away to his cousin on the grounds that she has a better right to it.

Lettice's childhood is a mixture of sunshine and demons. Her grandmother is a chronically angry, discontented woman who keeps a tight leash on her granddaughter while constantly criticizing her every move. In one horrific scene, Mrs Wynyate grabs a crudely carved doll out of Lettice's hands, yanks off its makeshift costume, and gets ready to throw it in the fire. Her hand is stayed by the gentle Amyas who sees no harm in letting Lettice have a toy.[3]

The 'dollie' incident is bad enough, but Mrs Wynyate, a joyless dissenter from the Church of England, disciplines Lettice by scaring her with stories about Satan and hell. The old, blind farmhand also frightens the girl with graphic demonic imagery and the news that such unseen beings are all around us at all times.

This catechism is enough to have Lettice literally watching her back, half expecting to see the devil sneaking up behind her. However, her native intelligence soon teaches her an iota of scepticism, and she double checks her facts against the testimony of her uncle Amyas.

Amyas intuits that Lettice has been steered toward a black hole of despair, and he refutes the notion that the devil is all around, trying to trip humans up. 'No; I don't believe in him one bit…' he explains, careless of whether his words are strictly canonical. 'Twoud be a good God and an evil God if he's so strong and powerful as all that … Ye needn't be afraid o' him nor any other bugs; God is about us in all our ways, both to will and to do; not that other one'.[4]

The above passage is not only redolent with the Unitarianism in which Parthenope was raised, but also reveals her own reflections on Christianity and its premises. Throughout her writings, and especially her novels, Lady Verney promotes the positive aspects of faith: unselfishness toward others, eventual unification with a loving God, and respectful stewardship of natural resources, while declining the notions of hell and malevolent spirits which reduce religious thought to a fear of the bogeyman.

But Lettice Lisle is mostly a tale of love and adventure, not a doctrinal text. Lady Verney's novel takes a romantic turn when the eighteen-year-old Lettice and Everhard, the young son of her landlord, fall in love and agree to be married.

The reader's immediate impression of Everhard is that he is a lovely, good-natured young man, unbeset by the malevolent materialism of his father. And so he is. But, as the novel progresses, it becomes evident that he is also *not* a Rochester, Byron, or Menaleas. His encyclopedic interest in the natural wonders of the world is charming, as is his love of fishing, but these pastimes also place him in the category of dilettante. He worries about his father's approval, he fusses over his horse much the way a contemporary suburbanite fusses over his minivan, and he stresses out over losing his desk job. He frequently reflects on what a hero of consistent loyalty he is. The reader never seriously doubts his attachment to Lettice. But if he had to launch a thousand ships to get her back, we suspect he would be forever buried in red tape trying to obtain them. Everhard is a realist's lover, not a Titan.

One does not have to look too far for the real-life model of Everhard. He was present all throughout Parthenope's childhood and young adulthood. Both of his daughters came to think that their father, William Edward

Nightingale, had not fulfilled his true potential. Content to enjoy his Lea Hurst and Embley homes and the beautiful acres surrounding them, WEN never quite distinguished himself outside the home, though he was obviously talented, educated, and smart. Even his Wikipedia page characterizes him mostly as a man who 'liked to hunt and fish'. This perception of WEN was unfair. He did, after all, leave both the Nightingale and Shore estates in better condition than he found them, creating opportunities for his descendants. But, to his daughters, he was something of an Everhard.

To return, then, to the tale of *Lettice Lisle*, almost as soon as the young people become engaged, they are discovered by Everhard's father and Amyas. Both men forbid the match with much anger and shouting. Everhard immediately reveals the flaws in his character by leaving with his father instead of standing by Lettice and fighting it out. Amyas is quick to point out this weakness.

Before anything can be done to save the lovers' breaking hearts, the infamous Norton Lisle shows up uninvited and unwanted at Woodhouse to reclaim his daughter. Against the protests of her uncles and grandmother, he invokes English law which says he has a right to his 'own girl'.

The next morning, Lettice finds herself travelling by carriage through the English countryside to a grim, dilapidated establishment set in a brickyard. The reader slowly learns that Norton bought this business as a way to establish respectability and as a cover for his real work which is smuggling. Norton is the head of a fluid ring of bandits whose fair trading takes place mostly with the passive consent of the people amongst whom they live, who frequently enjoy the spoils of such ventures.

The reader is slow to uncover the extent of Norton's piracy because we see it mostly from the point of view of Lettice who has only the vaguest idea of what her father does. She is not involved in his raids, but she knows from her other family members and from local gossip, that what he does is illegal. Meanwhile, her uncle Edward, the youngest of the Wynyate sons, has risen within the ranks of the civil service to a position of leadership within the coast guard. As her new friend Caleb jokingly puts it, 'What right have she to have a uncle as is a gauger, and her father in the fair-trading? Why didn't she see to it afore now?'[5]

Lettice only slowly comes to understand how precarious her own situation is by picking up information in bits and pieces from various new acquaintances. Around midway through the novel, she learns that a man has died from injuries sustained in a violent altercation in which Norton's men were involved.

Lettice takes refuge with an honest boat pilot and his wife, Mary. Though Mary is, technically, a Methodist, it's obvious that her version of the Christian faith is the one that Parthenope admires and subscribes to herself.

Mary's beliefs mostly manifest themselves in near-constant good works for her neighbours. While she is raising an orphaned boy named David, she also finds time to visit the sick and those giving birth, providing thread and other needful things to neighbours, sometimes from miles away. Her charity is so well known that people send messages to her from afar with their requests.

Through Lettice's perceptions, Parthenope makes an astute contrast between the scolding, judgmental, even hypocritical Mrs Wynyate and Mary. Mary, Lettice observes, 'seemed to have time and sympathy for everybody, and her work, of which she had plenty, to be always done quietly and quickly, so as to leave her at liberty for others, instead of the way in which Mrs Wynyate was miserable if she herself and everyone under her were not continually on the stir'.[6]

Mary is a model of the transformational Christianity that Lady Verney preferred. She exists in contrast to the negativity of the Mrs Wynyates of the world. Through these two characters, Parthenope emphasizes the importance of moral actions and de-emphasizes specific theology. Whatever she believes, Mary is a good Christian, while Mrs Wynyate's wrath reflects poorly on whatever faith she professes. Lady Verney implies, rather boldly, that the particular form of faith—Unitarian, Puritan, Church of England—matters little. What matters, she is at pain to note, is the way one translates one's belief into actions.

Estranged among fair traders, Lettice is still mourning the loss of Everhard Walcott, the boy she fell in love with back in Woodhouse. Everhard, himself, does not know where she is. Nor does Lettice know that Everhard's father has threatened to foreclose on Woodhouse at once if Everhard goes near it or any of its inhabitants.

It is in this state of uncertain mind that Lettice finds herself when she is blindsided by a declaration of love from a thoroughly unexpected quarter. Mary's brother-in-law, Caleb, surprises Lettice when she is meditating on the shore and tells her that he has loved her since the first time he saw her. Here is the Byronic lover that would have satisfied Tennyson, Burns, and Browning, Lady Verney's more fiery influences. His passion for Lettice is all-consuming and reckless. She is the only girl he has ever loved, and he will never be able to love anyone else. When he talks to his sister-in-law about it, he terrifies her and the reader. In describing his agony over Lettice, Caleb picks up a torn garment and notes that some tears are clean and easy to repair, so that the tear is nearly invisible. But other tears are 'rags out all round' and impossible to repair. The loss of Lettice to him is like the second kind of tear, he says: 'Tis all how the stuff's made, and I ain't one as can take up wi' folk, and set 'um down again so easy'.[7]

In creating Caleb, Parthenope surely considered Emily Brontë's Heathcliff and Rochester, wild, strong, menacing men, whose love is roughly expressed, but indelible. But it doesn't take a huge stretch to deduce that Parthenope also channels her own frustrated attachment to Florence in writing about Caleb's passion for Lettice.

Lettice tells Caleb that her heart belongs to another, and that there are lots of other girls who would have him. If anything, this only makes Caleb more reckless. He is half-mad with love and frustration when he goes off on a dangerous smuggling operation with Norton's crew. This time, however, the coast guard is prepared and monitoring the shore with multiple boats. Edward Wynyate, Lettice's uncle, is ambitious to catch the 'fair-traders' and advance himself professionally.

Caleb saves Norton from capture, but is captured himself, in the process of protecting the father of the girl he loves. He is handcuffed and put on a cutter and headed for prison, but a storm kicks up and Caleb takes command of the ship to prevent it from wrecking. When the storm quiets down, he jumps overboard and escapes. Toward the end of the novel, however, we learn that he did not long enjoy his freedom. The boat he boarded foundered and sank, drowning Caleb and others on board.

Edward chases Norton over land for days and finally captures him when the latter breaks his leg. It is only after Norton is in custody that Edward learns the infamous smuggler he has finally brought to assizes is his own brother-in-law. Though there is a great deal of worry about whether Norton will hang, he is, instead, deported to Australia where he thrives and raises another family.

Wallcott, Everhard's father, still opposes his son's marriage to Lettice, but a wonderfully modern scene conveniently dispatches him. Fresh from shouting at his son and forbidding his marriage, veins still bulging on his forehead, Mr Wallcott calls for a poorly behaved horse that he got at a steep discount. Surely the horse will throw him to his death, the astute and insufficiently compassionate reader may think. But Lady Verney goes for the more ironic and postmodern plot twist.

The horse does rear up, but it doesn't throw Wallcott. Instead, he slides off and then, overwrought with anger and stress, has a stroke from which he never recovers. He was only hours away from putting the final signature on Woodhouse's foreclosure.

Several plot twists then emerge which may seem more twentieth-century than Victorian. It turns out that Everhard's mother, Mrs Wallcott, is the true owner of Woodhouse. Since she never opposed the marriage to Lettice, she deeds it over to Everhard, who is more than content to live amid such a wealth of natural beauty and fish. His happy ending mirrors WEN's. He gets the estate and the girl he loves, mostly through luck. His happiness comes without a fight. Without having any Darwinian struggle to shape him, however, his character remains a little shallow.

On a beautiful spring day, Everhard reaffirms his love for Lettice in a manner that has come to typify him. He professes his undying devotion, then gets sidetracked by the landscape: 'I never saw such a place for wild daffodils as this is'.[8] At which point, the good-humoured reader may picture Will Ferrell playing him in the film version.

It also turns out that Everhard is nowhere near so wealthy as the Wynyates and perhaps he, himself, imagined. When the accounting is in, Woodhouse appears to be the only real asset of value. Everhard maintains his parents in modest comfort, and moves in with his bride. Because Amyas agrees to continue with the actual farming, the farm eventually reverses fortunes and starts making a decent living.

Up to this point, Lettice Lisle is a good read, ably plotted, replete with stylish, tongue-in-cheek humour, likeable characters, satisfactory brigands, and a gratifyingly selfish and money-hungry landlord/villain. But, as a whole, it adheres mostly to the template established for romantic novels by other nineteenth-century women writers.

That is, until we come to the last chapter. The concluding pages of Lettice Lisle depart boldly from nineteenth-century literary conventions which dictate that, however many mistakes the hero and heroine have made along the way to their union, at last they have made everything right.

At the beginning of the chapter titled 'Aftermath', Lady Verney rejects the 'happily ever after' conclusion on the grounds that too many stories end at the point that real life begins. Marriage itself is messy, she indicates with these words: 'the remainder is far more difficult and complex a subject—many more minor keys to be harmonized, more involved discords to be resolved'. The difference between courtship and marriage, Verney writes, is 'the difference between a melody and a symphony'.[9]

Verney finally comes right out and admits that her heroine is smarter than her hero. But Lettice never falls out of love with Everhard. Therefore, even though she sometimes questions his decisions, she cuts those thoughts short on the grounds that they are potentially treasonous.

The two have several sons and an only daughter, named Lettice. Mrs Wynyate has removed herself from the house, so this Lettice grows up without the constant scolding and nagging to which the elder Lettice was subjected.

When their little girl becomes sick and fails to recover, Everhard and Lettice take her to the seaside, and they end up in the same place where Lettice took refuge with Mary, Jesse, and Caleb. However, in the years since she was last there, the land has been developed as a resort, with new accommodations for guests. The beach is heavily dotted with sunbathers, sandcastles, hats, and spades.

Mary and Jesse have vanished, seemingly without a trace. And, finally, while she is looking out to sea as she did in the old days, Lettice reflects on her friendship with Caleb. Her busy life as a wife and mother had left her no time to reflect on Caleb's unfortunate passion. But now she takes the time to remember him, from the first time she met him to the last time she saw him, handcuffed, but looking at her with pleading eyes. The memory was 'as present to her as if it had been yesterday'.

This reverie is soon broken by the chatter and play of her daughter who is chasing her shadow down the beach. And, like the waves retreating on the shore, 'the traces of the old life seemed to be wiped away from her … as if they had been a dream'.[10]

The ambiguousness of the ending has more in common with a Jacques Demy or Eric Rohmer film than with any other Victorian novel. Up until the very last paragraphs, the reader is fully content with Lettice's choice of Everhard over Caleb, but, there, at the very end, we wonder if this is the best, most meaningful life she could have had. Everhard is blameless and loving, but did he ever love as passionately as Caleb? Are men like Caleb destined to self-destruct over the force of their feelings? Is it even possible to live with a man like Caleb, who is more like a tornado than a Victorian gentleman? Has Lettice traded a grand passion for someone safe and likeable?

Chapter 20

The Powers of Women and Class Morality

In the same year that Parthenope published *Lettice Lisle*, she also published 'The Powers of Women and How to Use Them' in a journal titled *Contemporary Review*.

'The Powers of Women' is the closest thing that Parthenope wrote to a feminist manifesto. And it will disappoint many women's studies scholars for its obvious failings. The most egregious of these is her failure to plead for universal suffrage.

Parthenope forges an argument that women should be trained as doctors, specifically midwives. Women were, she thought, better temperamentally suited to midwifery than men because of women's superior compassion and empathy. In this, she diverged from Florence, who thought women should stick to nursing and not aspire to be doctors. The sisters were in perfect unity, however, on the need for thorough training and establishment of credentials through testing for everyone in the medical profession.

In writing 'The Powers of Women', Parthenope drew inspiration from some correspondence she had with Florence about a workhouse that posed a danger to its inhabitants due to the management's lack of training. In a letter to Parthenope, dated March 1869, Florence stated definitively that nurses need at least a solid year's training before being sent into life or death situations. And she considered workhouses to be among those situations. 'For, however able the woman, one year's training is the very least that can give a person, without hospital experience, the slightest insight even into how to conduct such a work'.[1]

The immediate subject of concern, in this letter, is the Liverpool workhouse about which Florence granted several long meetings with one Miss Freeman, the interim workhouse matron. Florence felt that Freeman and a nurse, Miss Wilson, had undone all the good work of a previous matron in two years. The workhouse was now a 'deadlock' and 'total failure', according to Florence.[2]

Florence and Parthenope were in beautiful harmony on the need for better education and practical training for a wide range of women. But when it came to professions other than those of medicine, Parthenope betrayed a blind spot. She virtually laughed at the idea that there might ever be 'female lawyers'[3] or women members of parliament.

That does not mean that 'The Powers of Women' has nothing to offer history students or even contemporary women's rights advocates. The essay's greatest flaw stems from Parthenope's unwillingness to advocate for her own rights or, by association, the rights of women who were equally well off. She had attained a state of privilege, one that future Nightingale biographer Woodham-Smith would sneer at as that of a 'great lady'. It is obvious that, in writing 'The Powers of Women', she did not want to be selfish or draw attention away from the problems of women who were truly struggling to feed their children or find adequate housing.

By confining her argument to better education for women and better opportunities for the working poor, she steered clear of naysayers who would claim she was a whiner or ambitious for even more power than she already enjoyed as the wife of a baronet and Member of Parliament.

Within the limited argument that she does make, Parthenope makes devastatingly good points, many of which are as relevant today as when she wrote them. She notes, for instance, that mothers and employees engaged in early childcare are not legally required to have much education or training or, in some cases, any. And yet they are engaged in the most important work there is: they are raising the humans of tomorrow.

Parthenope also wishes that the education women *do* receive was more practical. Young women of good families are far too often, she writes, taught to play the piano when they should be learning how the boiler works. 'What young woman has learnt how to prevent the frost from bursting the water-pipes which flood hundreds of houses in London unnecessarily every winter? Or what has caused the cracking of the boiler, and how may it be avoided?' she laments.[4]

If these same young women are going to have children, they ought to also have good qualifications in health and nutrition. In fact, Parthenope advocates for something that looks a lot like a public school health class, if those classes were taken seriously, and not used as an opportunity for cigarette breaks by public school teachers:

Every girl ought to go through a course of training as to … how to bind up a cut, to put out fire, to treat a burn, the bad effect of air on a wound, its necessity to the lungs, the measures necessary to guard against infection—'common things', as they are called, but uncommonly little known at the present day.[5]

The call for better training makes the essay eerily relevant to today's audiences. Parthenope's principal argument is on behalf of poorly educated women of no independent means who have to support their own families through their labours. For them, there are nowhere near the opportunities that there are for men with an equal lack of resources.

To this argument, Parthe brings some excellent research. Citing the census of 1852, she notes that three and a half million women were then working for subsistence wages. Two and a half million of those were unmarried, many not by choice. She glosses over the difficulties of women born to or married to corrupt and abusive men such as those in her novels. But she notes the huge number of women who must support not only themselves, but also family members, on something less than a living wage: 'The pretty, pleasant, poetic view of life by which man goes forth to labor for his wife, while her duty is to make his home comfortable, is clearly not possible for this large portion of womankind'.[6]

The careful reader may see some equivocation (or perhaps tact) in Parthenope's feminist conclusions. She states, in so many words, that women like herself, i.e. married women of no financial hardships, should not 'press a claim' for better conditions. And she waives off the notion of professions for women at large.

But the title of the essay 'The Powers of Women, and How to Use Them' is a quip. It seems, at first, to promise that she will tell, exactly, what women's powers are. She does not. Instead, she says that women's powers have never been accurately or comprehensively measured.

She does this by taking a global view of women in the nineteenth century. In Native American culture, for instance, women do most of the hard, physical work while the 'braves' reserve their energy for fighting. Similarly, in Germany, the peasant woman 'digs, plows, manages the cattle, carries the fuel and hay from the mountains' while the men smoke and drink in the town 'platz'. And in Scotland, women run everything on land so that their husbands can focus on their boats and nets.[7]

In England, a woman was competent to be queen, but not a member of parliament. In India, men considered women capable of little more than farm animals. Yet, within that same country, women were often local government leaders.

Parthenope's research into women's 'powers' and 'uses' even dug up the obscure fact of women who served as an elite force in the army of Dahoney, present-day Benin. These special forces were called 'Amazons'.

Indeed, Lady Verney concludes, women 'have an extraordinary plasticity' that lets them 'adapt themselves to the ideal required of them by public opinion'.[8]

The powers of women, therefore, differ radically from one country to the next as well as one religion to the next. The implication could not be more clear or more elegantly crafted: Victorians had no idea what women were capable of, because they had allowed their women to do so little and educated them for even less. Thus, even though Parthenope did not advance the argument for equal rights, she questioned the very notion that, except for societal norms and laws, women have any real limitations whatsoever.

The Victorian period, in which Parthenope Verney lived, was in great part shaped by advances in transportation, especially train travel. The 1840s, 1850s, and 1860s were a time of frantic railroad building. Journeys that had previously taken days now took hours. England and Scotland were no longer distant neighbours with sporadic communication, they were now connected by a railway system. The world into which Parthenope was born had both expanded and contracted. New worlds and new experiences were now within easier reach. And faraway lands had been charted and documented.

But the railway system built in the mid-1800s had not been without its casualties. The most conspicuous of these was George Hudson, the 'Railway King' who came to epitomize bad business practices. Hudson was many things, among them a visionary, whose vision for connecting the world through trains far exceeded his resources. He is well known for paying investor dividends out of capital and then borrowing money that he would never be able to pay back.

By 1871, a broke and destitute Hudson hobbled back home to London to die, which he did, five days later. Only a brand new law, abolishing prison sentences for debt, gave him the opportunity to say goodbye to his home and wife before passing.

In that same year, Parthenope wrote 'Class Morality' for *Saint Paul's*. In it, she briefly holds Hudson up as the symbol of unethical business practices. She does not blame Hudson alone, but the worship of Hudson by the many people who had signed onto his dreams because they were promised huge returns on their investments.

The way railroad builders and investors considered the general public a rube to be swindled 'has been one of the phases of the nineteenth century of which, when its history is written, it will have least cause to be proud', she writes.[9]

While Hudson's business dealings were certainly the most high profile example of unethical practice, they were by no means unique. Business ethics, in general, had degraded in late years, threatening the nation on several levels, Parthenope posits. She cites a shipment of guns, manufactured privately in Birmingham, that were engraved with the letters 'TOWER 1870'.

This engraving gave the impression that the guns had been commissioned by the British government whose guns were similarly engraved with the year of their manufacture, and it was concluded that these guns were created to look like official government weapons in order to increase their value. When these weapons fell into the hands of the French who were fighting a war against Prussia, the Prussian government assumed that the British government had sided with the French. The subsequent British investigation proved their government had done no harm, the guns had been manufactured by a private company, with a forgery of the royal engraving. But continental forces were only half convinced. Parthenope sagely warns that this kind of thing could lead to a conflict with Prussia.

Again, Parthenope's concern for the most vulnerable of Britain's subjects, the rural poor, flames out in this essay. She decries the widespread practice of diluting food with sand and other substances, putting salt in beer to make bar customers thirsty, and diluting medications, especially quinine, which was used to treat malaria.

And these same shopkeepers who rob and cheat their customers make no bones about showing up in church every Sunday and putting on a show of piety: 'the English shop keeper, who half poisons his customers by adulterations, but is most particular in his keeping of Sunday, his church or chapel pew; and all his little dues of respectability are not at all infringed in his mind by such trifles as false weights and bad goods'.[10]

She quips that, while the 'The Turkish plan, by which the sinner's hand is struck off, is no doubt excellent, only we should scarcely by this time have a hand left to serve us amongst our trades folk if it were carried out'.[11]

It is also troubling to Parthenope that, when a merchant is caught red-handed, he is fined, but the fine does not necessarily discourage him from committing the same crime again. The obvious problem, she notes, is that the fine never goes up for second and subsequent offences.

The title 'Class Morality' is deceptive, just as is the title 'The Powers of Women and How to Use Them'. It might give the impression that the writer believes in a different scale of ethics for rich and poor. But that is not the case. Parthenope considers it axiomatic that there is one standard for good and bad and that it is essentially known by all classes. The title refers more to what we might today call 'flexible morals'.

The most glaring example of flexible morals is the selling of defective guns to customers in Africa by the British. She paints a horrific picture of these guns bursting in the hands of the purchasers while the seller chuckles over making an advantageous sale.[12]

Parthenope notes that, in the above example, the appearance of honour is all that merchants often seek and, so long as the goods they sell only threaten people in faraway lands, they don't see it as a crime: 'A sort of feeling seems to have grown up that international morality, like gravitation, diminishes as the squares of the distance increase, and that we may cheat without harm if it is only far enough off—among the savages'.[13]

In this essay, the Nightingale scholar can see that Parthenope is talking directly to Parliament, much more than she did in other articles or in her novels, and bidding them to make laws to remedy these crimes: 'With regard to the adulteration of food and drugs, and the question of short weights, it is to be hoped that the promised legislation of the present session may sharpen the blunted consciences of the class in fault'.[14] It is also interesting that, in taking credit for the article, she signed it only 'V' which suggests that she may have collaborated with her parliamentary husband in writing it.

In 'Class Morality', Parthenope does not hold Parliament to account, solely; she also beseeches ministers to quit preaching on obscure points of theology and, instead, instruct congregants that it is sinful to dilute a customer's grain or give him less than he paid for. And, while they are at it, these same ministers should definitely talk about the health benefits of sanitation, and instruct landlords not to charge tenants for uninhabitable dwellings. They should also explain that it's a sin to accept a bribe for a vote, and a greater sin to obtain office through bribery.

Chapter 21

The Miseries of War and the Pleasures of Home

In April 1871, shortly after the conclusion of the Franco-Prussian war, Parthenope published her great antiwar article, 'The Miseries of War', in *Saint Paul's*. Though she was not an embedded correspondent, she was a great storyteller. By collecting letters from the participants of war, both in the army and affected civilians, she crafted a tale of woe that examines the damages of war on several levels and then calls for something exactly like the European Union.

She focused this article on the Battle of Sedan, first showing what that midsize city looked like before the war. Located at the edge of the Forest of Arden and enjoying the beauty of the River Meuse, Sedan was, according to Parthenope, not too far off from being a utopia. It was well supported by an ancient, locally owned cloth industry, largely owned by families who passed down their manufacturing concerns from one generation to the next. Workmen and factory owners enjoyed a pleasant relationship, unfraught by the problematic labour relations in other parts of France.

The town benefitted from successful crops of tobacco, fruit, and corn as well as abundant timber. Arden was still the wild and magical world made famous by Shakespeare in his play, *As You Like It*. It harboured wild boars and wolves which made good hunting. The wild beasts claimed a few lives a year, but, on balance, the citizens of Sedan thought they were well out of the way of any battles. Surely those would be pitched in more populated areas, they thought, and went about drying their tobacco and threshing their grain. Meanwhile, the French Emperor Napoleon II had badly underestimated the size of the German army and had neglected to increase the French army for many years. Despite this, the French believed they would win the war, right up to and even past the moment that Napoleon surrendered.

By the time the Battle of Sedan produced a decisive victory for the Prussians, the town's food supplies had been completely looted by starving French soldiers, leaving the previously well-off civilians to starve themselves. The soil was saturated with the bodily fluids of injured and dead men and littered with dead horses. The grand town church was struck three times by shell casings, surrounding houses were destroyed, the nearby suburb of Bazeilles, which had sustained a thriving cottage industry, performing weaving for the cloth makers, had been burnt to the ground. A group of thirteen people had descended to their cellar for safety during the attack. They were all killed when the house collapsed in on itself.

Though all the fuel, food, and clothing had been ransacked, the defeated French soldiers had been abandoned at Sedan, left to plunder anything remaining that they could find. They had been half-starved when they arrived to fight, and now they were fully starving and desperate to the point of violence. Sedan's civilians were more scared to run into a French soldier than a German one. The Germans had provisioned their fighters a little better and also enforced better discipline. Nevertheless, the victorious Prussians did not hesitate to clear the forest, Sedan's last remaining resource, and sell its lumber.

The residents of Sedan, their crops ruined and plundered, entered a period of dire poverty. There was no food, no way to sow crops, no employment, no industry. Their economy collapsed, basically, in two days. The wealthiest were reduced to charity. Only the arrival of English-run soup kitchens prevented widespread death due to starvation.

Even so, there were examples of the poor taking the best care of each other, as Parthenope had so often witnessed and incorporated into her novels. Recipients of food and clothing would often return some of their donations, citing their worry for their equally poor neighbours.

On the military side, both armies suffered appalling casualties, and, as was true in the Crimea, the perils of bad transportation, disease, diarrhoea, and infection were as bad as the battle itself. A makeshift hospital was established in the Sedan cathedral. A few men died after bodies had been disposed of in the well and contaminated the water. The Meuse River was similarly defiled with dead bodies. Nearly every recorded amputation ended in the death of the patient.

The Miseries of War and the Pleasures of Home   141

There was little to no care taken of hygiene in any of the impromptu medical facilities established. Both the French and Germans were suspicious of fresh air and forbade adequate ventilation for their sick and wounded. Parthenope produced this shocking testimony from one of her sources, who tended to the injured:

> The danger of the hospitals was indeed such, from fever, gangrene, and erysipalas, and the torture of transport so great that the chances of recovery for the poor fellows who crawled under the cover of a hedgerow were greater than for those lying in the foul infectious atmosphere of overcrowded surgical wards.[1]

Parthenope would make another trip to continental Europe, this time as a mature, middle-aged woman, a successful writer, and a beloved wife. But the Europe she saw then would be a wreck of the beautiful continent she had travelled on the threshold of womanhood.

What conclusions could a writer reach about such a brutal conflict as the Franco-Prussian war? Parthenope never claimed the status of a prophet, but her recommendation at the end of 'Miseries of War' is somewhat clairvoyant:

A real congress of the United States of all Europe, where their common interests would be considered, and where they would be bound by laws of a federal connection among themselves [is] ... perhaps the only chance of escape out of the frightful state of mutual distrust—every man's hand against his neighbour—into which we have long been drifting.[2]

The year 1871 was another highly productive year for Parthenope. Not only did she research, write, and publish 'Miseries of War', she also saw the publication of *Fernyhurst Court*, her last full-length novel. *Fernyhurst Court* is simultaneously the most autobiographical of her novels and also the one that draws the least on extreme events. Unlike *Stone Edge* and *Lettice Lisle*, there are no murders, no piracy, no racketeering. The problems in *Fernyhurst Court* are the problems of young Victorian men and women born to the middle and upper classes. It is Parthenope's most realistic novel, her least melodramatic, and also the most nuanced.

Fernyhurst Court illustrates two of Parthenope's preoccupations. One is the devastating effect that estate entailment can have on women. The other is the state of English upper class and middle class marriages, which were so often made for social or financial benefit and upon the most superficial of acquaintances.

Florence Nightingale had decried the manner in which marriages were made in her seminal work, *Cassandra*, and her concerns there echoed the concerns of many young women, Parthenope included.

In *Cassandra*, Florence wrote that a woman, bored with her home life, would accept the proposal of a man she barely knew if he professed his love for her. 'Hence the vulgar expression of marriage being a lottery, which it most truly is, for that the right two should come together has as many chances against it as there are blanks in any lottery'.[3]

It's not a stretch to deduce that the young Florence had noticed the conflation of love and lust in these matches. Hence her use of quotation marks around 'falling in love'. And her conspicuous silence as to whether brides are ever in love, or even sporting a healthy lust, under this system.

Where Florence rails against the yoking for life of two young people after a few teas, picnics, and dances, Parthenope examines the peril of men who marry under these circumstances. The *Fernyhurst Court* characters of Hastings and Tom are the most comical examples. They make a kind of peace with their circumstances, returning the unearned entitlement and ignorance of their wives with a combination of patience, attempts to educate, but most of all, indulgence.

Fernyhurst Court takes up the story of a privileged family, much like the Nightingales, and it is set on an estate much like Embley, the Nightingales three-season home. The family name, 'Dimsdale', rhymes with Nightingale, and 'dim' is obviously a play on 'Night'. Mr Dimsdale, the patriarch, is a man whose intelligence and education have prepared him for a more public life than what he enjoys. But he happily spends his days on horseback, tending to his estate, much as William Edward Nightingale enjoyed doing.

The great joy of his life is his daughter, May, the last of his five children. She and her brother Tom were born years later than their three siblings, so they are, in many ways, like only children. As such, they mirror the lives of Parthenope and Florence, born in close enough proximity to function as peers as well as siblings.

In the opening pages of *Fernyhurst Court*, the reader finds that May is an exceptionally smart child who absorbs learning like a sponge. To an agile mind, just riding out every day with her father and taking in his natural history lessons and his critical analysis of events is an education. She reads newspapers like the *Edinburgh Review*. To that, she adds lessons with the local cleric, though those lessons are intended for her brother Tom. Tom mansplains things out of his lessons that May understands much better than he does.

As a young woman, May turns down proposals from two men. One of them, Lionel Wilmont, is a handsome and affluent neighbour who seems a near-perfect match. Though they are cousins, and the Dimsdales are opposed to cousin marriage in theory, even May's father is surprised to hear that she turned him down.

Her other suitor is Walter Scrope, a young man born into very few privileges. Despite his family's lack of wealth, he contrives to get a university education, alongside Tom. Though both Tom and Walter start law school together, Walter, the harder worker and more driven, is the only one who finishes. Tom, instead, trains for the ministry with the expectation that he will occupy the living afforded by the Dimsdale estate.

Scrope's proposal of marriage is the antithesis of romance. He begins by telling May how much work he has, and how much he needs her help with it. He believes she has the capacity to do good things. As an afterthought, he adds that she 'must know how much he loves her'.[4]

In fact, May is blindsided. Her entire relationship with Scrope has been characterized by arguments and his criticism of her. Though the reader can clearly see that these fights indicate sexual tension for Walter, for her they were just a sign of incompatibility.

It will be tempting for Nightingale scholars to say that, in creating May, Parthenope used Florence as her model. But it is equally possible that, in May, Parthenope created a character based on herself, if she had enjoyed perfect mental and physical health. Like Parthenope, May takes great pleasure in the beauty of her day-to-day life, walking and riding the estate, reading for mental stimulation and to be informed, and having intense conversations with her friends and family. Like Parthenope who declined a marriage proposal from the charming Spottiswoode, May turns down a perfectly eligible young man and declares that she will not marry. Like Parthenope, May is intensely interested in the visual arts. Like Parthenope, May is often the smartest person in a room full of men, unless challenged by either her father or Walter Scroggs. And, like Parthenope, May had rights in her father's estate only for the term of her father's life, after which it passed to her oldest brother. May assumes that she will go to live with Tom after her father passes, much in the way that, early on, Parthenope had counted on Florence to marry and provide a home for both of them on WEN's passing.

As she passes her mid-twenties, May second-guesses herself quite a bit. She finds she is no longer enamoured with learning for learning's sake. Women must live through their affections, the author insists, echoing some of the sentiments she put in 'The Powers of Women and How to Use Them'.

In fact, Parthenope ventures to make stronger feminist statements in *Fernyhurst Court* than she did in 'The Powers of Women'. If, she posits, men really considered to what extent their lives and thoughts were formed by their mothers, wives, and sisters, they would be appalled at the cursory education that even most upper-class women are afforded.

At one point in the novel, Parthenope illustrates the dangers of not educating women. May has allowed the schoolgirls, over whom she has management because she is the parson's sister, to study geography with the boys. Her sisters-in-law gang up on her and protest that it is way over the top to train girls in geography. Sophia insists that a study of Palestine might be in order, but she points casually to a map of England as an example of why no girl needs geography.

Again, because fiction writers get away with outrageous statements that could never be committed to non-fiction, Parthenope pulls this feminist gem out of a hat: 'Whereas their brains being larger in proportion than their bodies than those of men, and their temperaments more sensitive, they require good education for their guidance even more than the other sex'.[5]

Parthenope was saved from being unceremoniously evicted from Embley, via the Nightingale estate entail, by her marriage to Sir Harry. However, she always understood that Embley, the home in which she had lived most of her life, was not hers. She was only a tenant for the duration of her father's life. And such a woman could not help but imagine what it would be like to outlive a beloved father *and* be asked to leave her home all in one swoop.

That anxiety forms the basis for May's eviction from her home upon the death of her father, at whose bed she had sat for months, as he faded away.

The Miseries of War and the Pleasures of Home 145

The eviction scene is so horrifically detailed that it stands as possibly the best, the most lifelike part of the novel.

May's sister-in-law, Alicia, makes it well known that she doesn't want May staying on. Even though May's brother, Hastings, offers her the option to stay, May knows there will be no living with Alicia. On the day May is scheduled to go to Tom's house, Alicia says the horses are resting and not available to take her there. May says she will walk and that her things can be sent on at Alicia's convenience.

Then May hears raised voices and rushes downstairs to find Alicia fighting with May's servant. She learns that Alicia refuses to part with an inkpot and some vases that are May's personal property, gifts from her father and brother. May is near tears by this time but parts with these treasures in order to avoid a fight. Alicia's final parting insult transpires when a servant exits the manor with May's luggage in a wheelbarrow. Even the servants are outraged at the treatment May has received.

Thus it is that, in her late twenties, May finds herself sorely demoted from the darling of the household, cherished by parents and siblings as only the youngest of the family can be cherished, sought after by good men. Now she is a spinster of sorts with insufficient financial resources, no way to earn her living, and entirely dependent on the goodwill of her married brothers.

Parthenope had at least twenty single years to imagine this fate. But it would not be she who was thrust from a familiar home. It would be her mother, Fanny Nightingale, who was torn from her comfort zone by the Nightingale entail, just three years after the publication of *Fernyhurst Court*.

May's brother, Hastings, has made a terrible marriage by yoking himself to Alicia. He makes the common error of thinking he can marry for money, and also thinking he will be able to instil some sense into his wife. The reality, in Victorian England, is quite different. His wife commands the household via her temper. A man marries thinking he will be king in his own home, Parthenope quips, but he soon finds that he has married a prime minister who holds all the real power.

Sophia, May's other sister-in-law, is equally shallow. She strives to be a better person than she is, but falls under Alicia's influence. Parthenope cannot resist mocking Sophia's celebrity mongering. In every newspaper, Sophia turns directly to news of the aristocracy and immerses herself in the details of their fabulous lives. One might assume that those not acquainted with the 'Marchioness of Blankshire' would not care when she arrives home from her travels. But, wait, they do, the novelist quips. Fan worship was as bad in the nineteenth century as it is now. The aristocrats seem to supply a queer sort of imaginative romantic food agreeable to the humdrum,—glances into a glorified existence of beings, supposed to live in perpetual fine clothes and jewels, in a golden whirl of croquet parties and dances … and equally interesting whether considered as preternaturally wicked or preternaturally charming.[6]

By far, the most chilling mismatch befalls the charming and goodhearted Lamont Wilmot, who had hoped to marry May. When May learns that he has married her other cousin, Milly, she has a passing moment of humorous self-effacement. His feelings for her could not have been insurmountable if he 'fell' for so very different a woman, she thinks to herself.

But, when she visits the newlyweds, she finds a tragedy quickly unfolding. Milly is overwhelmed by the care of a new baby who cries constantly, while in her arms. Milly is miserable because she rightly suspects that Lamont does not love her. As if to illustrate just how difficult it is for Lamont to love Milly, Parthenope has her crumple up the pages of an important military report and use them to play ball with the baby.

Lamont uncrumples his report and leaves to attend the meeting where he is to present it, then Milly explains how she ended up married to him. Circumstances threw them together socially, but he didn't pursue her as did the other unmarried, eligible men. That was a challenge for her. When he came to say goodbye to her family—he was returning to Quebec—she burst into tears and gave him to understand that she loved him and would be devastated by his absence. Lionel, being a gentleman, proposed marriage because he couldn't stand to see her in such pain.

May is shocked to learn that this marriage is based on Milly's lie. She attempts to act as marriage counsellor for the two of them, coaching Milly to take more interest in Lionel's projects, especially reports he'd been working hard on. To Lionel, she recommends patience, and bends the truth a little in insisting that Milly loves him dearly. But it is clear that, to Parthenope, this marriage is the tragic outcome of contemporary manners, and that May is advising the doomed.

Upon marrying women who provided them with financial security, May's brothers discover that they enjoy the company of their sister much more than the company of their wives. And yet the wives drive May from their homes. May ends up going to live in London with her sister Celia and her husband, 'the admiral'.

In London, loneliness accomplishes for Walter Scrope what his protestations of love could not. May finds herself hoping to identify him in a crowd. She reviews her reasons for not loving him and finds them flawed. She has discovered how few good men exist in the greater world; even fewer of them would suit her.

She reads, in the newspaper, that Walter has saved the life of a young girl who fell on the train tracks. After returning her to her mother's arms, he found that the train was already too close, and he lay down on the tracks and let the train pass over him, emerging unharmed, after it passed, to an amazed audience.

May also learns that Walter's father has inherited an ancient estate, penniless, but noble. Tom informs her that Walter will need to meet and marry a nice girl with money that he can plough into resuscitating this inheritance.

Based on her reaction, especially her insistence that Walter is far too honourable to choose a woman for her wallet, Tom throws the two of them together again, at an exhibit of the Crystal Palace. They fall right back into their old comfortable conversations and find excitement in examining the art together. Walter proposes again, she accepts gratefully.

It is clear that the marriage of Walter and May, made after years of acquaintance, is meant to contrast with the other marriages in the book. The Scrope marriage will be a happy one because it is built, not on hopes of social advancement or greater riches, but on common interests and the essential goodness and compatibility of the two characters.

Just as the novel seems to be closing on this happy note, Parthenope springs Charlie's marriage on the reader. Charlie, May's middle sibling, appears not to have learned any lessons from the bad marriages his brothers made. May learns that Charlie is now engaged to his troop Admiral's daughter, having failed to make the admiral notice or promote him in any other way.

At the very end of her book, Parthenope dispenses with the usual 'happy ever after' ending that usually sounds like 'they would enjoy many happy years to come'. Instead, she issues a stern warning about the kind of marriages May's brothers have made.

It is a proof of the long-suffering of the human race that great numbers of wedded pairs do not 'cut each other's throats and their own afterwards every year ... as the happiest solution of the dead-lock in which they have engaged themselves, after an acquaintance founded on duly dancing a certain number of galops and waltzes together—too much out of breath to speak—a garden party or two, a few dinners, and a squeeze ...'[7]

Chapter 22

The Death of WEN; Entail Strikes

In the 1870s, marriage continued to be a symphony for Parthenope. She had learned that marriage was a rich, complex thing, much more engaging than the simple melody of courtship. But she had escaped the terrible fate of the heroes of *Fernyhurst Court*. Against the odds, she had made an excellent match, a union of two like-minded souls.

Though by all accounts, Harry and Parthenope made each other very happy, Sir Harry's sons provided some drama that marred their symphony with a few dissonant bars. Both brothers took an interest in politics, but their opinions and positions differed radically from that of their more moderate father.

Edmund, Harry's eldest and the heir to the Verney baronetcy, would become an MP in 1885. Frederick achieved the title of MP in 1906 after serving as a councillor for Buckinghamshire for eighteen years.

Parthenope's sons-in-law took the liberalism of their father to new lengths. Edmund and his brother, Frederick, sided with the fight for Irish home rule. Though Sir Harry and Parthenope were overtly liberal in their thinking, they disagreed, believing that Ireland should remain under British rule. Edmund and Frederick also identified with the liberation movement that wished to dethrone the Church of England as an official national religion. This they believed even though Frederick had served three years as a Church of England minister, after which he left the church to study law. These variances of opinion from their father's drove a wedge between the elder Verney generation and the younger. Florence happened to agree with Frederick and Edmund. However, she did not confront the older Verneys with her dissonance from their line of thinking.

The quarrel with Frederick and Edmund was offset by many blessings. Among other things, the publication of her books finally brought Parthenope the thing her heart most desired: the approval of her sister. Florence bought dozens of copies of her books and gave them as gifts to friends. It was her turn to run PR for Parthenope, and she did so gracefully.

It was meaningful to Florence that Parthenope had finally achieved something more substantial than being a genteel English lady. But it was even more noble that Parthenope did this work while she was so, so sick. In Florence's mind, Parthenope was recast as a tragic heroine, much like Florence herself.

When Parthenope was in London, she visited Florence on Sundays. She was, by this time, so disabled that she had to be carried to Florence's apartment. In their old age, they finally enjoyed the stress-free companionship that both had sought. They reminisced and traded jokes.

In 1872, Parthenope and Florence came together over their mother's illness. Though Fanny was still coherent enough to write letters to her daughters, it had become clear that her dementia would eventually rob her of her independence.

A very distressed Florence wrote to Parthenope at the end of 1872, implying that the latter had not taken good enough care of their mother. She begins by saying that Aunt Mai has 'written twice' to tell Parthe how serious the problem is. Then she goes on to note that she had to leave some 'harassing and pressing business' in London at 'ten minutes' notice' in order to deal with this situation.

The letter goes on to say that Mai and Florence are protecting WEN from any knowledge of their mother's condition, mentions that both Sir Harry and Aunt Mai have been advised of the problem, and that Florence has been sleeping in the music room, presumably to protect Fanny from all harm.

It emerges later in the letter that Florence believes Fanny's servant Webb has started abusing her by locking her in her room and possibly neglecting to bring meals. Florence also fears that the situation will lead to a fire, not an unreasonable fear in a home that would have employed candles and non-electric lamps.[1]

The history of women's liberation has never moved in any kind of straight line, obviously. Apparently, it occurred to neither of these nineteenth-century feminists that perhaps it was WEN's job to help his wife and find the necessary servants, companions, nurses etc. to supervise and comfort her. Florence's angry and alarmist letter would have been better sent to him.

However, Parthenope and Florence together faced the difficult task of dismissing Webb, the servant who had nursed them and had served their mother as a personal maid for fifteen years. The truth was that Webb, herself, was of advanced age and no longer fit to care for a patient with encroaching dementia.

Webb was incrementally replaced by a servant named Grace. Initially, Fanny would not allow Grace in her room. Then other cracks appeared in Grace's aptitude. She left Fanny in her bath too long, until the water was cold. Then there was the episode of the chamber pot. Fanny was left alone with two strangers, and would never ask them for the pot. Florence wrote in great distress about this; Grace's competence was definitely thrown in the shade.

Fanny's life would become even more difficult when her husband died. In 1874, WEN ascended the same Embley stairs that he had been going up and down for over forty years. This time, however, he slipped on the stairs, fell, and hit his head. He died upon impact. Parthenope was visiting Embley at that moment, so she was well placed to handle the next emergency.

Immediately upon WEN's death, Mai and Sam gave tactful notice of their intention to occupy Embley and Lea Hurst. Under the rules of the estate entailment, it was theirs the minute WEN's head hit the stair.

Officially, the estate fell to Mai's son, Shore Smith. But that meant that his parents inherited the right to do as they chose with the inheritance. The previous Smith tenants were universally exiled from Embley. Parthenope took offence at this action, but it was entirely legal. In fact, Mai and Sam allowed Fanny the use of Lea Hurst for several months after WEN's death, a charity they were not obliged to offer.

Eventually, William Shore and his wife took her in. She was, by that time, not capable of living on her own. Fanny would outlive WEN by six years, but they were not good years. She clung to life, even after she no longer recognized her own offspring.

Immediately after WEN's death, Florence briefly faced a problem that Parthenope quickly and tactfully resolved. With the death of WEN, the income that had maintained Florence in her London apartment came to a halt. Parthe convinced Harry to give Florence an allowance that allowed her to remain, without interruption, in the apartment she had chosen for its proximity to all the important people she needed to depose. This sufficiency was deposited four times a year, direct to the same bank where Florence had received money from her father. The Verneys thoughtfully increased this allowance to account for inflation.[2]

Chapter 23

Continental Travels

In the late 1870s, Parthenope and Harry travelled extensively in continental Europe. The official purpose of this trip was to take hot baths again, for Parthenope's health, especially her crippling arthritis.

But the secondary purpose for their travel was, by far, the more absorbing. Both Harry and Parthenope were intensely interested in the problems of poverty and how they were managed on the political, community, and individual level. We know about these trips in great detail because Parthenope subsequently published three articles based on her notes. These works were titled 'Autumn Jottings in France' 'Peasant Properties in Auvergne', and 'Peasant Properties in France'. They were published in magazines and then in a two-volume book titled *Cottier Owners, Little Takes and Peasant Properties*.

Any reader of these books can easily see that the hot water therapy, which is comically described, takes a distant back seat to Parthenope's interest in the social and economic conditions of the working poor. She and Harry were also both sad and anxious to see the domestic fall out of the Franco-Prussian war which had aggravated the poverty of many people, especially the rural French and Germans.

One important theme of these articles is the division of property amongst all the members of a family, upon the death of a patriarch. This Parthenope calls 'partage force', and today it is called 'forced inheritance'. These laws protect children from being disinherited by their parents. Such laws made it difficult to keep nineteenth-century businesses and farms going for multiple generations because all siblings had to share the inherited property. For farming communities, this often meant that a small farm had to support more siblings than it could realistically support. This partage force also resulted in severely fragmented plots of farmland, many of which were too small to yield an annual living. Many such farmers barely subsisted during the growing season and relied on charity in winter, just to prevent themselves from starving. One of the worst examples of partage force that Parthenope provides is that of a mill owner who cannot leave a mill exclusively to the one son who has learned to operate it.

Parthenope, herself, was a victim of the extreme opposite practice: estate entails which almost invariably disinherited women. But in her reviews of how the French poor live, she excoriates the French laws and practices that fragment properties which might otherwise provide sizeable livings. She conducted her research right in the field, visiting farm after farm and interviewing the inhabitants.

Parthenope's fluency in French gave her an entree to the lives of French and Swiss peasants that few English speakers could boast of. She was invited to share the most humble fireplaces, kitchens, and clothes washing circles. The peasants did not understand Parthenope's journalistic or political ambitions. They described her as a 'Madame' from Paris. They thought she was just visiting, and they showed her a great deal of hospitality.

In the preface to the 1885 book edition of *Cottier Owners, Little Takes and Peasant Properties*, Parthenope reveals a mixture of pride and uncertainty about the value of her observations. The title alone undermines the importance of the work by using the words 'little' and 'takes'. The writer goes on to note that she had to be asked to reproduce her 'little papers' in a 'cheap form'.

But, when she discusses her journalistic method, Parthe reveals the abilities of an undercover reporter. She used the fact that she was a woman (and therefore harmless) to ingratiate herself with country people. 'I was a woman and therefore supposed to have a right to an interest in household affairs'.[1]

Here, Parthenope reveals a theory that plain women make the best undercover agents, a theory that was exploited successfully by the allies in the Second World War. It would be around a century before newspaper reporters would think to show up at someone's house with a bottle of wine to get their subjects talking. Instead of wine, Parthenope offered patience, empathy, and pleasantry: 'I made it my business never to be in a hurry, and to listen attentively and sympathetically (always the surest manner of making oneself agreeable) in the seventy or eighty households which I studied near Aix and in Auvergne'.[2] As a field scholar, she also knew the importance of getting a good sampling.

On one hand, *Cottier Owners* is an important and possibly overlooked historical document. Parthenope's observations of rural western Europe were so astute, with such carefully selected detail, that this book will always be a precise record of its place and time.

On the other hand, *Cottier Owners* betrays the bias of its writer in favour of an English upper class life which was, after all, all she really had to compare to the lives of rural farmers.

When she finally published these memoirs in book form, she decided that the purpose of them was to show the disadvantages of small-scale farming. The principal disadvantage is that ownership of small flocks and land parcels fails to make the owners rich. Parthenope, in other words, is quick to condemn and even revile the poverty of the people who offered her so much hospitality. This sentence pretty much sums up the tenor of the work:

> I sat in the straw of the stable-houses with the mistress, the fleas, the cattle, and the chickens, or on a chair in the street with a group of old crones who preferred its cheerfulness to their dark and dreary dwellings—I stood chatting by the fountains to the women washing, to the men digging potatoes on the hillside, and the vine-dressers on the terraces above the lake—to the miller preparing his walnut oil, and the great man owning fifteen acres and a speechless clock.[3]

If there was any pride in being one's own boss, any satisfaction in being independent, any dignity in deprioritizing clocks and furniture, Parthenope did not see that. She saw misery and a lifestyle that was hard for her to stomach. She was offended by a simplicity that was that close to earth.

At the end of the preface, Parthe comes right out and declares that it would be wise for Englishmen to moderate their dreams of land ownership:

> If this little book can be the means of disabusing any of our working class of the exaggerated expectations which they have been led to form of what can be done for them by small ownerships of land, by seeing what are the effects of such possessions in France, Switzerland, and Germany, I shall indeed be abundantly satisfied[4]

The first trip started out in Paris where Parthenope was dismayed by the new construction. Her laments have been echoed through the ensuing decades by people who deplore the cookie cutter nature of suburban developments and cheap urban housing projects. All the buildings looked the same, she noted. Even their windows lined up. Nothing was built to lovingly live in, but to sell. The 'old Paris' of Parthenope's imagination featured buildings that were all different and individualistic. She longed for the Paris of yesteryear just as much as Woody Allen's hero in *Midnight in Paris*.

Parthenope also exercises her wit on the Paris weather, noting that it's really no better than in England, but it has better self-marketing:

> Indeed, we have seen an amount of bad weather there at different times, wet, cold, windy, snowy, such as would have ruined the reputation of any English town. But it is always useful as well as agreeable to praise oneself, and Paris has done this to such good effect that the world at large believes that her climate is as pleasant as some of her other characteristics[5]

From there, the Verneys travelled through the centre of France to Dijon. Here, too, Parthenope was mostly displeased with what she saw. The flat landscape was monotonous. The villages were a study in squalor. All the houses in this part of France looked alike also.

In Dijon, Parthenope quickly got to work on her thesis: the difficulty of making money with any small farm. Each small landowner she interviewed expended a huge amount of energy ploughing and fertilizing his individual acres. These farmers did nothing communally. They used the most rudimentary equipment instead of investing together in machines that could be used on several plots, making everyone's harvest more successful.

The end result of this individualization was small harvests, half of what could be harvested on big English farms even with worse weather. What Parthenope was describing here are, of course, the drawbacks of any small business. Corporations can do more, exploit resources more successfully, trim fat, and force labourers to specialize. It was galling to Parthenope to see so much effort go to creating relative poverty.

She perked up a little as they entered wine country. Here was more colour. But Parthenope was also aware that the Burgundy-producing vineyards undertook a good deal of risk. In a good year, the owners made a 12% profit; in a bad year, they took a loss. The smaller the vineyard, the greater the risk.

As the Nightingales travelled south, Parthenope's mood improved with the more beautiful landscapes. The villages had more colour, and Medoc grapevines covered rocky surfaces against all odds, prompting the local adage that the grapes keep growing even after all the weeds have died.

Her trip to France gave Parthenope many excellent opportunities to exercise her wit on wealthy American travellers. Their skewed values and lack of self-awareness were almost always good for a laugh, no matter where she encountered them: 'Vulgarity is very amusing when it is French or German, it is part of the day's experience; but when it speaks English one feels a sort of unpleasant responsibility for it'.[6]

Parthenope may not have been the first European to notice the cultural blindness of American travellers, but she touches on all the notes that would be sounded for the next century and a half. Why do they travel if all they're going to do is complain about the food, the clothes, and the shopping?

A well-dressed American woman in Dijon came under fire specifically. She was in the same neighbourhood as the magnificent gothic Cathedral of Saint Benignus and went back to her hotel complaining that there were no shops. '… "and I felt so lonesome that I came back," she said, with a twang, enough to electrify one'.[7]

Finally, Sir Harry and his wife arrived in Aix-les-Bains. The chief work there was to take the baths which Parthenope irreverently described as 'parboiling'. The Aix featured a natural hot spring around which the infrastructure of therapeutic baths had evolved. In the bathhouses, the patients were alternately inundated with hot, then cold water while assistants, called baigneuses, gave massages and shampoos, and steam baths.

Parthenope admired the strength and stamina of the baigneuses that waited on her. One was a grandmother, the other a young mother with babies. Both were tireless in executing their duties and complained of the off-season when they had nothing to do. They made good money and were well-nourished.

By contrast, the small farmers in the surrounding fields could not survive on their crops and the meagre income that those harvests brought in. They were subsidized by charity and outright begging. Their nutrition mostly came from rye bread. Most of these landowners, according to Parthenope, were underweight and in poor health. The further away from the town they lived, the more likely they were to be starving.

Women routinely left their children uncared for at home while they went out to work the fields. This caused a high rate of accidents and poor health for the children, according to the doctors that Parthenope interviewed.

On a drive, one day, Parthenope located a stone farmhouse and dropped in. Where artists like Jean-François Millet and poets like John Clare saw peasant life as a noble thing, with its own dignity and beauty, Parthenope saw nothing but poverty. The farmhouse had an earthen floor, the chairs and chest of drawers were broken and the table wretched. The farmer and his wife did not own the land; instead they rented it from their neighbour who, according to Parthe, lived in just as much squalor.

Parthenope was equally horrified by the family's diet which did not include meat. They did not drink the wine they produced, but the children ate some of the grapes and they drank some of the buttermilk that could be processed from their cow milk. In fact, a doctor today might not think this the worst diet, especially considering the absence of refrigeration. But Parthenope was horrified by what she saw as destitution. Such a household would be considered abjectly poor by English standards, she protested.

Cottier Owners is, luckily enough, many things. Where the writer focuses on the poverty of rural farmers, she seems like a snob. But the book is also a feminist treatise. And in this, it is strong and still relevant. Parthenope is frequently outraged by what she sees as an unequal distribution of labour. For instance, outside Aix, she saw a woman carrying a bushel of leaves on her head. The woman's husband was walking behind her, carrying nothing.

On a day trip to Chambery, she noticed four men riding on a bullock cart, while three women, presumably wives, walk alongside the cart. In the same neighbourhood, she saw three women doing all the agricultural work of hoeing, ploughing, and harrowing. One of them was quite old, another had left her baby on a pile of sticks. Nearby, another woman had paused from fieldwork to nurse her baby while her other three children stood nearby. The pathos of this situation: four juveniles so far from the safety of their home while their mother worked full time and attempted to keep them safe and fed, was not lost on the writer. Though Parthenope does not decry the male of the species or ask 'where is the father in all this?' She does write: 'The fatigue and anxiety to a woman of dragging such tiny feet to such a distance, where they had to be kept and fed the whole day, perhaps only a woman can rightly understand'.[8]

More than once, Parthe uses the term 'beasts of burden' to describe farm women. The stark difference between the over-protection of wealthy women and the exploitation of poorer women was an inexplicable injustice.

Parthenope conceded that the bath town had some of the best natural scenery of anywhere in the world. A small lake was within view. The purple grapes hung low, and the long-leaf corn grew high with oxen grazing nearby. All this was framed by mountains.

However, one theme of *Cottier Owners* is the contrast between the beauty of the landscape and the poverty that existed within the outwardly charming cottages. On one road trip to the north, Parthe notes that the children are wallowing in dirt, barefoot, and sickly. She describes the women as stunted, ugly, and overworked. Despite the external beauty of the stone cottages, the lives within them were miserable, Parthenope concluded. Once again, the floors were hard mud, the women's clothes were torn, and their legs and feet bare.

Another earmark of poverty that offended Parthenope was the lack of distinct boundaries between agriculture/industry and home life. At one point, she visited a home where the hay, rope, and wine press all existed side by side with the people who lived there. Upon leaving the first room and entering the second, she saw a number of farm tools only a few feet away from the newly baked rye bread. In the bedroom, chickens were allowed to run about. Altogether this dwelling resembled a barn more than a place to live, Parthe felt.

She was also horrified by the production of wine. Men trod the grapes with dirty feet, and they had to work in pairs lest one of them pass out from the fumes and die. Even with this precaution, there was an average of one death or a close call every winemaking season. Despite this liability, the possession of a wine press was considered a sign of affluence.

The farm folk worked on Sundays, often going straight from church to the fields in their slightly better clothing. Their houses were all abject in almost identical ways. There was no such thing as a private room. All rooms opened onto the other rooms.

In addition to the lack of proper floors, Parthe was horrified by the lack of back doors, the lack of books or other reading material, and children sitting on the earthen floors because most families had so little furniture. In her opinion, this life was so desperate that it was not life: 'The struggle for life is so severe, the wolf of starvation is so close to the door, that the effort to get bread enough to eat seems to exhaust their energies. They simply preserve life at the expense of all that makes life worth having'.⁹

It is not entirely lost on Parthenope, however, that the people who lived this way thought it was a bona fide way of life. They pitied her for coming from a country with no grapes. And when she told them that the English had beer, they expressed disdain for such a poor drink. They thought their wine indispensable even though she considered it vinegary.

One day, she discovered a home on a hill with a view and around eighteen acres. But, upon being invited inside, she saw that it was just as squalid as the poorer homes nearby. And the owners were desperate enough to offer it to her for purchase. She had a good chuckle about this with Harry, to whom she refers only as 'H—', when she took him there to see what she had been offered.

Nearby, a successful miller lived without any kind of parlour or wall art. His sitting-room featured a bag of flour and a stove rather than a fireplace. Parthe had observed that, in general, the oven doubled as a cooking and heating implement, dispensing with the need for fireplaces. She was not impressed with the efficiency. The lack of wardrobes and dressers distressed her. Instead, these French farm folk hung their clothes from ropes.

Back at the hotel, Parthe met a middle class French traveller who revealed another reason for the poverty of French farmers: even at that time, the profit from their crops was being undermined by even cheaper wheat, cheese, and pork imported from North and South America.

In fact, some of the indigence that Parthenope witnessed in the French countryside was the result of a small insect called phylloxera which attacked the grape industry so brutally that eventually half the vineyards in France would be impacted. Some scientists believe that the insect was brought over to France on specimens of American grapevines.

The cure came, ironically, from the original source of the problem: American vines. These turned out to be proof against the insect, and so most French vineyards owe their survival to the timely grafting of American vines onto the French scions: 'The phylloxera is very bad and widespread, and no cure has yet been found against this almost microscopic insect, except to plant the American vine, whose bark is tougher and cannot be gnawn away'.[10]

Parthenope was also correct in noting that it was an almost insurmountable hardship to implement this solution. Newly-planted grapevines typically take two or more years to produce. Anyone who applied the grafts, then, had to do without a crop for at least two market seasons. This was untenable for many of the small landowners who were already living hand to mouth.

The phylloxera was not the only insect that had wreaked destruction on continental Europe. In the year that the Verneys travelled to southern France for the baths, the silk industry had collapsed because of *Beauveria bassiana*, a fungus that spread among the native silkworms. It took less than a generation for this blight to destroy a thriving silk industry.

The Nightingales continued to explore the Chambery region, and Parthenope praised its beauty at every turn. But she also explored attitudes toward the Catholic Church. Post-revolution, the Catholic schools had reopened under secular names. Education, generally, was so languishing among the children she met that she had to concede that any schools were better than no schools. However, despite multiple reform movements, the people to whom Parthenope gave ear complained about ongoing corruption. There was a visceral hatred of the monks. A statue of Peter the Hermit had been badly defaced by flying bricks and bottles. A passer-by said that it should be pulled down and broken up.[11]

Many were resentful of sums paid to the church even when the community had no use for the church's presence. One man reported that his wife complained about him to the local priest and the latter had interfered in their business. As a consequence of this privacy invasion, many husbands had forbidden their wives and daughters to go to confession. The same man said that, for three francs, anyone could get a document stating that he or she was up to date on devotion without going near the church.

In the French Catholic Church of the nineteenth century, curates were the local, very poorly paid priests who did most of the church's leg work in the community. These minor clergy generally came from poor homes and had little education, Parthenope notes. However, their humble origins did not make them one with the poorest farmers. Instead, the curates rubbed shoulders as much as they could with the more prosperous members of the community. In comparing the French clerics to the English, Parthenope may have nursed some bias and optimism about England. English ministers, she insisted, would never abandon their poorer parishioners to their own devices.

The hotel where the Nightingales stayed was packed to capacity with guests, to such an extent that they ended up sleeping in an outbuilding that the hotel chose to call a chalet. There was little wind whistling through the town, and Parthenope became very sensitive to the scents which gathered outdoors, but mostly indoors. She categorized these, on a scale from the honest smell to the suspicious to the underhanded to the downright tyrannical smell, 'which keeps no terms, and is always present and asserting itself; the gas smell; the burnt - fat smell, where the ghosts of five daily tables … rise in evidence against the eaters'.[12] The Verneys changed their rooms five times, trying to find a cleaner one.

Strong female employees augmented the water therapy with what we would today call massage and sauna therapy. The only joy she seems to get from this experience is the ability to witness the bath employees who administer the steam and baths and also provide massage. Parthenope notes, with no obvious envy, how strong these women are. She also notes that they are scantily dressed. Though she attempts to adopt an anthropological objectivity to this state of undress, it's pretty obvious that it offends her. Nevertheless, she notes, from conversations with these women, that they are well paid, therefore well-nourished, and happy to have this work. By their own testimony, they were only happy when busy.

Never once in her memoirs of this trip does Parthenope note any relief from the water therapy. On the contrary, she uses terms that suggest she considered this treatment a form of mild physical abuse. Hot water, then cold is alternately 'fired at the unhappy patient' she writes. She also uses the word, 'violent', to describe the therapy she underwent. Upon their imminent departure from Aix, she writes, 'At last our bathing purgatory came to an end'.[13]

The Verneys moved on to Annecy, a city in the southeast alps of France. Annecy is built right up to a lake of the same name. They took a steamboat around this lake stopping at many points.

Annecy was, at that time, best known as the resting place of Saint Francois de Sales. Of this man, Parthenope gives a pleasant portrait. He was humble, and pilgrims, at that time, sought out his resting place. However, we see Parthenope's Unitarian convictions in the way she describes de Sales' persecution of Protestants: 'a good logical Catholic must be a persecutor—it is his duty to torment unbelievers well in this world, however unwillingly; it would be a cruel kindness to spare a little pain here, according to his creed of salvation, if by any means he may save their souls in eternity'.[14]

And that, in a nutshell, is the Unitarian point of view on religious intolerance. Even the humblest, holiest man can become a monster if his theology is skewed enough. The fault is in a theology that authorizes persecution as a sign of faith. In this, Parthenope is the theological mother of many atheists today who, like Bill Maher, would first ask, 'Does your religion require you to harm people who do not believe it? If so, that's just a bad religion'.

Parthenope did not, however, universally condemn Catholics. As a good Unitarian, she took them as they came on an individual basis. While touring the nearby lake, she met and talked to an old priest who agreed with her that winters were difficult for the local poor to survive. A younger priest in his company, however, objected to the old man chatting with 'heretics'. This younger priest kept trying to separate Harry and Parthenope from the older priest by changing his seat, claiming that his current seat was too exposed to the wind or uncomfortable in some other way. The older priest enjoyed his conversation with the Verney's, however, and declined to move.

The Verneys then travelled on to Chamounix. On the road to their hotel, Harry pointed out Mont Blanc, off in the distance, looking as poetic as always. It might be impossible for any writer not to attempt a poetic description of Mont Blanc, as the famed poets Percy Bysshe Shelley and Samuel Taylor Coleridge had done. There is little doubt that Parthenope would have read the two poems which, together, constitute a dialogue about ideas. There was something unreal about this mountain, Parthenope noted, and, no matter how many times one has seen it, it is 'fresh in its novelty of beauty' every time. To Parthenope, this famous mountain appeared uncommunicative, strong, and almost harsh: 'This day, through the deep dark gorge, with mighty silver furs clinging to the almost perpendicular rocks; the Arve dashing unseen, but not unheard, below, and the lofty cloudland, with the sun on it above, the effect was saisissant (striking)'.[15]

The Verneys were in Chamounix during the off-season, and the hotel was casually neglected. Parthe encountered some more Americans. These particular gentlemen were consciously ticking off all the great sights that they felt obliged to see, so they could say they saw them before returning home. Much to Parthe's amusement, they referred to Mont Blanc as 'Mount Blank' and pronounced 'glacier' as 'glazier'.

These gentlemen were accompanied by 'flocks' and 'herds' of women with rude children. The children, in particular, appalled Parthe. One of them ate too much at dinner, taking two slices where others took one, grabbing extra pickles, and flooding her food with sauce. One boy asked Harry how old he was, and a teenager interrogated Parthenope, non-stop, over three consecutive meals. At one point, he asked three questions in a row, without waiting for an answer, at which she could not help but burst into laughter. He believed he must have said something very clever. 'The young of no other species are so unpleasant', Parthenope concluded. But then she compassionately backpedaled enough to acknowledge that some Americans are 'agreeable and excellent': 'they must somehow shed this their first exceedingly unpleasant husk'.[16]

At the Swiss border, Parthenope and Harry saw only the second agricultural 'machine' they had seen since leaving England. Parthenope had read enough about global agriculture to know that machinery had made farming much more profitable in America and Britain. But, to her mind, another terrible disadvantage of the small farm was that such machines were mostly unviable. Food was planted in such tight rows and so close to neighbouring plots as to make use of a mechanical device virtually impossible. How would it take the corners? Where could it turn around? She noted that even an ordinary plough would inflict damage on a neighbour's crop. But ploughs were used nevertheless. Neighbours inflicted damage on each other reciprocally, reducing the number of lawsuits. 'A steam plough would be a bull in a china closet'.[17]

Parthenope also discovered that many farmers were renting their land, not just from one, but from multiple landlords. One Belgian farm of fifty acres was stitched together from the land of fifteen different owners. Landlords whose only asset was a few acres of farmland, like small-scale farmers, lived with their hands close to their mouths. They demanded high rents and could not afford to accept late rent. Where landlords like the Verneys and Nightingales, for instance, could afford to let their tenants slide on the rent during a bad growing season, these smaller-scale landlords could not.

She heard of one small-scale grower who adopted two nephews whose parents had died and was also supporting his mother. He decided never to marry because he believed the small profits from his farming would not support any larger family.

Parthenope could see no way of improving one's lot in life through such small-scale farming. With the amount of money, time, and hard labour people put into subsisting on the land, they could have made respectable sums of money in trade. They could have then bought their own houses and had their own families. A stubborn and proud attachment to land kept French farmers from thriving and building wealth, she observed. In these observations, we see that Parthenope held an expansionist, Horatio Alger view of wealth and economy. It was not enough to survive and maintain the family assets, held sometimes for centuries. One must improve his lot.

Parthe also analyses why properties cannot be consolidated. Buyers and sellers rarely could come to terms. Offers were refused, and pride kicked in. Sometimes, a badly needed acquisition would go unpurchased and unsold during the lifetimes of the buyer and seller who could never reach an amicable purchase price.

From Chamounix, the Verneys crossed the Swiss border into Geneva. There, Parthenope enjoyed poking fun at a badly executed monument to the Duke of Brunswick. The artists, she thought, should have paid more attention to proportion. Also, when visitors see a monument, it would be a good idea if they had some clue as to who it is in memory of. Parthe also got a laugh out of the fact that the duke had financed a huge, ungainly memorial to himself, but the town had no memorial to its most famous resident: the Protestant reformer John Calvin. Not that Parthenope liked Calvin. He was the most famous of Geneva's notables, but not the most agreeable. She took a line out of Shakespeare's Hamlet to complete the joke: 'Thrift, thrift, Horatio. Calvin left no money to the town to build a monument to himself'.[18]

In Geneva, Parthenope was pleased to see that the watch-making industry was holding its own, even against the competition offered by Americans and their shortcuts. Of particular note for Parthenope was how many Swiss women found employment in the detailing of watches: engraving, painting, adding the hours, and making hinges. As watch artisans, these women were able to make their own independent incomes and needed not to rely on their parents. It was also impossible for Lady Verney not to compare the dignity of the watchmakers with the enforced uselessness of wealthy English tradesmen's daughters, many of whom really weren't cut out for watercolours and the piano: 'striving after gentility by practising bad music, ugly drawing, and useless woolwork'.[19] Even when their lives were harsh and bitter, poor women still had an inherent honour, an honour born of working, raising their own children as well as orphans, and helping out people in their communities. Women of Parthenope's station were mostly deprived of that, she felt.

In Switzerland, Lady Verney saw examples of thrift and prosperity more or less side by side with miserable poverty. She was, of course, more sensitive to the poverty. At one point in her memoirs, a female child chased her down the street, begging. This child had a pronounced goitre, the result of poor nutrition, which nearly prevented her from breathing. At tea, one day, Parthenope met a woman who told her that the begging in that part of the country began at seven in the morning. She also noted the proximity of some households to the odours of cattle and how, in general, people who most needed fresh air, failed to ventilate their homes, even when such ventilation was possible.

Verney points out that, for small-scale farming to succeed, there must be a trifecta of good soil, a market for produce that can be grown on that soil, as well as thrift and good work habits. She goes on to note how rarely these elements actually all come together on one farm. As a consequence, some of the wine regions in Switzerland and nearby French provinces thrive, while others fall into poverty. All of these grape farms are at the mercy of the weather. And nearby Mont Blanc, so cherished of poets and artists, is a source of terror for the vineyard owner who may lose a crop to the frosts and hail that surround that beautiful, but also dreadful mountain.

Lady Verney noted that the only reason any forests remained in France was because of a few old families that owned vast stretches of timber which they managed in a manner that today we would call 'sustainable'. In other words, they cut one section of trees at a time, systematically leaving other trees to stand after their lifetimes. In both France and Germany, experts had deduced that the average tree took 125 years to grow to maturity, a longer time than a man's life. Therefore, the only way to realize the immediate value of a forest is to cut and sell all of it. However, such clear cutting often produces poor soil for farming.

It is fascinating that Lady Verney was familiar with all the fundamentals of climate change as it relates to deforestation. Destruction of mountain forests was a disaster, she wrote: 'the deterioration of the climate, which alternates between too great dryness and devastating torrents after heavy rains, the stripping of soil which leaves only bare rocks and dry ravines in the place of meadows with streams and meadows, has done incalculable harm to society, both in France and Italy'.[20]

While Lady Verney focused her criticism of deforestation on the long-term timber shortage, it is clear that she sees the big picture. Farmers were burning the manure of their livestock instead of being able to use it to fertilize their crops. And, all over the world, she noted, deforestation had injured 'rainfall' and 'dew moisture'.[21] Parthenope considered the problem on a global scale, noting that in India, trees were cut without replanting and that in America, forest resources were wasted on a grand scale, to the point where forests were even burned down to produce farmland, and the wood imported to Europe from America came from further inland every year.

And this is a problem that can only be solved either by government intervention or rich landowners, Lady Verney sagely warns. Small landholders (peasants, as she calls them) cannot be expected to plant a crop that cannot be harvested for a hundred years. They must plant fruit, grains, and vegetables which can produce income every year. Only very wealthy timber owners can afford to consider the long-term benefits to their nation of preserving trees. Therefore, they must.[22]

Throughout *Cottier Owners*, Lady Verney alternates between descriptions of nature, analysis of the local economy, and political commentary, which she gets from her wide reading and from conversation with the people she meets during her travels. The theme of the political commentary is usually the unfortunate amount of corruption inherent in nearly every system and department. People who have lost their livelihood are denied the vote in Switzerland; nepotism prevails in Paris; hope triumphs over experience, and people reinstate kings out of desperation for stability, and men placed in positions of leadership, whether through inheritance or an election, rarely have any common sense. Again, readers may find her political commentary, with its emphasis on the ludicrous and the comic, to be very modern. It verges on a Kafka-esque cynicism at points.

In Paris, Lady Verney visited the Louvre and did an analysis of the Venus de Milo, which she sees as an otherworldly production, not the least bit explicable. She declares it impossible to discern the thoughts of the artist[23] and declares that Venus looks like she stepped out of the marble in the form she takes now. Lady Verney marvels that this masterpiece was located on a small, rocky island in the Aegean Sea. 'What a wealth of artistic power there must have been in Greece thus to sow her masterpieces, as does nature, on some barren rock'.[24] She then free associates on over to the topic of objectification of women in art. Most artistic representations of women are executed by men who, in general, just put together an assemblage of features that they consider ideal with no attempt at individuation. By contrast, the Venus de Milo is an individual with a strongly conveyed individual personality. The writer goes on to praise art which captures individuality rather than simply generalizing. When the heads and hands of artistic subjects are flawless, the work loses 'what alone is valuable in art'.[25] But, once again, Parthenope's thought train turn to the lives of the poor, in whose cottages she never sees any artwork, even a print.

And then Lady Verney tells a story in which all the worst aspects of French economy come together to starve people right out of their homeland. In an unnamed Protestant village, the property was subdivided to a terrible degree, and the peasants also deforested. When the snows came, they carried off so much soil that the land was completely infertile, and the locals were in danger of starvation. Only through the efforts of charitable organizations in England and France were the peasants able to survive by being moved to a region of Algiers.

To further illustrate the poverty in rural France, Parthenope tells the story of a friend from her teen years, Monsieur Julius Mohl. Mohl planned a walking tour through a part of France, but he discovered that the food served in inns was a thin mixture of water and cabbage. The proprietors of these inns often filled a pot with water and cabbage, kept it over a fire, and refilled the water several times a day, ensuring that the cabbage lost all its nutrients. This and black bread were all that could be found. Mohl was, as Parthenope notes, a 'man of very simple habits', but he gave up his travel plans when he discovered how little food was available to the traveller.[26]

The women of France, Parthenope writes, are overworked to the point that infant mortality, under the age of one, is at 50%. By contrast, a French doctor was surprised to note how relatively healthy young British mothers of the same class were. To understand how the severe poverty of French peasants impacts their morals and intellects, Parthenope refers readers to the Balzac novel, 'Les Paysans', which takes up the subject of French farmers in poverty.

The Verneys then travelled to Royat, another bath town. Only a few years previously, a hot spring had been discovered in Royat. But when it was unearthed from layers of snow and earth, the excavators found remnants of a Roman bath installation. Almost immediately upon the rediscovery of these waters, there sprung up a spa town where the three month tourist season alternated with months of economic stagnation. As usual, Lady Verney finds this bath town a mixture of beauty, exploitation, and sadness. The lava cathedral in nearby Clermont is beautiful, she concedes, but the tourist enclave itself is a hodgepodge of: 'hotels, flies, booths, sedan-chair porters, fruit and flower women, donkeys'.[27]

Lady Verney indulges in some very cruel, but devilishly comical observations about the financially comfortable bourgeois who come on Sundays to listen to the garden band play. They were, she thought, 'squat', ugly, and abominably dressed in over-feathered hats. But the thing she found most offensive about these (most likely perfectly respectable) middle class denizens was their air of superiority which clashed mightily with the outrageous hats: 'a whole panache of feathers, seven or eight red roses as big as saucers, and a simpering, conquering look under them inexpressibly comical: "Look at me and learn; I am the pink of the fashion"'.[28]

Parthenope concludes that 'French taste in dress is confined absolutely to Paris'.[29] Of course, literary trends have changed and few publishers would currently publish non-fiction that was so specifically sarcastic about private individuals who currently exist. Today such observations would have to be carefully embedded in fiction, where they would bring the same joy. It is interesting to note that Lady Verney practised the opposite. In her non-fiction, she holds back no punches, especially against the well-off. But in her fiction, she is always compassionate, even to the most desperate characters.

Parthenope suffered from the lack of ventilation in the Verney's Royat hotel as she so often did. She reports that 'the English' dared to open a window in the common area, and 'the Frenchwoman' ran up and slammed it shut right in their faces.[30]

As usual, Lady Verney quickly turned her attention to the farming community. Here, again, she found that the partition of once-great homesteads had wrought havoc with the economy and with any individual's chances of amassing wealth. One of the wealthiest grape growers in the vicinity was a man who sold wine to the hotel where the Verneys were staying. He owned ten acres, a princely amount of land in those parts. But he had had to patch together that estate with parcels here and there. No one owned a continuous stretch of good farmland. Parthenope asked why the locals didn't trade lots with one another in order to have continuous land, but she learned that there was too much jealousy and rivalry to make that happen. Struggling landowners would even drive up the cost of land at auction to prevent a neighbour from becoming rich. Furthermore, the weather had been cruel to the grapes, always a more vulnerable crop than hardier grain. The latest season had produced grapes the size of peas when they were not spoiled altogether by rot and mould. Lady Verney saw a woman feeding grapevines to her cows. Once again she was informed that the women did all the really hard farm work while the men did the lighter work.

Lady Verney also learned, to her great dismay, that some of the locals slept with livestock in the winter to keep warm. She also met a woman who lived in a house with the loft in the bedroom, but, in the absence of an indoor staircase, she had to go around the house, using the street and enter the loft through a separate door.

Despite the tawdriness of the rural existence in France, Lady Verney was surprised to learn that these poor French people rarely ever would voluntarily leave France. They looked upon emigration as not just a last, but a tragic resort. By contrast, she finds the Swiss and the English much readier to abandon their homelands to pursue their fortunes. (From this, Lady Verney might have extrapolated that the French farmers did not find their lives as miserable as she found them, but the potential beauty of severe minimalism was not a point of view she entertained.)

Just outside Clermont, the Verneys journeyed to a village entirely occupied by washerwomen. When the couple arrived at this site, they found four long rows of women beating clothing with paddles using river water as the cleaning agent and stones of the river as platforms. The women downriver received only the nasty water that had already soaked up the dirt from clothing that had been cleaned upstream.

Lady Verney sat down to sketch this enterprise which she found both curious and barbarous. The fifty or so women greeted her and asked if she were there to take their portraits. Not all of them, she explained.

She asked what time they started work, and they merrily replied that they began at six AM and usually worked until dark and sometimes by torchlight, all seasons of the year, including winter. The women were dressed in cotton gowns with white caps and yellow handkerchiefs. Lady Verney surmised that they must be wet all the time from their work.

Once again, the writer paused in describing the landscape and the people to decry the lack of civilizing forces. She accused the French of living only to save money and of living in more squalor than necessary in order to save. The people of these small French villages are in competition with each other to remain at the exact same level of apparent poverty as their neighbours: 'their level of taste and civilization sinks to the capacity of the lowest; any advance on this is regarded as pride and absurdity'.[31]

Chapter 24

Germany

During a trip to Germany with Harry, Parthenope had the singular fortune to see Germany's Cologne Cathedral just as it was being completed, a venture that took 632 years of starts and stops.

Parthenope was mostly unmoved by the cathedral's majesty. She was, however, acutely aware of the nationalism surrounding its completion and the upcoming celebration which would be attended by the Protestant German emperor.

> That majestic building, begun with the idea of glorifying and pleasing God ... is now completed with little reference to God at all, but as a patriotic tribute to the unification of Germany and to the honor of the German race, the work of men of all creeds, by a national instead of a religious enthusiasm.[1]

Though Parthenope was generally sceptical of all religions, she had a strong belief in God and in living according to the tenets of the Sermon on the Mount. But the patriotism she saw on display in Cologne, having supplanted faith, made her nervous without an ability to see the comical side of it. Again, the biographer must make an effort not to see Parthenope as a sort of Nostradamus, here predicting the rise of Nazism.

She and Harry arrived in Cologne via a very unpleasant coal-powered boat ride; 'we came into Cologne looking almost black', she writes. And they arrived to see that the cathedral was still surrounded by building scaffolds.

As they entered the cathedral, Parthenope noted that the newer parts of the building had a 'cut and dried look' and that the statues were badly executed, looking like the work of journeymen who sold their work 'by the yard'.[2] Likewise, she found the new stained glass to be ugly. One magenta and green panel, in particular, looked like a carpet 'from Shoolbred's'.[3]

Parthenope acknowledged that the need to represent a story in glass interferes with the main purpose of such windows which is to delight the viewer with light and colour, a delight that the writer admitted is sensuous. Ideally, the colour is melody, and the story is harmony, she adds.

Parthenope took some unbecoming potshots at the 'Rhinelanders' who attend Sunday services at the Cologne Cathedral; she called the women 'ugly, ill dressed, in colors hopelessly wrong' and went on to say that French women with the same assets make themselves beautiful, and that the Italians would be dirtier, but at least they would be 'more picturesque'.[4]

She also could not resist aiming her comic radar at an opulent statue of the Virgin Mary, arrayed in 'a crown and very fine brocade gown, over a crinoline'. About this queen of heaven, dressed like a German noblewoman, Parthenope wrote, 'She was evidently much in fashion for a whole gallery of *ex votos* [votive offerings] hung over her'.[5]

But Parthenope was not all sceptical sarcasm. She saw positive signs of true faith and humility. A poor woman dressed all in black and carrying a heavy basket sat down near Parthenope, closed her eyes, and counted her rosary beads; 'a look of peace stole over her worn face'.[6] Parthenope also found it pleasant to see that the churchgoers of Cologne moved freely around the cathedral, believing it belonged to all of them and not just the church sexton and beadle.

She waxed lyrical about the sound of the church organ which, she stated, sounded like the sonorous voice of the church while the choir sounded like all humanity, petitioning heaven. The organ and choir sounded like they were in dialogue.

But, before leaving the subject of the church, Lady Verney made another satiric point about Catholicism. When everyone in the church (save the Verneys, apparently) got up to attend the eucharist, she saw it as a follow-the-leader, mindless act that had nothing to do with the individual's relationship with God:

> You had only to follow your leader and do as you were bid, and you were washed, 'clean and done for' by the priest in the lump ...[7]

Parthenope could not know that the prominent matching towers of this celebrated monument would help guide the allied pilots in flattening most of Cologne during the Second World War or that the cathedral would take multiple bomb hits, but remain standing, the only vestige of history that would remain in this large German city.

The Verneys hopped a steamer and travelled to other parts of Germany. Parthenope again bewailed the ugliness of modern architecture. In her mind, every old building in every village was more beautiful than the modern dwellings. And each town's old architecture was individual to that town where all the modern buildings were the same. The same trend existed in clothing, she noted. Gone were the beautiful and sturdy velvets and brocades that could last a family for multiple generations. These lovely garments had been replaced by cottons.

On this trip, the Verneys were accompanied by a wine merchant's sister. The merchant himself was visiting his vineyards. Through the information supplied, presumably by this woman, the couple learned that every inch of German soil that could be used for good grape growing was already occupied by grapes. Any remaining plots of land were too sunny or otherwise not conducive. From their travel guide, they also learned that all the winemakers were in debt. Any year that the crops did not do well, they survived by taking out another loan on their land.

Chapter 25

The Defense of Science

The 1880s were Parthenope's last decade, and for most of the decade, she continued to write both fiction and non-fiction articles, that might today be called editorials rather than essays. She was, in fact, so prolific during the last ten years of her life that two of her novellas and a collection of short stories and essays were published after her death.

In 1880, Fanny finally died, after a fierce struggle. Her nephew, William Shore and his wife sat at her deathbed. She was buried at the same East Wellow churchyard, where Florence would be buried, near the Nightingale's Embley home. Parthenope was unable to attend the funeral. Florence sent her a bouquet of flowers that had decorated Fanny's coffin, but Parthenope probably enjoyed the kind letter that accompanied it more than the flowers.

The next thing the sisters collaborated on was the text that would adorn Fanny's grave. There was a surprising amount of drama and polite disagreement over this enterprise. In the end, they produced a text that represented both sisters' ideas, but Parthenope's editing skills prevailed in producing a more concise wording than Florence had originally planned. The inscription reads: 'Devoted to the memory of our mother Frances Nightingale, wife of Edward Nightingale, Esq … God is love … Bless the Lord, oh, my soul and forget not all his benefits'.

The two also had extensive correspondence over the exact wording of some memorial cards that they distributed to poor neighbours after the death of their mother. One might question whether it was a good use of either woman's time to spend so much energy on these cards. But their disagreements were very polite, and they finally arrived at a compromise. During this debate, Florence refrained from putting Parthenope's words in quotation marks while throwing them back at her.

The renewed goodwill between the sisters continued to the end of Parthenope's life and mellowed as they aged. It appears that, with the vantage of time, Florence was able to regain some of the fonder feelings she had nursed for Parthenope before that sister became a burden to endure. It helped that Parthenope herself had gained so much self-confidence through her writing, her successful marriage, and her productive relationship with her stepchildren. Being able to provide financial resources also put Parthenope on a more equal footing with her younger sibling. Parthenope would send clothes to Florence when the latter was too ill to shop. The Verneys also sent tree branches from their grounds to use for wreaths in the hospitals and training centres with which Florence worked.

This is not to say that there were no more disputes between the sisters. But the occasional spats were much more gracious, and Florence, in particular, found it possible to write with compassion and to ask for her sister's input, even when she frequently refused visits.

After Fanny's death, the Verneys created an 'F wing' (short for 'Florence') in their Claydon mansion. This consisted of a bedroom and dressing room, replete with bells that could summon a servant at any hour of day or night. This became Florence's summer residence. She loved spending time at Claydon and managed to praise Parthenope's hard work at restoring it to its original grandeur.

Florence had the status of a hotel guest at Claydon. She owed nothing to her hosts, yet her every need was wordlessly met. She sometimes went days without speaking to either Verney. She even declined to attend entertainment events that the couple staged, on the grounds that going downstairs would be too much for her. On one occasion, Florence wrote that she would like to have joined Parthenope in the library for a conversation, but doctor's orders told her to keep her feet on the bed.[1]

The Verneys staged an annual day's outing for Florence's nurses in training. On these occasions, the nurses would come to Claydon House for some rest and relaxation in a rural setting. During these field trips, Parthenope would accompany the young women in a carriage. Florence did not always interact with these guests.

The Verneys also made their London home available to Florence, who had priority use of it. The Verneys used it only when Florence had no more need for it. The Verney carriage was available to Florence and for all her travel needs. And Harry Verney, himself, was often available to do errands. For instance, when Florence's dear friend, Selina Bracebridge fell mortally ill, Verney was dispatched to pay her a visit in Florence's stead.

For the rest of their lives, the Verneys would support Florence and her work in many other ways. Florence's London accommodation was modest by design; she stayed unequipped to entertain the important people that she often needed. So it fell on the Verneys to host these friends in their more spacious home. One such guest was Benjamin Jowett, an Oxford don whose heretical theology resonated with Florence and with Parthenope. Several biographers believe that Jowett was in love with Florence. He gave her substantial help with her work, but eventually distanced himself when her demands seemed excessive. Another important guest at Claydon was Georgina Hurt, a neighbour of the Nightingales at Lea Hurst with whom Florence wished to correspond on the abysmal state of medical treatment at Buxton Hospital.

In 1880, correspondence between the sisters shows that Parthenope had continued her practice of reaching out to help the rural families who lived nearby. Lady Verney had become concerned about the welfare of an unnamed woman, the daughter of a man named 'Joseph'. This girl had a medical problem that was not disclosed in the sisters' correspondence, but Parthenope wished for advice on where to send her for the appropriate treatment. Flo recommended Dr Armitage on Audley Street. However, Florence warns that there is no point in 'sending a girl to any doctor' without first corresponding with the doctor or somebody going with the patient.[2] Florence Nightingale understood the importance of patient advocacy well before the term for it was invented.

In 1882, Parthenope collapsed. She had been beset by rheumatoid arthritis pretty much her entire adult life. Her poor condition brought Sir Harry to tears. He was in his eighties and not strong enough to nurse his wife full time, but her frequent cries of pain were a torture to him. As usual, when a friend or relative was sick, Florence swung into action.

During this crisis, it was discovered that Parthenope had frequently changed doctors, possibly looking for one who could help her or at least diagnose her. She came under the care of one Dr Ogle, who met Florence's standards.[3]

However, the decisive factor in Parthenope's recovery was probably the arrival of her stepson's wife, Margaret Verney. Margaret took up the job of providing full-time care for Parthe. The road to recovery was slow, however, and it was two years later that Florence commented that Parthe seemed like her old self.

Upon her recovery, Parthenope wrote so prolifically that it can be difficult to date some of the work she produced during this decade. Her publishers could not keep up with her output, and reams of her work were published after her death. This spate of productivity was all the more impressive considering that she had almost completely lost the use of her hands and was reduced to dictating her thoughts to the friends and relatives who helped her put her thoughts on paper. It is a testament to these young people's zealous attention that Parthenope's last writings were so marvellously well organized, cogent, and always well supported by her research and keen observation.

This keen observation was, in fact, the subject of her editorial, 'Evidence For Opinions, Events, and Consequences'. This essay explores the problem of evidence as it was acquired and invoked in the late Victorian age. Parthenope had developed her ability to observe and process minutiae from the teaching of her father, from her walks around the countryside with Florence, and from extensive, voracious reading. As witness to Parthenope's almost supernatural observational powers, we have her unique ability to reproduce dialect and her ability to speak French like a native.

One thing she had noticed was how often eyewitness accounts are not reliable. Eyewitnesses, even when giving testimony in court, are often influenced by the excitement they felt at the time of the event. They are also influenced by their own interests and temperaments. She gives the example of a group of people on a 'pleasure outing'. One of the group is an artist who mostly only notices the landscapes and the play of light and shade; the group's naturalists notice the flora and fauna; the maid notices how people are dressed; the cook notices how the food was cooked and cut; and only people who are familiar with the arguments for sanitation notice the smells.[4]

As a contemporary example of how people differently perceive facts, she cites the then well-known Tichborne case. Now lost to history, the Tichbornes made the news when a man claiming to be a long-lost family member, Roger Tichborne, the heir to the family fortunes, showed up and claimed his inheritance. His rough manners, more like those of a butcher (which, in fact, the imposter was) than a gentleman, led most of the family's friends and members to conclude that he was not who he claimed to be. And, eventually, he was tried in court and found guilty of impersonation. Toward the end of his life, he confessed to not being a Tichborne. But his mother, who had never stopped believing that her son was alive, stood by him for quite some time and upheld his claim.

Parthenope's point is that people often see what they want to see. Today, we call this confirmation bias. She could have invented the term, her definition of it is so precise.

In part through her research on the Verney family, and in part through the research she did on art, society, women, and morals, Parthenope had developed a keen sense of what kind of evidence should be relied on as solid and how frequently no evidence was required to back a well-accepted convention.

She notes that the standards for what is acceptable evidence have changed. This explains the decline in miracles in the eighteenth and nineteenth centuries, she notes, trying hard not to expose the tongue that pokes out of her cheek so clearly to someone who has read the rest of her work.

In discussing the miracles that turned ordinary Christians into saints, she notes that, in the cases of both Saint Augustine and Saint Francis, that they did not claim to have performed miracles or to have had any part in them. Saint Francis, she notes, was not the one who drew attention to his supposed stigmata, nor did the observers of it make any attempt to understand a possible scientific cause for it.

When new standards for proof went into effect, the number of miracles declined steeply. But Parthenope cautions that the standards of proof are in further need of improvement, and where proof exists, policy needs to be implemented based on it.

Her most poignant application of this principle is in the health sector. Science, she writes, has given us plenty of proof that people need clean water, nutritious food, ventilation, and sanitation. The evidence is not lacking, it's the implementation: '[E]very case of zymotic disease and of small-pox can be traced to our national neglect ... The adulteration of food, drink, and drugs, is distinctly shown to be poisoning our poorer neighbors, ... yet year after year, any interference was carelessly postponed'.[5]

But public policy on health is not the only target of Parthenope's wit and sense of the ludicrous. She also targets superstition, one good, historical example of which is witch identification. She gives the example of a woman who seemed to be spitting pins. She is declared a witch, but no one bothers to question whether she could have simply pulled them out of her dress with her mouth.[6]

'Evidence For Opinions, Events, and Consequences' was published in 1885, five years before her death and three years after her terrible collapse and long recovery. The extreme bravery of the essay suggests that Parthenope may have known she did not have long to live. There is a 'damn the consequences' scepticism and free commentary about organized Christianity that she was more hesitant about expressing in the 1860s and 1870s.

In *Stone Edge* and *Lettice Lisle*, for instance, Parthenope confined her scepticism to the dialogue of her characters. Through them, Parthenope made gentle fun of doctrines like predestination that had no relevance to the average believer who vaguely understood them, if at all. When she seriously wanted to criticize the way Christianity was practised, she limited herself to indicating that people should not terrify children with the Bible or indicate that God is a malevolent presence waiting for us to mess up.

But in 'Evidence for Opinions', she flat out questions the 'evidence' for God, quoting Voltaire's line, 'God made man after his own image, and man has returned the compliment'. She goes on to point out that a mean man will invent a mean god, a weak man a weak god, and a tyrant a tyrannical god.

The 'evidence' for God, throughout history, has been found in natural catastrophes: earthquakes and destructive storms, the writer notes. Parthenope always hated the alignment of God with terror and, in 'Evidence', she suggests that we look for God in 'that still small voice' that is synonymous with conscience[7] instead of looking for him in the worst tragedies that befall humanity.

Though Parthenope reaffirms her belief in a God 'in whom there is no variableness, neither shadow of turning',[8] it is obvious from this essay that Parthenope's disenchantment with the leadership of Christian highest institutions runs deep.

While mocking the miracles that have been offered as evidence for God, Parthenope also writes about the importance of scientific inquiry. Where the 'evidence' for God is inevitably subjective and should be sought in one's conscience, science follows strict rules for making conclusions that are based on fully-vetted evidence.

The corruption of Christianity and struggles of science are such weighty matters, the contemporary reader of Parthenope's 'Evidence' might be left feeling that nothing could be done. Just at that point, however, she offers a simple thing that everyone can do: encourage children to develop their skills of observation by taking them on walks and then asking them questions about what they have seen.[9] Children can also be asked to give a summary of events they witness. Here we see the influence of Fanny Nightingale who trained her children to take notes on church services.

Parthenope's last years were a flurry of industry. It's as if she were aware that she got a late start on her destiny, and was rushing to fulfil it in the time she had left.

In May 1884, Macmillans published Parthenope's 'In a Great Town Hospital'. Though the hospital in question is not identified, nor is the 'great town', it is obvious that the article refers to a London hospital for paupers. It was a teaching hospital, and might well refer to Saint Thomas' Hospital which was built using Florence Nightingale's ideas of hospital design. Saint Thomas' was also where, in 1860, Florence founded her Nightingale School and Home for Nurses.

The article describes a public hospital of the era, mostly by depicting several of its more extreme patients. In this piece, Parthenope examines both the progress made in Victorian medicine and also the limits of available medical treatments.

Many of the hospital patients behave horribly, she observes. Possibly the most shocking example is the one Parthenope leads with. A drunk Irishman arrives with a head wound that he obtained from falling into the river. He resists care to the point of assaulting four doctors and has to be handled by the porter. (At that time, the hospital porter was a combination of janitor and security guard.) The porter holds the patient down so that a doctor can apply a carbolic spray to the wound. The next morning, having sobered down, the Irishman is a completely changed man: grateful, cooperative. He tries to help the nurses, and entertains his fellow patients with song and dance. The rather heavy-handed message is that the problems of many patients originate in their own moral failures. This is a theme running through the article.

The article next examines two attempted suicides, the most pitiful of which is a mother of six children whose husband died and left her destitute. She had tried to support her offspring, one of whom was still a baby, but when they started starving, she attempted to take herself out of the picture by drinking vitriol. It burned her mouth and throat badly but left her well enough to recover in the hospital. The nurses allowed her to slip out, unseen by the law enforcement agent waiting to arrest her. She disappeared back into the crowds of London, never to be followed up on.[10]

At another point, a valued bed is occupied by a fifteen-year-old boy who seems to have descended into insanity. His symptoms are twisting, twirling, throwing his legs in the air and frequent fainting spells, during which he does not respond to stimuli. After a few days, however, the doctors and nurses discover that he is faking. He did not like his apprenticeship and was dodging it by faking madness.

Parthenope uses a couple of cases to underline the plight of some Victorian women, married to unreliable or even violent men. A successful shoemaker appears in the hospital, so drunk he can barely breathe. The hospital staff rally to put him back together. Upon his release, his wife and baby show up to visit him. Parthenope hints that the shoemaker will relentlessly drag her down along with her child.[11]

Another patient is a seven-year-old boy whose father tossed him headfirst onto a stone floor, much like the child in *Stone Edge*. One might think that *Stone Edge* was inspired by this case, except that the novel predates 'In a Great Town Hospital' by over a decade. No legal action is taken against the father who comes to visit the boy, along with his wife. The boy's fellow patients are outraged that no consequences will ensue for the father to whom the child was eventually released, Parthenope noting that 'the mother seemed to be a tolerably respectable, quiet woman'.[12]

The child patients are, predictably, the most pathos-inducing of Parthenope's medical portraits. At one point, a child comes into the hospital having been burned from smoking in bed. At another point, a child comes in with welts all over her body. 'Measles,' says the doctor. 'Fleas,' says the nurse. It turns out the nurse is right.[13]

It seems unlikely that Parthenope, who was in poor to terrible health throughout the 1880s, directly observed all of the goings-on that she reports on in this article. However, as is true for other writings she put together from primary sources, it reads as if she were an eyewitness. She was reasonably well reconciled with Florence by this point, and may have benefitted from the wealth of testimony that Florence accumulated, concerning all things medical, hospital, and nursing.

Parthenope notices that having children mixed in with the adults in a ward has a civilizing effect on even the roughest patients. Almost magically, the cursing and singing of obscene songs diminish, and the adult patients participate in the care and coddling of the youngest patients.

Perhaps the most amazing thing Parthenope reports on in 'In a Great Town Hospital' is the role of nurses, who have been transformed from characters little better than Charlotte Brontë's mad nanny, Grace Poole, to the colleagues in good standing of doctors.

Parthenope gives testimony to this when doctors identify a case as something that can be handled by the nurses alone. The nurses have all undergone training. They are respectable. The doctors listen to them. This is a 180-degree change from what they were in 1850, before Florence Nightingale's reforms.

The reporter closes out her article by noting the bitter underfunding of many hospitals, especially those that heal the poor at no charge. She calls for both more charitable contributions and also for something that, today, we would call 'co-pays': 'Probably also some small payments should be exacted from many who are perfectly able to contribute'.[14] The worst horror of underfunded hospitals, Parthenope noted, was empty beds, badly needed by the sick but untenanted, because the hospital has such limited funds for treatment.

'In a Great Town Hospital' betrays, more than Parthenope's other writings, a limited global perspective that will jar the sensitivities of the modern reader. She used the words 'negro' and 'Chinaman' which were not yet the pejoratives they would later become. While this might be excused based on historical context, her humorous description of an African sailor and two Chinese patients really cannot be, especially when she describes the existence of Black sailors as evidence of an unreliable factor in the British trade: 'It shows that the whole nominal strength of our merchant service is not to be relied on as a reserve for the navy in time of war, on which we sometimes seem to count'.[15] Sadly, Lady Verney finds it humorous that the African patient keeps taking off his shirt when none of the medical staff is around. Equally unfortunate is Parthenope's story about a white woman who gives birth to a black child which the writer refers to as a 'surreptitious addition' to the hospital's 'black population'.[16]

While it is true that Parthenope also enjoys a good laugh at the expense of several presumably white drunks, the tone is different. In her descriptions of bad white male behaviour, there is an implication of tragic waste, a life that could have been virtuous and useful but has been squandered in this way by someone who knew better. There is none of this feeling in her description of those who come from beyond Great Britain and Europe. Instead, they are caricatured. In writing about people of colour, Parthenope hit the glass wall that surrounds a brilliant education encompassing only the achievements and languages of Britain and continental Europe.

Chapter 26

Last Years with the Verneys

Parthenope wrote very little about her own life and work, and the care she took to preserve all of Florence Nightingale's letters was not reciprocated. In fact, no one was systematically saving Parthenope's letters. This poses a difficulty for the biographer of Frances Parthenope Verney, née Nightingale. Florence knew, from an early age, that she had a great destiny to fulfil. She often saved copies of her own letters. Recipients of Florence's letters generally cherished them. And, at times, Florence would demand the return of her letters, if she thought they had fallen into the wrong hands. As a consequence, Florence's life is well documented at nearly every turn.

Parthenope never enjoyed that level of confidence or popularity. As a consequence, it can be very difficult to date some of her works, especially the stories that were published posthumously.

The novella, *Grey Pool*, is such a work. It was published posthumously and may have been dashed off in a few free evenings, or she may have come back to it over a period of years.

Grey Pool takes up the story of three women, all of whom suffer at the hands of one bad man, Mark Ogden. Mark's wife, Joan, was a serving girl when she met him. He struck her as an entertaining man, but far too rough to consider marrying, even though a proposal was forthcoming on the same day as their acquaintance.

Joan serves in a strict, one might say puritanical, household with rules that govern not just the family but all its staff as well. The sanctity of the Sabbath is one of the family's strictest rules. Simultaneously, Sunday is the only day off work that Joan ever gets. Joan takes a chance on going out with some friends one Sunday, and they end up in a public house. Time passes quickly when enjoyment is afoot, and Joan soon discovers, to her fright, that she has been out several hours later than her employer allows. She might have gotten away with it. However, as she sets out on foot, alone, for the big house, she runs into a church elder who knows who she is. Scandalized, this man immediately tells Joan's employer of her wayward behaviour, where she had been and with whom, on a Sunday!

Joan is scolded but not dismissed. She is retained on the condition that she never leave the house on Sundays. The terms of her employment are now intolerable to a young woman with a free spirit. At this point, Mark Ogden's proposal starts to look good. He has flagrantly lied to her about his prospects. She will have her own home to lord it over, he claims. Joan has one moment of triumph in her life, when she tells her 'mistress' that she is leaving her position as a servant to get married.[1]

That is Joan's backstory. When the reader first sees Joan, she is unhappily trying to feed her two children with leftover potatoes while her husband is off at a nearby tavern, spending what little money he makes on booze.

Joan, Mark, and their two daughters, Rowan and Nelly, live on a rented barge with which Mark ekes out a living, transporting various goods up and down the river. He uses his daughters as unpaid labour. It is they, mostly, who pull the horse who pulls the barge along the towpath.

Ogden's work takes him to Joan's home region, and there she finds work and lodging with a washerwoman, Mercy Gaunt, who is her maternal cousin. The elder daughter, Rowan, works alongside her mother while little Nelly attends school.

Mercy takes in laundry for many households, but mainly for the great Squire's hall, whose walls and woods lie nearby. This is the home of Mrs Heron, the widow of Colonel Heron. Since the death of her husband, all her affection has been focused on her son Lawrence. When the reader first sees Mrs Heron, she is busily preparing welcome home festivities for her son and several friends, including a young lady who is obviously a candidate for Lawrence's wife. Mrs Heron's love for her son is so unadulterated by selfishness that she never once pauses to reflect that, when Lawrence marries, his wife may well wish for his mother to vacate the premises.

Parthenope's own mother was a victim of English heredity laws that frequently ousted women from the homes they had occupied from their first day as young brides. Here again, *Downton Abbey* provides a ready example. The dowager countess, played by Maggie Smith, formidable as she is, does not live in the Abbey, but in the nearby and much smaller 'dower house'. *Downton Abbey* fans may never think to pity the Lord's mother. Her imperiousness seems always to guarantee her comfort, but we must also note that not all mothers-in-law had such lavish accommodations to fall back on. These women were mostly dependent on the goodwill of their husbands and, when those died, their sons, daughters, and daughters-in-law.

Awaiting Lawrence's return is the preserved game in the Herons' woods. And Lawrence has promised his friends an opportunity to shoot pheasants which have been carefully fed so that gentlemen can shoot their pets while enjoying the illusion of hunting wild animals.

It may be difficult for twenty-first-century readers to understand the controversy surrounding private game preserves at the time Parthenope wrote this novella. Farmers bitterly resented what were essentially the sports fields of the rich, when the well-fed rabbits and game birds settled on nearby crops, sometimes devastating a farm's produce.

The Game Act of 1831 gave such farmers the right to shoot animals that strayed onto their land and also legalized the buying and selling of game. However, in 1862, the Poaching Prevention Act further privileged the owners of game preserves by giving law enforcement officials the right to search the persons of anyone leaving a game preserve to see if he had illegally killed his supper.

It is against this political backdrop that Lady Verney brings together Mark Ogden and Lawrence Heron in a violent exchange that changes the course of three women's lives. Through his gamekeeper, Lawrence learns that a group of men plan a poaching party on his preserve, just in advance of his intended shooting party. The surrounding community already suspects Mark Ogden of shooting fish on property that doesn't belong to him. The gamekeeper has seen Mark hanging around the private woods. Even Joan sees Mark stalking Herons' game, though she convinces herself it could not be him.

Upon learning of the poaching party, Lawrence and his friends team up and go out to stop the invaders. When the two groups clash, Lawrence takes off after Mark and catches up to him. Mark hits Lawrence on the head with a rock, and the young man dies shortly thereafter, breaking the heart of his mother who had begged him not to confront the poachers, on the rather sensible argument that a few pheasants were not worth getting killed over.

Mark is tried for murder, but the judge is well known to be pro-poacher and is on record saying he will never convict a poacher. Meanwhile, the evidence against Mark is thin, there were no eyewitnesses to the murder, and Mark has an alibi. Joan, in a state of agony, invokes her right not to stand as witness against her husband. As a consequence, Mark is found not guilty and set free to pursue his ongoing ignoble deeds.

Mrs Heron retreats to the inner rooms of her lonely hall, rarely to be seen again. Joan and her daughters are now saddled with a known murderer for a husband and father. But their fortunes finally take a turn for the better when Mark lights up some tobacco while carrying a load of dynamite. He blows himself and his barge to smithereens.[2]

Joan, then, is finally free to rise in the world on the strength of her own hard work. She leaves town and changes her name along with the name of her children. To provide for them, she takes in laundry with which Rowan helps her.

Nelly, however, has other plans; she convinces Joan to spend all her hard-won savings on private education for Nelly at the Pelham Boarding School. There, Nelly achieves just enough tone to attract the honourable intentions of a grocer. And it is at this point in the tale that Parthenope introduces the comical sub-narrative of Nelly.

When Nelly announces her engagement, it comes out that the Ogden women, Joan, Rowan, and Nelly, have been living under an assumed name and that they are the spawn and moll of the famous poacher and murderer Mark Ogden.

Nelly's fiancé is given pause by this news. He needs some time to think about it. But not that much time. His intense attraction to Nelly wins out, and he takes her out of town to get married, so as not to have to face his mother's anger.

Nelly, who is now Nelly Robinson, finds a worthy adversary in her mother-in-law. The elder Mrs Robinson believes her son could have married much better. And, while she no doubt overestimates Johnny's appeal, it is probably true he could have married someone who brought some money to the table. This Mrs Robinson, Sr. cannot so easily be dismissed from her own home as a woman of the more elegant class could be. She is a co-owner of the grocery, into which she has put her own labour and money. Hers, too, is the furniture that graces the neat little house into which Nelly moves with her new husband. Nevertheless, the elder Mrs Robinson is no match for Nelly's beauty and sex appeal. During their first encounter, Mrs Robinson, Sr. ushers her son and new bride into the parlour of the house. This gesture is meant to symbolize that she regards Nelly as a guest.

Nelly responds by taking off her bonnet, a gesture that says she is right at home. Then she gives a nearby maid orders to get her luggage out of the carriage and take it upstairs. Nelly forcibly suggests that tea be served because she and her husband have had quite a journey and 'We could hardly discuss business so late at night, could we?' she concludes with a smile.[3]

Nelly's list of encroachments is the comic relief badly needed in an otherwise painfully hard-hitting novel. And Parthenope trots out all her talent for comedy in painting the picture of Nelly settling in with the Robinsons. When Mrs Robinson declares that there's no room for the couple in that house, Nelly unpacks her things and takes over the guest room. By the time Nelly has demanded clean sheets for the guest bed and seated herself at the dinner table in time for fresh-baked muffins, even the servant has defected to Nelly's side, as the handwriting could not be clearer as to who will win this match.

Lady Verney tucks in the corners of Nelly's story by having her wonder if she had really married as far up as she could have. Considering her charm and great beauty, might she have aimed higher than a grocer? Maybe she had been in a little too much of a hurry to get herself properly settled into a well-off home.[4]

Joan finds it difficult to be content with having a daughter so well cared for. Nelly was always her favourite daughter to the point that she often neglected Rowan who frequently and privately wiped her own tears at her mother's indifference.

Nelly had always been the sole ray of sunshine in Joan's bleak life. For her, Joan made or bought pretty hats and dresses. Nelly was always beloved by everyone who met her, and a source of great pride. As a married woman, settled in her own home, with money for all the bows and ribbons she will ever need, Nelly rarely finds time for Joan or her sister. Her visits are typically limited to fifteen minutes.

However, in her bitterness and rejection, Joan finally turns to Rowan, the daughter who has been at her side through every trial and ordeal. And the reader is left hopeful that the two women now will find comfort and refuge in one another.

Lady Verney certainly had her own experience as the less loved sister to draw on while writing *Grey Pool*. Like Rowan, she was there for Florence, working collaterally with her in everything that Florence chose to do, silent and in the shadows. In having Joan finally turn to Rowan with a heart of love and appreciation, Parthenope was perhaps imagining such an ending for herself and Florence.

It was an ending that she would get, at the very end. In the last years of her life, Parthenope was often in London. The Verney house was very close to Florence's apartment. And, even though she became too badly disabled to make the short walk, servants were found to carry Parthenope to Florence's place. Florence lifted her restrictions against family visits, so that these get-togethers were pleasantly frequent. The sisters reminisced about their childhoods and youths, exchanged jokes, and made each other laugh.

But neither sister would ever abandon a moral duty to serve others. As late as 1887, three years before Parthenope's death, the sisters were corresponding about the best treatment for Mrs Robertson who needed to be fitted with some kind of 'truss'. Parthenope underwrote the cost of a bed for her at a London hospital. Florence agreed to pay the doctor for her diagnosis. Florence recommended the two doctors she would most trust with this case.

In 1888, the two sisters tag teamed each other on the care of John King, another patient who needed a truss. Parthenope had sent him to London to be measured and fitted with a better device. There he was treated by Doctor Croft, one of Florence's favourites. She then sent King back to Parthenope for nursing and mothering because he didn't yet know how to manage his new truss. Florence jovially referred to King as Parthenope's patient.[5]

Memoirs of the Verney Family in the Seventeenth Century was Parthenope's magnum opus. That book gave form and narrative structure to the massive archives that sat in Claydon Hall, waiting for the right historian. This was, after all, a family that traced itself back four centuries and saved every document that could be saved.

By the time she was finishing the work on this history, Parthenope was very disabled. She was beset with insomnia and took opiates for pain and to sleep. Her hands were so deformed by arthritis that she had to use a stylographic pen, a type of fountain pen that was easier for crippled hands to wield, to write the Verney history. As the work progressed, however, she became unable to write by hand at all. Her step-daughter-in-law, Margaret Verney became her assistant. Margaret would eventually complete the work, writing two out of the three volumes. Today, this history is still in print, and justly considered a culturally important document.

By this time she was pushing through the pain to finish the *Memoirs*, Parthenope's relationship with Florence was so cordial that the latter offered several editorial notes on the rough draft. Florence proposed deleting phrases like 'magniloquent nonsense' on the grounds that respondents might get sidetracked by language and name-calling instead of engaging the ideas.[6]

Because she was so disabled, but also working at the fastest possible pace, Parthe came to need more help than what Margaret could offer. So Lady Verney enlisted the help of the young Frederica and Catherine Spring Rice, daughters of Thomas Spring Rice, first Baron Monteagle of Brandon.

With the help of these three young women and through sheer determination, Parthenope was able to keep writing, producing almost the same output in the 1880s as she had in her prolific 1860s and 1870s.

In her preface to *Memoirs of the Verney Family*, Parthenope writes that the original Verney documents were in surprisingly good shape when she embarked on her project. Some of the papers had gotten a little damp, others were rat nibbled along the margins, where the rats found any kind of grease that had transferred from the hands of the writers onto the pages.

She sought and received help from the famed British historian Samuel Rawson Gardiner. Gardiner, himself, was the author of a multi-volume work on the English Civil War and the concurrent rise of Puritan influence. Like Parthenope, he had a familial connection to his subject matter. Gardiner was a descendant of Oliver Cromwell, the famed seventeenth-century Lord Protector of England.

To Parthenope, Gardiner provided a role model of the historical biographer: someone enthusiastic to discover details of a time to which the biographer is connected while also maintaining a strict impartiality toward the events. Inspired by this example, Parthenope wrote a book that in many ways complemented Gardiner's. Her *Memoirs* are also organized around the Civil War in England, but they focus on the contributions and actions of the Verneys, a family divided by political loyalties.

Parthenope's history takes up, first, the story of Sir Edmund Verney, her husband's direct ancestor. This Verney was both a courier and also a close personal friend of King Charles I. However, Verney was also a Member of Parliament for Wycombe. When Parliament fell out with the king, launching the civil war, Verney reluctantly sided with his monarch. Verney was at odds with himself, however, and wished that Charles would accede to at least some of Parliament's demands.

Parthenope quotes Verney soliloquizing: 'For my part, I do not like the quarrel and do heartily wish that the king would yield and consent to what they desire'.[7] In portraying Edmund, Parthenope gives us an anti-hero who goes against his own political conscience out of personal friendship: 'I have eaten his bread and served him near thirty years, and will not do so base a thing as to forsake him; and choose rather to lose my Life (which I am sure I shall do) to preserve and defend those things, which are against my conscience to preserve and defend'.[8]

Like many other reforming Protestants, Edmund was also dismayed by the way Charles clung to the vestiges of Catholicism that, at that time, lingered in the Anglican Church. The failure of the Anglican leadership and the crown to truly separate itself from the rituals and corrupt practices of the Catholic Church was an ongoing public concern, starting with Henry VIII. And Parthenope, a Unitarian by birth and breeding, would have understood this tension.

In her memoirs, Parthenope paints Sir Edmund as an almost Shakespearean character. Like Hamlet, Edmund clearly sees the correct course of action, but fails to act upon it at a time that action is most needed.

Verney did, indeed, foretell his own death. When conversations between king and parliament failed in 1642, both sides amassed armies. The king's forces faced those of the Earl of Essex on Edgehill. It turned out that both armies were composed of raw recruits who did not have the stamina to hold their ground. Many deserted their armies right then and there; others took to looting. The armies were equally matched in incompetence, so neither side won the day. However, according to Verney family documents, Sir Edmund's hand was found on the battlefield, separated from his dead body. His hand was still holding tight to the king's standard.

Parthenope traces a direct line between Sir Edmund's divided soul and the actions of his two sons, Ralph and Edmund. As the war waged on, Ralph sided with parliament, of which he was a member, while his younger brother, Edmund, sided with the royal forces.

Parthenope's accounting of the Civil War is a good story. It also upholds a solid standard of journalistic objectivity, and Gardiner praised its accuracy.

The eighth of December 1889 was a red-letter day in Parthenope's life. Less than five months before her death, she had completed the first volume of the Verney memoirs. She would never see it within the covers of a published book, but she bundled the hand-written pages together and presented them to her beloved husband with the label 'a birthday gift for my dear Harry'.

This series was mass-produced in 1892 by Longmans, Green & Co. It received a glowing review by the esteemed historian Charles Harding Firth, who wrote, 'The history of these four brothers is traced and their characters described with the greatest clearness and vividness. The five sisters and their matches and fortunes are treated with the same skill'.[9]

A positive review from Firth was meaningful as he was a leading historian of his time, though not as acclaimed as Gardiner. Firth was the author of several histories pertaining to Oliver Cromwell and Scotland. He was also one of the founders of the Historical Association, president of the Royal Historical Society for four years in the early 1900s, and the Regius Professor of Modern History at Oxford.

But, in the twentieth century, opinion turned against the *Memoirs*. They were reissued by Barnes and Noble in 1970, and they met with a rather scathing critique from John Ferguson who reviewed the series for the *Social Science Quarterly*. Ferguson finds the series reliable only where Parthenope used secondary sources that had already compiled some of the letters, especially John Bruce's compilation. Parthenope's own prose, which stitches these more reliable sources together, is reminiscent of Charlotte Yong's novels, he notes. This is not meant as a compliment, even though Yonge is still widely read today. Yonge wrote books mostly meant to convey palatable moral lessons to young women on the Anglican faith.

By thumping Yonge, Ferguson managed to insult two women writers for the price of one.

Ferguson goes on to accuse Parthenope of taking quotes out of context, writing too few footnotes and not making them more informative, and a failure to provide dates. Finally, he tells readers that the series is unreliable because it was written by a disabled woman: 'one's confidence diminishes when the "Introductory Note" tells us that the author's hands were so badly crippled by arthritis and rheumatism that she was unable to turn over the letters she was reading'.[10]

Despite that rather cruel assessment, *Memoirs of the Verney Family* has remained relevant to historians through the years since Parthenope's death in a way that her novels and essays have not. The *Memoirs* have reverberated in later writings. For instance, the popular BBC series, *By the Sword Divided*, took up the story of a seventeenth-century family much like the Verneys, though Lady Verney was never credited as a source.

Chapter 27

Death and Epilogue

Margaret Verney was a huge source of comfort and companionship to Parthenope in her last years. Though Parthenope had not been able to carry a child to term, here was a young woman who nursed her with all the love and care of a daughter. It must have pained Parthenope and Harry Verney when Edmund, Harry's eldest son, was the centre of a scandal.

Edmund shot his own foot off shortly after marrying Margaret. As a consequence, she found herself yoked for life to an amputee. She bore this setback with good grace, but it was not the last time that Edmund would be a disappointment. In 1889, he was accused of seducing a number of young women. One of them pressed charges. This lady had been led to a hotel. Though it appears the two did not have sex, Edmund was found guilty of moral turpitude and spent a year in prison.[1] Such a thing was not easy to live down in the Victorian era, and this scandal threw a shadow over the happiness of the Verneys.

Parthenope finally succumbed to cancer at the age of seventy-one. She died at Claydon on May 12, which was, coincidentally, Florence's birthday, in the year 1890.[2] On the following Ascension Day, she was interred on the Claydon estate. There is a plaque in her memory in a nearby church, but her grave is unmarked.

When he died four years later,[3] Sir Harry was buried with his first wife and one of their daughters. Parthenope's husband would outlive her by many years, as would her sister and Queen Victoria of England.

When Frances Parthenope Verney died, the landscape of opportunity for women of Britain had been transformed. Parthenope had played her part in the great fight to qualify women in medicine. Florence had, with Parthenope's help, transformed nursing into a noble and respected profession. They did not work in isolation. Many other women drove the movement to educate women and provide opportunities in medicine. By 1869, the Edinburgh Seven had prevailed on the University of Edinburgh to educate women in the medical arts. In 1874, Sophia Jex-Blake and others were able to launch the London School of Medicine for Women. That is not to say that the playing field was level. It would not be until 1920 that the first women students were admitted to Oxford University.

Parthenope played no small part in educating the public about the plight of working women and women living in poverty in England and other parts of the world. Her calm and lucid demands for better conditions, better education, and better training would reverberate in minimum wage laws and the structure of the work week in the decades following her death.

Parthenope's role in creating Florence Nightingale should not be underestimated. The two girls shaped and challenged each other growing up, as they competed to be the best and brightest student of their father and their various tutors. Without Parthenope's determined public relations campaign, which raised Florence into the public limelight, the latter's achievements might not have captured as much of the public imagination.

Parthenope has been unfairly demonized, especially by her earliest biographers and then, later, by twentieth-century feminists who turned Parthenope into a representative of all the evils that the Victorian era inflicted on women of talent and intelligence. Parthenope, for these writers, represented all the prim, conventional societal forces that held Victorian women, such as Florence Nightingale, back, and prevented them achieving their full potential.

In fact, Parthenope herself was a victim of those societal forces, not a perpetrator of them. Like her sister Florence, Parthenope chafed at having no great work to do. Her career, as a journalist and novelist, was delayed, as was Florence's. Parthenope found the space and emotional support she needed to pursue her real work only in the last twenty-five years of her life. And she had no golden retirement years. She worked almost until the day she died.

The writings of Frances Parthenope Verney have stood in the shadow of Florence Nightingale, just as much as Parthenope herself stood in that shadow. Future historians will need to re-examine *Stone Edge*, *Lettice Lisle*, *Grey Pool*, and *Fernyhurst Court* to determine their true place in the canon of English Literature. In particular, Parthenope's elegant use of whimsy and irony can hold its own against that of any political commentator today.

It is hoped that this book has done its part to pull Parthenope out of the shadow cast on her, first by the greatness of her sister, and next by Nightingale scholars eager to find a villain for Florence's narrative. While it may be unusual for one family to produce two siblings who make their mark on history, it is not unheard of. Lady Frances Parthenope Verney, née Nightingale, was as eminent a Victorian as John Ruskin, Thomas Carlyle, and Mary Clarke. She both represents and transcends her age.

Notes

Introduction
1. Showalter, p. 397
2. Ibid, p. 401
3. Ibid, p. 397
4. Cassandra, p. 28
5. Ibid, p. 29
6. Ibid, p. 30
7. Strauss, p. 72
8. Ibid, p. 78
9. Gill, xiii
10. Woodham-Smith, p. 68
11. Ibid
12. Mackerness, p. 131
13. Ibid
14. Ibid

Part I: Ancestry and Childhood

Chapter 1: The Shores
1. Michie, p. 2
2. Bostridge, p. 18
3. Bowers, pp. 29-90
4. MacDonald, Intro, p. 829

Chapter 2: The Smiths
1. MacDonald, Intro, p. 829
2. Wallace, p. 599
3. Gill, p. 27
4. Ibid, p. 28
5. Ibid, p. 34
6. Ibid, p. 47-48
7. Ibid, p. 49

Chapter 3: Born on a Honeymoon
1. Bostridge, pp. 20-21
2. Ibid, p. 21
3. Ibid
4. Gill, p. 56
5. Ibid, p. 55
6. Ibid, p. 56
7. Ibid, p. 57

Chapter 4: The Shore, Smith, and Nightingale Brew
1. Bostridge, p. 562
2. Ibid p. 24
3. Gill, p. 75
4. Ibid, p. 68

Chapter 5: Embley
1. Gill, p. 79
2. Ibid, p. 82
3. Ibid, p. 86
4. Ibid, p. 64
5. Reef, p. 11

Chapter 6: Educating the Titans
1. Gill, pp. 102-103
2. MacDonald, Intro, p. 113
3. Gill, p. 102
4. Crawford, p. 35
5. Gill, pp. 98-103
6. Ibid, p. 114
7. Ibid, p. 93
8. Cook, p. 232
9. Gill, p. 128

Chapter 7: Second Tour of Europe
1. Bostridge, p. 59
2. Ibid, p. 65
3. Ibid, p. 61
4. Gill, p. 151

5. Cook, p. 9
6. Gill, p. 64
7. Ibid, p. 154
8. Bostridge, p. 77
9. Peasant Properties and Other Selected Essays, pp. 248-260
10. Gill, p. 112

Chapter 8: Florence Refuses to Marry
1. Gill, p. 183
2. MacDonald, Intro, p. 296
3. Ibid, p. 297

Part II: In the Shadow of Florence Nightingale

Chapter 9: Florence Breaks Away
1. MacDonald, Volume 7, p. 131
2. Keele, p. 87
3. MacDonald, Volume 7, p. 158
4. Cook, p. 28
5. MacDonald, Intro, p. 128
6. Ibid, p. 305
7. Ibid, p. 306
8. Ibid, p. 128
9. Ibid, p. 308

Chapter 10: Parthenope Breaks Down
1. Rappaport, p. 188
2. Markel
3. Bostridge, p. 176
4. MacDonald, Intro, p. 134
5. Ibid, p. 133
6. Ibid, p. 313
7. Ibid

Chapter 11: WEN Gives In
1. Bostridge, p. 188
2. Ibid, pp. 188-189
3. MacDonald, Intro, p. 314
4. Ibid
5. Ibid, p. 317

Chapter 12: Gaskell Friendship, Spottiswoode Refusal
1. Gaskell, p. 307
2. Ibid, p. 322
3. Bostridge, p. 181

Chapter 13: 'All things have ... fitted her for this'
1. Gill, p. 317
2. MacDonald, Volume 5, p. 484
3. Gaskell, p. 322
4. Ibid, p. 317
5. Ibid
6. Ibid, p. 319
7. Bostridge, p. 209
8. Ibid, p. 211

Chapter 14: The War at Home
1. Latimer, p. 149
2. MacDonald, Intro, p. 318
3. Cook, Volume 1, p. 240
4. MacDonald, Volume 14, pp. 249-250
5. Ibid, pp. 265-66

Chapter 15: The Great Divorce of Pop and Flo
1. MacDonald, Volume 5, pp. 233-34
2. Bostridge, p. 328
3. Ibid, p. 329

Chapter 16: 'I never thought to marry anyone but F'
1. Lodge, p. 785
2. Bostridge, p. 347
3. Ibid, p. 348
4. Annan, p. 66
5. Ibid, p. 239
6. Ibid, p. 216
7. Ibid
8. Ibid, p. 75
9. Bostridge, p. 348
10. Ibid, p. 349
11. Ibid

Chapter 17: 'Principle Object'
1. MacDonald, Intro, p. 838
2. MacDonald, Intro, p. 323
3. MacDonald, Volume 6, p. 536
4. MacDonald, Volume 5, p. 146
5. MacDonald, Volume 8, pp. 973-974
6. MacDonald, Volume 12, p. 353

Part III: Ink-bottle

Chapter 18: Novelist
1. Bostridge, p. 460
2. MacDonald, Volume 6, p. 72
3. Verney, Parthenope, *Stone Edge*, p. 6
4. Ibid, p. 62
5. Ibid, p. 64
6. Ibid, p. 69
7. Ibid, p. 67
8. Ibid, p. 249
9. Ibid, p. 314
10. Ibid, p. 27
11. Ibid, p. 309
12. Ibid, pp. 154-155
13. Ibid, p. 109
14. Ibid, p. 190
15. Ibid, p. 95
16. Ibid, p. vi
17. MacDonald, Volume 5, p. 148

Chapter 19: Lettice Lisle
1. 'The Powers of Women and How to Use Them', p. 212
2. Ibid, p. 213
3. *Lettice Lisle*, p. 19
4. Ibid, p. 47
5. Ibid, p. 141
6. Ibid, p. 137
7. Ibid, p. 254
8. Ibid, p. 311
9. Ibid, p. 321
10. Ibid, p. 328

Chapter 20: The Powers of Women and Class Morality
1. MacDonald, volume 6, p. 315
2. Ibid, p. 318
3. *Peasant Properties and Other Selected Essays, Volume II*, p. 235
4. Ibid, p. 221
5. Ibid, p. 222
6. Ibid, p. 212
7. Ibid, p. 214
8. Ibid
9. Verney, Parthenope, 'Class Morality', p. 262
10. Ibid, p. 264
11. Ibid, p. 261
12. Ibid, p. 260
13. Ibid
14. Ibid, p. 268

Chapter 21: The Miseries of War and the Pleasures of Home
1. Verney, Parthenope, "The Miseries of War," p. 515
2. Ibid, p. 524
3. Verney, Parthenope, *Fernyhurst Court*, p. 47
4. Ibid, p. 61
5. Ibid, p. 211
6. Ibid, p. 241
7. Ibid, p. 337

Chapter 22: The Death of WEN; Entail Strikes
1. MacDonald, Intro, pp. 197-198
2. Ibid, p. 342

Chapter 23: Continental Travels
1. Verney, Parthenpe, *Cottier Owners, Little Takes and Peasant Properties*, p. vi
2. Ibid, p. vi
3. Ibid, p. vi
4. Ibid, p. vi
5. Ibid, p. 1

6. Ibid, p. 7
7. Ibid, p. 7
8. Ibid, p. 17
9. Ibid, p. 18
10. Ibid, p. 21
11. Ibid, p. 24
12. Ibid, p. 10
13. Ibid, pp. 27-28
14. Ibid, p. 27
15. Ibid, pp. 29
16. Ibid, p. 32
17. Ibid, p. 32
18. Ibid, p. 37
19. Ibid, p. 37
20. Ibid, p. 48
21. Ibid, pp. 47-48
22. Ibid, p. 48
23. Ibid, p. 56
24. Ibid, p. 57
25. Ibid, p. 57
26. Ibid, p. 59
27. Ibid, p. 65
28. Ibid, p. 65
29. Ibid, p. 65
30. Ibid, p. 65

Chapter 24: Germany
1. Verney, Parthenpe, *Cottier Owners, Little Takes and Peasant Properties*, pp. 96-97
2. Ibid, p. 97
3. Ibid, p. 98
4. Ibid, p. 97
5. Ibid, p. 98
6. Ibid, p. 98
7. Ibid, p. 98

Chapter 25: The Defense of Science
1. Bostridge, p. 487
2. MacDonald, Volume 6, p. 637

3. MacDonald, Intro, p. 359
4. *Peasant Properties and Other Selected Essays, Volume II*, p. 170
5. Ibid, p. 170
6. Ibid, p. 165
7. Ibid, p. 157
8. Ibid, p. 152
9. Ibid, p. 170
10. Verney, Parthenope, "In a Great Town Hospital", p. 16
11. Ibid, p. 17
12. Ibid, p. 20
13. Ibid, p. 21
14. Ibid, p. 22
15. Ibid, p. 19
16. Ibid, p. 19

Chapter 26: Last Years with the Verneys
1. Verney, Parthenope, *Grey Pool*, p. 8
2. Ibid, p. 70
3. Ibid, p. 86
4. Ibid, p. 89
5. MacDonald, Volume 6, p. 654
6. MacDonald, Volume 7, p. 343
7. Firth, p. 580
8. Ibid, p. 580-81
9. Ibid, p. 581
10. Ferguson, p. 432

Chapter 27: Death and Epilogue
1. Bostridge, pp. 489-90
2. Bostridge, p. 508
3. Mackerness, p. 132

Bibliography

Annan, Noel, *The Dons: Mentors, Eccentrics, and Geniuses*, (University of Chicago Press, 1999)
Bostridge, Mark, *The Making of an Icon*, (Macmillan, New York, 2008)
Bowers, J.D. *Joseph Priestley and English Unitarianism in America*, (Penn State Press, 2010)
Edward Cook, *The Life of Florence Nightingale*, volume 1, (London: Macmillan, 1913)
Crawford, P., *Florence Nightingale at Home*, Springer International Publishing, New York, 2020), online
Dependent Personality Disorder. Cleveland Clinic.
Ferguson, John, 'The Memoirs of the Verney Family by Frances Parthenope Lady Verney and Margaret Maria Verney,' *Social Science Quarterly*, Vol. 52, No. 2, September 1971, pp. 431-432. Published by Wiley
Firth, C. H., 'Review of Parthenope Verney's Memoirs of the Verney Family', *The English Historical Review*, Vol. 8, No. 31 [Jul., 1893], pp. 579-581. Retrieved through JSTOR
Gaskell, Elizabeth, *The Letters of Mrs. Gaskell*, (Harvard University Press, Cambridge, 1967)
Gill, Gillian, *Nightingales, the Extraordinary Upbringing and Curious Life of Miss Florence Nightingale*, (Random House, New York, 2004)
Gilpin, William, *Observations on the River Wye and several parts of South Wales*, fifth edition, (A. Strahan, London, 1800)
Keel, Mary, *Florence Nightingale in Rome*, (American Philosophical Society, 1981)
Latimer, Elizabeth Wormeley, *Russia and Turkey in the Nineteenth Century*, (McClurg & Co., 1903)
Lodge, Edmund, *The Peerage and Baronetage of the British Empire* (28th ed.), (London: Hurst and Blackett, 1859).
MacDonald, Lynn, *Collected Works of Florence Nightingale*, (Wilfrid Laurier University Press, 2010)
Mackerness, E.D., 'Frances Parthenope, Lady Verney', *Journal of Modern History*, Volume 30, number 2, June 1958
Markel, Howard, 'How Poet John Keats Met His Early End', PBS.org.
Michie, Helena, *Victorian Honeymoons: Journeys to the Conjugal*, (Cambridge University Press, 2007)

Nightingale, Florence, *Cassandra*, (The Feminist Press at the City University of New York, 1979)

Porch, Douglas. 'Not the Good War.' *New York Times*. 7 January 2001.

Rappaport, Helen, *Queen Victoria: A Biographical Companion*, ABC-CLIO, 2003.

Reef, Catherine, *Florence Nightingale: The Courageous Life of the Legendary Nurse*, (Houghton Mifflin Harcourt, 2016)

Scamahorn, Alexandra Virginia, 'Feminine Realism in Cornhill Magazine: Anne Thackeray Ritchie and Frances Parthenope Verney', University of Denver Digital Commons, 2012.

Showalter, Elaine, 'Florence Nightingale's Feminist Complaint: Women, Religion, and Suggestions for Thought,' *Signs: Journal of Women in Culture and Society*, (University of Chicago, vol. 6, no. 3, 1981)

Simpson, M.C.M, *Letters and Collections of Julius and Mary Mohl*, (Keegan, Paul, Trench & Co., London, 1887)

Strauss, Sylvia. 'Florence Nightingale and the Bonds of Sisterhood,' *The Sister Bond*, (Pergamon Press, New York, 1985)

Tooley, Sarah, *Florence Nightingale*, (Kessinger Publishing, LLC, 2009)

Verney, Frances Parthenope, 'Class Morality,' *The Saint Pauls Magazine*, Vol. 8, 1871. pp. 259–268

Verney, Frances Parthenope, *Cottier Owners, Little Takes and Peasant Properties*, (Longmans, Green, and Co., London, 1885)

Verney, Frances Parthenope, *Fernyhurst Court*, (Strathan and Co., London, 1871)

Verney, Frances Parthenope, *Grey Pool, and Other Stories*, (Simpkin, Marshall, Hamilton & Co., London, 1891) (print facsimile)

Verney, Frances Parthenope, 'In a Great Town Hospital,' *Macmillan's Magazine*, Vol. L, May to Oct. 1884. pp. 14–22.

Verney, Frances Parthenope, Letters to Mrs. S.C. Hall, (Auchincloss Florence Nightingale Collection, Columbia University Irving Medical Center)

Verney, Frances Parthenope, *Lettice Lisle*, (Smith, Elder & Co., London, 1870) (print facsimile)

Verney, Frances Parthenope, *Memoirs of the Verney Family*, (Dalcassian Publishing Company, 1892)

Verney, Frances Parthenope, 'The Miseries of War,' *The Saint Pauls Magazine*, Vol. 8, 1871. pp. 509–524

Verney, Frances Parthenope, *Peasant Properties and Other Selected Essays*, Volume II, (Longmans, Greene, and Co., London, 1885)

Verney, Frances Parthenope, *Stone Edge*, (Smith, Elder & Co., London, 1868) (print facsimile)

Wallace, Robert, *Antitrinitarian Biography, Or, Sketches of the Lives and Writings of Distinguished Antitrinitarians*, (E.T. Whitfield, 1850)

Woodham-Smith, Cecil, *Florence Nightingale: 1820-1910*, (Avon Books, New York, 1951)

Index

Albert, Prince, 96
Acropolis, 60
Athena, the owl, xiii, 60-62
   Rescue by Florence Nightingale, 60
   Death, 78
   Subject of Frances Parthenope's
     published tale, 85

Bonham Carter family, 29, 34, 69
Bonham Carter, Helena, xiii, 29
Bostridge, Mark, vii, 201
Brontë, Charlotte, 114
   Jane Eyre, 182
   Death in childbirth, 50
Browning, Elizabeth, 64, 117, 128

Calvin, John, 97, 165
Calvinism, 98
Cassandra by Florence Nightingale, xii, x, 46
Christie, Sarah, 33-35, 49
Death in childbirth, 49-50
Clarke, Mary
   Salon, 42
   Lifestyle, 43
   Marriage to Julius Mohl, 54
Clark, James, 67
   Treatment of Flora Hastings, 67
   Treatment of John Keats, 68
   Treatment of Frances Parthenope
     Verney, 68-70
Claydon, 101, 104, 110, 176, 189, 194
   Inheritance of by Sir Harry Verney, 94
   Restoration by F.P. Verney, 102-103, 105
   Second home to Florence Nightingale, 109, 175
Clough, Arthur Hugh, 91, 117
Cornhill Magazine, 111, 123
Crimean War, viii-ix, xii, 26
   Causes, 79
   Reason for popularity with the British, 80
   Sevastopol, 80, 85
   Scutari, 80-87, 90
   Outcome, 80

Darwin, Charles, 97, 129
Dependent Personality Disorder, 62, 63
Dickens, Charles, 86, 118
Dupin, Amandine Aurore, *see* George Sands

Eliot, George, 4, 64, 114, 118
Embley, xi, 25-29, 55, 60, 65, 71, 88, 93, 126, 142, 144, 151, 174
   Bought by William Edward Nightingale, 25
   Expansion, 40, 44, 47-48

Feminism
   Florence Nightingale's feminist
     limitations, viii-ix
   F. P. Verney's feminism
     'Feminine Realism,' 111, 116
     'The Powers of Women and How to
       Use Them,' 122, 132-135
Franco-Prussian War, 123
   Subject of F. P. Verney's 'Miseries of
     War,' 139-141
   Effects on France and Germany, 152

Gaskell, Elizabeth, xv, 22, 120, 122
   Relationship with F. P. Verney, née
     Nightingale, 76-78, 81-82, 101
   Novels
     North and South, 76-77
     Mary Barton, 111
Gardiner, Samuel Rawson, 190-192
Gill, Gillian, vii, xii, 34, 47
Gilpin, William, 32-33

Institution for Ill Gentlewomen on Harley Street, 72-75

Jowett, Benjamin, 176

Lea Hall, 21
Lea Hurst, xi, 6, 21-26, 29, 43, 55, 70, 76, 78, 93, 111, 117, 126, 151, 176

Manning, Cardinal Henry Edward, 88
Marianne Evans, *see* George Eliot

Memoirs of the Verney Family in the Seventeenth Century, 106, 189-193
Milnes, Richard Monckton
  Rejected suitor of Florence Nightingale, 54-55, 59, 72
  Party in honour of Florence Nightingale, 86
Mohl, Julius, 54, 168

Nicholson, Harry, 48, 73
Nicholson, Marianne, 73
Nightingale estate entail, 5, 16, 55-56, 145
Nightingale, Florence, viii-xvii
  Birth, 19
  Childhood relationship with Parthenope, 26, 28-39
  Education, 13, 30-39, 41, 60, 100, 195
  Travels with her family, 40-44
  Trip to Greece, 59-60
  Trip to Egypt, 59-61, 63
  Studies nursing, 60
  Directs Harley Street establishment, 72-75
  Sent to manage nurses in Crimean War, 80-88
  Breaks from mother and sister, 90-92
  Relationship with Harry Verney, 93, 103-105
  Wing at Claydon estate, 175
  Reconciliation with F. P. Verney, 174-176
Nightingale, Frances (Fanny), xvii, 10-11
  Upbringing, 11-13
  Marriage to William Edward Nightingale, 14-15
  Relationship with her mother-in-law, 23-24
  Social ambitions, 25-26, 35, 40, 62
  Relationship with Florence and Parthenope, 28-34, 44, 47, 56
  Dementia, 109, 150-151
  Death, 174
Nightingale, Peter II
  Businesses, 4-5
  'Mad Peter' moniker, 4
Nightingale, William Edward (WEN), xvii, 9
  Heir to Peter Nightingale's estate, 5-6, 8
  Marriage to Frances Smith, 14-15
  Honeymoon trip to continental Europe, 16-19
  Births of Parthenope and Florence Nightingale, 16-19
  Construction of Lea Hurst, 21
  Purchase of Embley, 25
  Education of his daughters, xv, 35, 37-38
  Run for Parliament, 36
  Second trip to continental Europe, 40-44
  Reaction to Florence Nightingale's bid for independence, 59, 72-73
  Death, 151
Nursing
  State of, before Florence Nightingale, 65, 83
  Professionalism of, in the aftermath of the Crimean War, 89, 182
  Training of nurses, 80, 132-133

Plato's Republic, 37
Phylloxera, 159-160

Reeve, Hope, 49, 51
Ruskin, John, 4, 196
Russell, William Howard, 80

Sand, George, 44
Saint Paul's Magazine, 202
Shelley, Mary, 50
Shore, William Edward (father of William Edward Nightingale) 5-6, 20
Shore, Mai *see* Mai Smith
Sinclair, James, 13-14
Sismondi, Jean-Charles-Leonard, 41-42
Smith, Benjamin,
  Engagement to Mai Shore, 20-21
  Illegitimate children, 29, 35
  Not welcome at Embley and Lea Hurst, 46
  Financially supports unmarried sisters, 17
Smith, Frances *see* Frances (Fanny) Nightingale
Smith, Frances Coape, 11-12
  Scafell Pike, 12
Smith, Julia, 17, 28, 56
Smith, Mai,
  Engagement to Benjamin Smith, 20-21,
  Marriage to Samuel Smith, 24
  As Florence's companion and gatekeeper, post Crimean War, 90-91
  Inherits Embley and Lea Hurst by way of her son, 151
Smith, Mary Evans, 6, 23-24
Smith, Martha Frances (Patty), 56
Smith, Samuel
  Marriage to Mai Shore, 24
  Son becomes heir to Nightingale estate, 151
Smith, Shore, 35, 55, 151
Smith, William, 10-11, 13-14
  Unitarian Relief Act, 11

Sugar imports, 13
Bankruptcy, 17
Spottiswoode, William, 78
Stanley, Mary, 88

Thackery, William Makepeace, 119

Unitarianism
  Theology, 6-8, 94, 125
  Influence on culture, 7
  Influence on women's rights, 7, 46
  Influence on F. P. Verney's religious beliefs (reason for not marrying Verney), 95
  Influence on F. P. Verney's writing, 125, 162, 191

Verney, Edmund (Sir Harry Verney's son), 101-102, 149, 194
Verney, Eliza Hope, 94
Verney, Harry, xii, xiv, xvii, 92
  Military career, 93-94
  Inheritance of Verney estate, 93, 102
  Parliamentary career, 94
  First marriage and children, 94
  Marriage to Parthenope Verney, 92, 101-105, 122, 194
Verney, Frances Parthenope
  Ancestry, 3-15
  Birth, 16
  Inability to nurse feed, 17-18
  Childhood illness, ix, xii, 29, 38-39, 62
  Education, 31-3813, 41, 100, 195
    Excellence in drawing, xi, xiii, 61, 84-85
    Excellence in French language, 36-37, 41, 100, 110, 153

Nervous breakdown, 67-71
Treatment by James Clark, 67-70
As Florence Nightingale's secretary, 84-89
Denied access to Florence Nightingale, 89-92
Engagement to Harry Verney, 95, 99-101
Religious differences from Church of England, 95-99, 179-180
Restoration of Claydon, 102-103
Works
  Avenhoe, 110
  Llanaly Reefs, 111
  Stone Edge, 64, 98, 111-121
  Lettice Lisle, 97, 120-131, 141, 179, 195
  Fernyhurst Court, 110-111, 141-149, 195
  'The Miseries of War,' 123, 139-141
  'The Powers of Women and How to Use Them,' 122, 132-135
  'In a Great Town Hospital,' 180-183
  'Evidence for Opinions, Events, and Consequences,' 179-180
  'Class Morality,' 135-138
  'Cottier Owners,' 98, 152-170
  'Peasant Properties,' 153
Verney, Margaret, 176, 190, 194
Victoria, Queen, 50, 67, 95
  Birthday, 3
  Petitioned for donations for soldiers of Crimean War, 87
  Donation of painting, 85

Walker, Thomas, 8
Wollstonecraft, Mary, 7, 11, 12

About the Author

Lynn Hamilton is a writer who divides her time between Louisville, Kentucky and Blue Ridge, Georgia. She is the author of *Florence Nightingale: A Life Inspired*, *The Dalai Lama: A Life Inspired*, *Gandhi: A Life Inspired*, and *Clay-foot Titan: An Agenda For Improving Wikipedia*. She holds a Ph.D. in English Literature from Loyola University of Chicago where she specialized in the Victorian period. She is the publisher of AnimalRightsChannel.com, a website devoted to saving wildlife and pet welfare. She lives with her husband, Joel Worth and their companion animals.